Saved by Grace...
for Service!

Saved by Grace... for Service!

Evangelistic Preaching in Ephesians

By Evangelist Robert L. Sumner, D.D.

Biblical Evangelism Press
Brownsburg, Indiana 46112

Copyright © 1979
BIBLICAL EVANGELISM
ISBN 0-87398-797-7

Printed in the United States of America

Dedication

In sincere gratitude for their gracious willingness to listen to *small* preaching from *big* texts, the author dedicates this volume of sermons to the faithful congregations where he pastored in days gone by:

      1943-1945: Calvary Baptist Church
                      Pontiac, Illinois

      1947-1949: California Heights Baptist Church
                      Long Beach, California

      1949-1954: Morningside Baptist Church
                      Graham, Texas

      1962-1964: Temple Baptist Church
                      Portsmouth, Ohio

Table of Contents

	Author's Preface	9
I.	Paul's High Calling and Ours	11
II.	Work of the Trinity in Our Redemption	33
III.	"Lord, Open Our Eyes!"	53
IV.	From Depths of Depravity to Summits of Grace	69
V.	Saved by Grace. . .for Service!	89
VI.	Things Are Different Now: We've Got It "Made"!	107
VII.	The True Church, God's Hidden Mystery	123
VIII.	"Lord, Open Our Hearts!"	143
IX.	Walking Worthy of Our Calling and Commission	165
X.	Walking Worthy of Our Creation and Cleansing	189
XI.	Walking as Imitators of God	217
XII.	Walking in Light and Wisdom	237
XIII.	"Be Filled With the Spirit"	253
XIV.	God's Ideal Marriage	273
XV.	Heavenly Orders for Home and Business	297
XVI.	Christians At War!	315

Author's Preface

In releasing this book we feel empathy with the Christian newspaper editor who pointed to his desk and said, *"On one side is the Bible and on the other is the typewriter. I try to make the two sides of this desk say the same thing. I know that if what I write in my editorials coincides with what is in that Book, it will live on; but if it is not in harmony with that Book, it will perish."*

This sums up our philosophy exactly! If our evangelistic preaching is in harmony with what the Holy Spirit has inspired in the Book of Ephesians, it will live. Anything out of harmony will—and should—perish.

We have tried to keep three things in mind, each of which is typified in a passage of Scripture:

(1) *We have a definite motive:* **to produce and develop strong Christians.** As Paul said, in explaining why the ascended Christ had given evangelists:

"For the perfecting of the saints, for the work of the ministry, for the edifying of the body of Christ: Till we all come in the unity of the faith, and of the knowledge of the Son of God, unto a perfect man, unto the measure of the stature of the fulness of Christ: That we henceforth be no more children, tossed to and fro, and carried about with every wind of doctrine, by the sleight of men, and cunning craftiness, whereby they lie in wait to deceive; But speaking the truth in love, may grow up into him in all things, which is the head, even Christ: From whom the whole body fitly joined together and compacted by that which every joint supplieth, according to the effectual working in the measure of every part, maketh increase of the body unto the edifying of itself in love."—Eph. 4:12-16.

The ministry of an evangelist is not only to get people saved, it is also to build them up in the most holy faith.

(2) *We have a determined aim:* **to make it plain.** In the words of Jehovah to His prophet, Habakkuk: "Write the vision, and make it plain upon tables, that he may run that readeth it" (Hab. 2:2). We want our readers to understand the truth in a manner that will effectively enable them to pass it on to others.

(3) *We have a deep need:* **the help of the Holy Spirit.** As Paul wrote to the saints at Corinth: "For what man knoweth the things of a man, save the spirit of man which is in him? even so the things of God knoweth no man, but the Spirit of God. . . Which things also we speak, not in the words which man's wisdom teacheth, but which the Holy Ghost teacheth: comparing spiritual things with spiritual" (I Cor. 2:11,13). Since man's wisdom is of no avail in teaching the things of God, we have earnestly sought the Spirit's anointing and instruction.

Ephesians is considered, perhaps, one of the most doctrinal books in the Word of God. We trust this volume will prove to preachers everywhere that doctrine does not need to be dry or dull, and that doctrinal preaching can be—*and often should be*—evangelistic preaching as well.

Paul's High Calling and Ours

Paul, an apostle of Jesus Christ by the will of God, to the saints which are at Ephesus, and to the faithful in Christ Jesus:

Grace be to you, and peace, from God our Father, and from the Lord Jesus Christ.

Blessed be the God and Father of our Lord Jesus Christ, who hath blessed us with all spiritual blessings in heavenly places in Christ.—Ephesians 1:1-3.

This high calling is for R.F.D. people.

We are thinking of the high school boy who drove a very delapidated car to school each day. One of his teachers, with a laugh, inquired, "What in the world kind of car is that?"

The youth, without even as much as a glance in the instructor's direction, responded, "R.F.D."

"R.F.D.?" was the surprised reply. "I never heard of that make."

The boy looked up and grinned, saying, "Rescued from dump!"

The high calling which Paul experienced, and the high calling which he outlines in this passage as being the inheritance of every child of God, is tremendous indeed. Yet through it all he continually emphasizes that it is for people who have been rescued from the dumps of human depravity and whose lives have been revolutionized through the dynamic power of the Son of God.

I. THE WRITER OF THE EPISTLE

Ephesians opens abruptly with a terse statement of identification: *"Paul, an apostle of Jesus Christ by the will of God. . . ."* (vs. 1). As you probably know, there are thirteen New Testament epistles which begin with a similar salutation.

We are quick to point out that this was not Paul's original name. He was born Saul of Tarsus and was of the tribe of Benjamin, just as was the first king of Israel who bore the same name of Saul. Paul's name had been changed as a result of a revolutionary meeting with Jesus Christ on the road to Damascus. That was an experience he never got over and he repeatedly testified to others about what had happened.

Years ago, a small family of Italian immigrants settled in an American coal mining region. One day there was an explosion. The father lost his life and a son lost his arm. To help assuage the grief, the family moved from the community where the tragedy had occurred.

But that was not enough. One day the son announced he was going to change his name to Giovanni Sperandeo. When they asked why he had selected that name, he replied: "Well, Giovanni simply means 'John.' But Sperandeo comes from a word meaning, 'My hope is in God.' After all the heartaches we passed through, I came to the realization that there is no hope except in God. From now on, I want everyone to know that 'my hope is in God.' "

Saul of Tarsus took a new name to let everyone know he had become a new creature. Something happened to him in that Damascus experience. If Lecky, the historian, could write of John Wesley's experience at Aldersgate on May 27, 1738, *"This day in the life of John Wesley meant more to England than all the victories under Pitt,"* then that day on the road to Damascus in the life of Saul of Tarsus surely meant more to the world than all the military victories in the history of mankind.

This man with a new name could express his emotions with the poet:

> O glory of the lighted mind!
> How dead I'd been, how dumb, how blind.
> The station brook, to my new eyes,
> Was babbling out of Paradise;

> The waters rushing from the rain,
> Were singing Christ has risen again.
> I thought all earthly creatures knelt
> From rapture of the joy I felt.

In a single moment of time Saul of Tarsus lost all his self-righteousness, all his fond ambitions, all his valued achievements and everything else he once so highly esteemed. As he wrote to the saints at Philippi: "But what things were gain to me, those I counted loss for Christ. Yea doubtless, and I count all things but loss for the excellency of the knowledge of Christ Jesus my Lord: for whom I have suffered the loss of all things, and do count them but dung, that I may win Christ" (Phil. 3:7,8).

The man whose name opens this epistle is the one who bore "in my body the marks of the Lord Jesus" (Gal. 6:17). He had the scars of imprisonments, persecutions, beatings, stonings, shipwrecks, plus a thousand-and-one evidences of the world's hatred of the Gospel of Christ. Yet he not only *experienced* them, he *enjoyed* them. As he told the church at Rome, "And not only so, but we glory in tribulations also" (Rom. 5:3).

How opposite is today's generation of servants. What a soft, satisfied, shiftless generation of Christians are we! Most of our scars are from football, fistfights, auto accidents, and kindred incidents. Not many can show any scars from service.

A. His Authority

Immediately after announcing his name, Paul offered his credentials: *"an apostle of Jesus Christ."* Just as Paul was not his original name, even so he was not initially an apostle. Quite the contrary, he was a persecutor. Acts 9:1 pictures him as "breathing out threatenings and slaughter against the disciples of the Lord." What amazing grace was manifested in transforming Saul the persecutor into Paul the apostle!

One of Scotland's great evangelists was Brownlow North. A treasured book in our library is his biography, written by K. Moody Stuart. Before his conversion, North lived a very profligate and wicked life. After experiencing the new birth, he immediately began giving his testimony in churches all around the area.

On one such occasion he was seated on the platform waiting for the time to speak when an usher slipped down the side aisle and handed him an envelope. Thinking it might be a prayer request or an announcement, he opened the envelope immediately. To his utter amazement and chagrin, he found it catalogued a long list of vicious and heinous sins. Furthermore, the anonymous writer charged that he had committed them right in that very city.

His first impulse was to flee. But by that time the host had finished the introduction and turned the service over to him. Mr. North stood beside the pulpit, opened the envelope, and said to the audience: "I have just received a letter that has upset me tremendously. Let me read it to you." He then proceeded to read the long list of charges, pausing after each one to say, "That is true. I am guilty."

When he had finished, he placed the letter back in the envelope, put the envelope in his coat pocket, stepped behind the pulpit and said: "No doubt you wonder how I would have the nerve to stand before you, guilty of such terrible sins in your own community, and talk to you about righteousness and purity. I have but one explanation." He then proceeded to quote I Timothy 1:15.

Thus it was with Paul, the former persecuting Saul. As a matter of fact, in that passage to Timothy he wrote:

"And I thank Christ Jesus our Lord, who hath enabled me, for that he counted me faithful, putting me into the ministry: Who was before a blasphemer, and a persecutor, and injurious: but I obtained mercy, because I did it ignorantly and in unbelief. And the grace of our Lord was exceeding abundant with faith and love which is in Christ Jesus. This is a faithful saying, and worthy of all acceptation, that Christ Jesus came into the world to save sinners; of whom I am chief. Howbeit for this cause I obtained mercy, that in me first Jesus Christ might shew forth all longsuffering, for a pattern to them which should hereafter

believe on him to life everlasting."—I Tim. 1:12-16.

What an illustration was Paul of Romans 5:20: "Moreover the law entered, that the offence might abound. But where sin abounded, grace did much more abound." Well might he burst forth singing:

> Grace, grace, God's grace,
> Grace that will pardon and cleanse within;
> Marvelous grace, infinite grace,
> Grace that is greater than all our sin.

When Dwight D. Eisenhower was in the White House, he opened a news conference on a beautiful day following some very severe weather with his typical grin, remarking that there had been a real revolution in Washington weather. He suggested to the reporters that they read Song of Solomon 2:11,12. It says: "For, lo, the winter is past, the rain is over and gone; The flowers appear on the earth; the time of the singing of birds is come, and the voice of the turtle is heard in our land."

Saul of Tarsus had finished a cold, bitter, stormy winter of persecution against Christ, now a blessed spring of warmth, beauty and blessing had begun.

As the songwriter, George W. Robinson, expressed it:

> Heav'n above is softer blue, earth around is sweeter green!
> Something lives in every hue, Christless eyes have never seen.
> Birds with gladder songs o'erflow, flow'rs with deeper beauties shine,
> Since I know, as now I know, I am His—and He is mine!

Paul called himself "an apostle." This means a "sent one," or a "special messenger." There is one sense in which all Christians are apostles, since all are sent ones. The Great Commission of Matthew 28:19,20 is for every disciple. In the same manner, all the saints are to be evangelists (bearers of good tidings), pastors (shepherds), and teachers (instructors in doctrine). But these offices are gifts of the ascended Christ above the normal sense in which all Christians are involved.

Thus Paul was an apostle in a superior sense. He was specially, personally commissioned by Christ to do a definite work. Immediately after his conversion, God described him to Ananias: *". . .he is a chosen vessel unto me, to bear my name* before the

Gentiles, and kings, and the children of Israel: For I will shew him how great things he must suffer for my name's sake" (Acts 9:15,16).

Note, too, that he was not merely a special messenger. He was a special messenger of Jesus Christ!

B. His Sponsor

But Paul was not satisfied to identify himself as an apostle. He pointed out that this calling was "by the will of God." When he wrote to the churches of Galatia, he said in Galatians 1:1: "Paul, an apostle, (not of men, neither by man, but by Jesus Christ, and God the Father, who raised him from the dead.)."

Many today seek the ministry because of personal ambition. Sometimes mothers want their sons to be ministers because they think "it would be nice." Down South they call such preachers "Mama called and Papa sent." I know of one mother of two who wanted her son to be a minister and her daughter a movie star!

Paul received his calling "by God's choice." Dr. Hyman Appelman tells of a conversation he had with his First Sergeant in the Army, shortly after his surrender to preach. After he explained that he wanted to leave the Army, his superior wanted to know why. The conversation went something like this:

"I want to preach the Gospel of Jesus Christ."

"Well, that's a good job, too."

"It is the best job in the world."

"Appelman, are you really sure you want to be a preacher?"

"Sarge, it is a whole lot better than that. I am really sure **God** wants me to be a preacher!"

Do you know what that First Sergeant said then? He said, "Appelman, I would give everything I've got in the world if I knew what God wanted me to do."

Whatever you are, it should be "by the will of God." Paul called that will "good," "acceptable" and "perfect" in Romans 12:2. Oswald Chambers once wrote, "I have learned that when God says something—never dispute it, do it."

I laughed aloud when I read the incident of a very dignified clergyman and a very uneducated cobbler being introduced. The cobbler didn't catch the other's name and said, "I didn't get your name." The clergyman replied, "The Reverend Dr. Blank, by the will of God." And the cobbler said, "I am John Doe, cobbler, by the will of God. I am glad to meet you."

That is the way it ought to be with everyone, no matter whether he be apostle, housewife, grocery clerk, farmer, teacher or whatever. When the English government sent Henry M. Stanley to Africa to find David Livingstone, the former told the great missionary: "If you will return to England with me, the Empire will honor you as no man has ever been honored before. You will be entertained by royalty and acclaimed by all the inhabitants of the Empire." And Livingstone is said to have replied, "I had rather be in the heart of Africa, in the will of God, than to be anywhere else on earth out of it."

Someone expressed it:

> Sweet will of God
>   I cherish only Thee.
> None other will could be the best for me;
>   In Thee my all, my only need, I see,
> Be Thou my Guide.
>
> If I could choose my task
>   I would not dare;
> What seemed to me as best
>   Might prove a snare
> To call me from Thy side
>   And from Thy tender care.

II. THE READERS OF THE EPISTLE

After identifying himself, the author described his readers by both position and practice. As to their position, he called them "the saints which are at Ephesus."

What is a saint? Or, rather, *who* is a saint? Some say a saint is one who has reached a place of sinless perfection. Others say a saint is some dead hero of the faith who has been canonized by a certain church. Still others have other ideas.

However, according to the Word of God, a saint is simply a believer in Christ. Nothing more; nothing less. That he may not always be characterized by a personal holiness, I sadly acknowledge. For example, the Christians at Corinth were called saints in I Corinthians 1:2, yet Paul went on to berate them for divisions in their church, carnality, permitting immorality among their membership, going to law against each other before ungodly judges, marriage disorders, and even gluttony and drunkenness at the Lord's table!

Believers are saints because they are *in Christ*. His holiness is imputed at the moment of salvation and we are "made the righteousness of God in him" (II Cor. 5:21). Since our position is that of saints, however, it behooves us to live like saints and manifest saintliness.

The late Dr. Ernest Reveal, whom most people affectionately called "Pappy," told of a redeemed derelict of society who attended his Rescue Mission in Evansville, Indiana. This fellow had lived a wild and wicked life before his conversion and, in a drunken brawl, on one occasion, had lost one eye. His companions in sin referred to him as "Old Bill." When he got saved, however, the revolution in his life was so tremendous that no one ever called him anything again but "New Bill."

Thus it is with every sinner saved by grace. Second Corinthians 5:17 says, "Therefore if any man be in Christ, he is a new creature: old things are passed away; behold, all things are become new." And that new creature is called *a saint*.

After describing their **position** as saints, Paul pinpointed his readers' **practice** as "the faithful in Christ Jesus." That is literally, "full of faith." The thought is not necessarily "trustworthy"—although that should certainly be true—but it is a sense of believing, of "having faith" in Him. It is simply another way of addressing those who "walk by faith, not be sight" (II Cor. 5:7).

The poet expressed it:

> Faith is a living power from Heaven
> Which grasps the promise God has given!
> A trust that cannot be o'erthrown,
> Securely fixed on Christ alone.
>
> Faith finds in Christ whate'er we need
> To save and strengthen, guide and feed;

> Strong in His grace, it joys to share
> His cross, in hope His crown to wear.
>
> Faith to the conscience whispers peace,
> And bids the mourner's sighing cease;
> By faith the children's right we claim,
> And call upon our Father's Name.
>
> Faith feels the Spirit's kindly breath
> In love and hope that conquer death;
> Faith brings us to delight in God,
> And blesses e'en His smiting rod.

Since Paul is addressing his readers as "the faithful in Christ Jesus," it makes the epistle apply to believers in our day. This is for any group of the faithful in any church, in any land, in any age. *If you are a Christian, the Book of Ephesians is for you!*

We think here of a lad who, while playing on a pier at a summer resort, slipped and fell into deep water. A man some distance away saw what happened and ran to the water, plunged in, and dragged the boy to the shore. Artificial respiration was applied and the boy's life was saved.

Later, in childlike language but with obvious sincerity, the youth warmly thanked his benefactor for saving his life. The hero did not respond immediately, but stood looking into the eyes of the boy, a strange expression on his face. When he finally spoke, he said, "That's all right, Son. I'm glad I was able to do it. Just see to it that you are worth saving."

We pass on an identical admonition to all the redeemed who read these lines. You have been saved from the bitter consequences of sin and its eternal damnation. You have been made a saint in redemption. Heaven is your home. Now prove that you were worth saving by living a life "full of faith" in Christ Jesus.

III. PAUL'S SALUTATION: GRACE AND PEACE!

Paul saluted these who were saints in position and faithful in practice: "Grace be to you, and peace, from God our Father, and from the Lord Jesus Christ" (vs. 2).

A. Grace

This word is found thirteen times in the six chapters of Ephesians. D. L. Moody, the great soul winner and evangelist, is said to have walked up to a stranger on the street one day, inquiring, "Good morning, my friend. Do you know Grace?"

"Grace who?" the startled stranger responded.

"The grace of God!" said Moody, then began immediately to talk about our Lord's "so great salvation" (Heb. 2:3).

What is grace? A common definition is "unmerited favor," but it is much more than that. Grace is unmerited favor *where punishment is due*. Someone has described it as **G-R-A-C-E**, meaning, **G**od's **R**iches **A**t **C**hrist's **E**xpense. John Henry Jowett defined grace as "the energy of divine holiness issuing forth in love to the unlovely, creating in the unlovely its own loveliness continuously." What a beautiful description!

In one of Manford George Gutzke's many books he relates an experience of a missionary friend serving in what was then the African Congo. Busy translating portions of the New Testament into the dialect of his people, he had been stymied in trying to discover a native word for grace. During an audience with the tribal chief he observed a maid accidentally step on the king's leopard skin. In this tribe it was a definite "no no" to even touch the monarch's leopard skin, to say nothing of stepping on it, and the act made the girl liable for serious and dire consequences.

However, the tribal chieftan merely picked up his scepter and held it out to the maid, she touched the tip, and the ruler spoke a single word of forgiveness. The girl smiled with relief, freed from all fear of reprisal, and continued about her duties. The excited missionary realized he had discovered the word he wanted, had the chief repeat it to make sure he had it right, then explained, "That is what God does for us in salvation!"

Wondering why he had not heard the word used by any of the tribesmen about forgiveness before, he learned from the chief that it was a word only he could use, since it meant, "The king pardons you." The missionary had found the perfect word in the native dialect to indicate the divine pardon from the hand of the heavenly King.

Perhaps a good illustration from the Bible of grace being a king's pardon is seen in David's action toward Mephibosheth, recorded in II Samuel 9. It is what David called "the kindness of God" (vs. 3). Note three things:

(1) This "kindness of God" was help for the helpless. In the case of Mephibosheth, he was lame in both feet. In our case, we stand before God as hopelessly helpless sinners, completely bereft of anything and everything that would gain us favor in the sight of a holy God.

(2) This "kindness of God" was help for another's sake. In the case of Mephibosheth, David was showing kindness because of his love for Jonathan. In our case, the grace of God is extended to us by the Father in behalf of His Son. As I John 2:12 explains it: "I write unto you, little children, because your sins are forgiven you for his name's sake."

(3) This "kindness of God" resulted in a place at the king's table (vs. 13), the position of honor usually reserved for the king's family. In the case of Mephibosheth, it was a seat at King David's table. In our case, we have a seat reserved at the banquet table of the King of kings. No wonder John was instructed to write, "Blessed are they which are called unto the marriage supper of the Lamb" (Rev. 19:9).

This is grace, indeed.

However, the grace of which Paul speaks in the salutation of Ephesians is primarily *daily* grace, not *saving* grace. This is the kind of grace outlined in Hebrews 4:15,16, where we are told: "For we have not an high priest which cannot be touched with the feeling of our infirmities; but was in all points tempted like as we are, yet without sin. Let us therefore come boldly unto the throne of grace that we may obtain mercy and find grace to help in time of need."

One time the famous Rowland Hill found an elderly Scotch gentleman looking very intently upon his face. Hill inquired, "My good man, why are you studying my face so seriously?"

The observer replied, "I am examining the lines."

"And what do you make of them?"

"Why, I make out," said he, "that if the grace of God had not changed your heart, you would have been a great rascal."

"Ah," said Hill, "you have made out the truth indeed."

So it is with every one of us! It not only takes grace to save us, it takes grace to keep us and to make us victorious.

Someone asked D. L. Moody, when he was in Milwaukee for a weekend of special services, "Do you think you have grace enough to be burned at the stake?"

Moody replied, "No, I know I do not."

His interrogator went on, "Don't you wish you had?"

"No," the famous revivalist replied, "for I do not need it. All I need right now is grace to live in Milwaukee three days and conduct meetings for my Saviour."

B. Peace!

Years ago an art institution offered a prize for the best picture on the subject of peace. One gifted artist painted a remarkable picture of a battlefield. He vividly portrayed cannons and guns muted, the dead and wounded being carried away, and the triumphant soldiers happily started on their journey home.

It did not win the award.

The painting given first place portrayed a robin in her nest among some branches overhanging Niagara Falls. Ignoring the danger of the dashing cataract beneath her nest, seemingly oblivious to the roaring rush of water, the red-breasted bird was a perfect picture of contentment and peace.

It is that way with the peace God offers. It matters not that troubled waters rage about the individual, or that alarming dangers threaten on every side. The soul right with God has peace, perfect peace, regardless of outward circumstances.

Not many today experience such peace. On the contrary, millions are gulping down tranquilizing pills—"Happy Pills," they call them—in record numbers, seeking to relieve multifold worries and tensions. Although one psychiatrist called them "peace-of-mind" pills, they usually leave their users in much worse shape than they were before the remedy had been prescribed!

Dr. Walter L. Wilson tells of interviewing a bank vice-president who told him he had been earnestly and honestly seeking peace for many years. He said, "I have joined five different denominations seeking peace. I have not found it. I am about to give up hope. It seems as though God does not want to give me peace. What can you tell me?"

Wilson replied, "My friend, you will never find peace as long as you are seeking it. You are seeking the wrong thing. You want God's *gift*, but God wants you to take the *Giver* of the gift. Christ Jesus is the Prince of Peace and peace is His prerogative. He will not give you the gift unless you take Himself, for 'He is our peace.' "

The banker broke down in tears and exclaimed, "Why didn't any of these people tell me to take Jesus Christ? I would have taken Him long ago." And then and there he made his surrender to Christ.

Christ is the *only* source of peace. As the poet exulted:

> He giveth peace!
> Though storms may rage, the billows roll
> And beat upon thy weary soul;
> Though skies be dark and overcast,
> The storm will not forever last.
> He giveth peace!
> Dear restless heart, be still and know
> That He who walked life's path below
> Will surely understand and care,
> And all thy heavy burden share.
> Thy loving Father knows thy heart;
> He sees the tears that often start;
> With arms outstretched He yearns for thee
> To come to Him that you might see—
> He giveth peace!
> Whatever He may send, 'tis best;
> It may be that it's meant to test
> Thy willingness to follow Him.
> Press onward then, though faith be dim!
> He giveth peace!

Dr. John R. Rice tells of a man who came to his home after an unsuccessful suicide attempt. He was in bad shape. His wife and family had left him, he had no home or job, his health was broken with an incurable disease, and he felt like he could not go on. After the preacher had pointed him to Christ, the new convert sat up and exclaimed, "Isn't it strange?"

Dr. Rice asked, "What is strange?"

He said, "I was so worried, so fretful and despairing; I thought I couldn't live, couldn't face another day. But now that is all gone and I feel so peaceful and happy, just like I didn't have a care in the world. Isn't that strange?"

And, of course, Dr. Rice replied, "No, that isn't strange at all. Jesus said, 'Come unto me, all ye that labour and are heavy laden, and I will give you rest. Take my yoke upon you and learn of me; for I am meek and lowly in heart: and ye shall find rest unto your souls.' You have found rest for your soul." Thus it is.

Here, just as in other passages in Scripture, grace is mentioned before peace. Why does peace always *follow* grace in scriptural order? Because there can be no peace until grace is experienced.

Isaiah 57:20,21, describes a soul apart from God's grace: "But the wicked are like the troubled sea, when it cannot rest, whose waters cast up mire and dirt. There is no peace, saith my God, to the wicked." But after grace has been manifested in salvation, we are able to say, "Therefore being justified by faith, we have peace with God through our Lord Jesus Christ" (Rom. 5:1). People today are frantically seeking peace. But it does not come of itself; it is the result, the fruit of grace.

Again, however, this is not primarily peace *with* God, it is the peace *of* God. This is daily peace, not saving peace. It is the kind of peace our Lord had—*and the disciples should have had*—during the storm on the sea (Mark 4:35-41). Mark tells us "there arose a great storm of wind, and the waves beat into the ship, so that it was now full," but when the disciples aroused the Master with the accusation, "Carest thou not that we perish?" He rebuked them as fearful and faithless.

Why?

Because they should have trusted the Saviour's word! He had said to them, "Let us pass over unto the other side." He did not say, "Let us go out into the middle of the sea and drown." They had His word that they were going "to the other side." They could not go *under* for going *over*! When that truth grips the soul, all the storms of this world's seas cannot trouble the heart or fill the soul with anxiety. Such a believer has, instead, what the hymn writer, W. D. Cornell, exultantly described as

> Peace! Peace! Wonderful peace,
> Coming down from the Father above;
> Sweep over my spirit forever, I pray,
> In fathomless billows of love.

C. From God Our Father

The apostle describes the Source of this daily grace and daily peace as "God our Father."

Whose Father?

Ours!

He is the Father of "the saints." He is the Father of "the faithful in Christ Jesus."

Incidentally, this is another manifestation of grace—that we are permitted to call Him "Father."

D. From the Lord Jesus Christ

Actually, the second "from" is not in the text; it was supplied by the translators, as indicated through their use of italics. This is a case where the supplied word would have been better omitted. The source of grace and peace is not twofold, it is singular.

Dear friend, let me warn you that there is no other source of grace and peace. These twin blessings can be secured from no one else, from nothing else. Dr. R. A. Torrey tells of an infidel judge to whom Moody witnessed, but did not win. However, the judge could not get away from the tender words of earnest warning the evangelist had given him and, one night when his wife was in prayer meeting, he became extremely agitated about his lost condition. When his wife returned home, he explained that he did not feel well and was going to retire for the night.

The next morning he felt even worse and excused himself from breakfast, saying he was still ill and would go immediately to the office. After arriving at work, he felt so miserable he told his clerks they could have the day off. After they left, he went into his inner office and sat down, feeling more and more miserable as he thought of his sins. Finally, he threw himself on his knees and cried out, "O God, forgive my sins."

Since he was a Unitarian and did not believe in the atonement, his petition was just in a general sense. Repeatedly he cried out in anguish, "O God, forgive my sins." But there was no answer; there was no peace.

Finally, he became in such distress of soul that he cried out, "O God, *for Jesus Christ's sake*, forgive my sins!" Immediately, as he later testified, he experienced God's wonderful peace.

There is no other *source* of peace and no other *basis* of peace. In John 14:27, Jesus said, "Peace I leave with you, my peace I give unto you: not as the world giveth, give I unto you. Let not your heart be troubled, neither let it be afraid." And Isaiah 26:3 adds, "Thou wilt keep him in perfect peace, whose mind is stayed on thee: because he trusteth in thee."

Before leaving Paul's salutation, we might emphasize the Redeemer's full title: *"the Lord Jesus Christ"*! As Sir Robert Anderson once said, "Never again speak of 'Jesus,' it suits the Unitarian too well, and the critical student as well; employ the biblical phrase 'the Lord Jesus Christ.' Defend His claim; decry His critics; declare His deity."

IV. THE APOSTOLIC BLESSING!

Paul said: "Blessed be the God and Father of our Lord Jesus Christ, who hath blessed us with all spiritual blessings in heavenly places in Christ."

A. "Blessed Be the God and Father of Our Lord Jesus Christ"

Actually, this is a doxology. It is the start of a grand hymn of praise that continues through the 14th verse. Some have called it the "benedictus" of the New Testament.

Since this doxology is properly the beginning of the epistle, we think it is significant that Ephesians starts with praise. A Christian's communion with his Lord should always start thusly, whether it be in prayer, in worship, in service, or in something else.

Why is the Father described as the "God" of our Lord? The answer lies in the fact that Christ became man!

Why is God described as the "Father" of our Lord? The answer lies in the fact that Christ is God the Son from all eternity. This same relationship is seen in our Lord's words to Mary in the Garden, after the resurrection: "Touch me not; for I am not yet ascended to my Father: but go to my brethren, and say unto them, I ascend unto my Father, and your Father; and to my God, and your God" (John 20:17).

Why did the Saviour go to the trouble of saying "unto my Father, and your Father; and to my God, and to your God"? Why didn't He simply say "unto our Father and to our God"? Because His relationship to God the Father is a different relationship than ours.

B. "Who Hath Blessed Us"

Note that this is not something that is going to happen—not some benefits we are to receive in Heaven. This is something *now!* This is blessing provided at Calvary and available immediately through His "so great salvation."

Spurgeon said that whenever he thought about his redemption, he felt like shouting in the language of Charles Wesley,

> "Oh, for a thousand tongues to sing
> My great Redeemer's praise!"

Then he told how his friend, Dr. Alexander Fletcher, had met a man one day who had just been released from prison. He was running, jumping, turning cartwheels, shouting, and waving his arms. Fletcher said, "What has happened to you? You seem to be tremendously happy."

And the man replied, "Ah, Sir, if you had been locked up for six months, and had just gotten out, you would be happy, too!"

That is exactly the point. When a soul is freed from the awesome prison house of sin, his life is filled with praise. He is indeed a "happy" man, which is what the word "blessed" means.

It is like the story told in verse:

> Not far from New York, in a cemetery lone,
> Closely guarding its grave, stands a simple headstone
> And all of its inscription is one word alone—
> **"FORGIVEN!"**
>
> No sculptor's fine art hath embellished its form,
> But constantly there through the calm and the storm,
> It beareth this word from a poor fallen one—
> **"FORGIVEN!"**
>
> It shows not the date of the silent one's birth,
> Reveals not his frailties, nor lies of his worth,
> But speaks out the tale from his few feet on earth—
> **"FORGIVEN!"**
>
> The death is unmentioned, the name is untold,
> Beneath lies the body, corrupted and cold,
> Above rests his spirit, at home in the fold—
> **"FORGIVEN!"**
>
> And when from Heaven the Lord shall descend,
> This stranger shall rise, into Glory ascend,
> Well known and befriended, to sing without end—
> **"FORGIVEN!"**

No wonder the angel who announced the Saviour's birth to the shepherds declared: "Fear not: for, behold, I bring you good tidings of great joy, which shall be to all people. For unto you is born this day in the city of David a Saviour, which is Christ the Lord" (Luke 2:10,11).

C. "With All Spiritual Blessings"

This is reminiscent of Peter's words, "According as his divine power hath given unto us ALL THINGS THAT PERTAIN UNTO LIFE AND GODLINESS, through the knowledge of him that hath called us to glory and virtue" (II Pet. 1:3).

The inheritance of the saints of the Lord is certainly different from the relatives of one man whose safety deposit box was discovered to contain nothing but a sandwich and a note: "For my hungry relatives!" How we need, as the writer urged us, to count our many blessings—*name them one by one.*

Years ago I clipped from an unknown source someone's evaluation of what actually happened the moment he trusted Christ.

He wrote: "I was received by a Person (John 6:37). I was accepted in the Beloved (Eph. 1:6). I received a Person (Col. 2:6). I was incorporated into the body of Christ (I Cor. 12:13). I was born from above (Titus 3:5-7). I became a child of God (John 1:12). I became a partaker of the divine nature (II Pet. 1:4). I became an heir of God (Rom. 8:17). I received pardon (Eph. 1:7). I was justified in His sight (Rom. 5:1). I was counted righteous before God (Rom. 5:19). I became free from condemnation (Rom. 8:1). I became a saint in Christ (Rom. 1:7). I became reconciled to God (Rom. 5:10). I became free from fear of death (Rom. 8:2). I was delivered from the law (Rom. 7:6). I became a spiritual priest (Rev. 1:6)."

Yes, **all this and Heaven, too!**

Paul, in the Ephesian passage, especially emphasizes the fact that we are chosen (vs. 4), sanctified (vs. 4), foreordained (vs. 5), adopted (vs. 5), accepted (vs. 6), redeemed (vs. 7), forgiven (vs. 7), enriched (vs. 8), enlightened (vs. 9), heirs (vs. 11), and sealed (vs. 13).

There is nothing lacking. We have all the Spirit-bestowed blessings. All things that pertain unto life and godliness are ours. As J. Hudson Taylor once wrote to a friend, "We are getting along well; we have 87 cents, plus the promises of God."

Now it is up to us to possess the possessions that are ours to possess in Christ. Their availability means nothing if they are not claimed. Some one tells of a miserable old man who lived in a shanty and subsisted on whatever he could beg. Eventually his condition deteriorated to the place where it was necessary that he be hospitalized. The nurse who removed his clothing found a worn paper hidden in an inner pocket. Examination showed it to be an order on the United States Treasury, granting the man a comfortable pension in lieu of his service as a scout during the war between the States.

The old man excitedly called to the nurse, "Please don't take that away from me! President Lincoln gave me that and I value it above everything else." He *valued* it, but he never *claimed* it. He had never cashed in its worth or availed himself of its blessing.

Many Christians are like that. They have an invaluable inheritance for this life, yet it is treated as an object to be admired rather than an instrument to be used.

D. "In Heavenly Places"

This phrase is found five times in Ephesians, yet it is used nowhere else in all the Word of God. It is literally "in the heavenlies," and the expression has been called "the masterkey to the meaning of the epistle."

Paul wrote in the same vein to the saints of Colosse, saying: "If ye then be risen with Christ, seek those things which are above, where Christ sitteth on the right hand of God. Set your affection on things above, not on things on the earth" (Col. 3:1,2).

E. "In Christ"

Right here, dear friends, is the secret, the sum of it all: **IN HIM!**

This word "in" occurs in the original eighty-nine times in this epistle, and it is supplied an additional four times by the translators as being in harmony with the sense of what Paul was saying.

Note that it is not "with" Christ, but "in" Christ. This is the believer's *continual* position "in the heavenlies in Christ." What the Negroes meant when they sang in their spiritual, "sometimes I'm up, sometimes I'm down," has nothing to do with this. We are always up. It is the *fact* of our position in Him. Christ is there in the heavenlies and God sees us in Him. This is why all the treasures of Heaven are at our disposal.

Did you hear about the minister who preached on the theme, "Dressed Up in Jesus"? It wasn't much of a sermon, but he repeated the phrase again and again, "Dressed Up in Jesus." Even when he said something that was not related to it, he would exclaim, "I'm dressed up in Jesus!" By the time he had finished his discourse, the hearers were rejoicing in the fact that they were clothed in the righteousness of God, with all the inheritance of redemption at their disposal.

Conclusion

Surely the most important question anyone could possibly ask another human soul is: "Are you in Christ?" Second Corinthians 5:17 says, "Therefore if any man be in Christ, he is a new creature: old things are passed away; behold, all things are become new."

This is not a question of works; it is not a matter of self-righteousness; morals are not the issue; baptism and church membership are not the determining factor. It is: **"Are you in Christ?"**

While we are asking questions, here is one to Christians: Are you possessing the wealth, the riches that are yours to claim in your Saviour and His so great salvation? Oh, that we might enter fully into the blessings provided for us at Calvary.

One time a preacher of extremely modest means was asked to perform the wedding ceremony for a very rich man. Quite naturally, the clergyman and his wife speculated on what kind of a fee he would receive. While the wedding was a huge affair and gifts from the groom were in keeping with the event, instead of a check or an envelope containing cash, the preacher was presented with a pair of kid gloves. Suppressing his disappointment, he went home and showed the gift to his wife. They half-jokingly made some light banter, then the preacher tossed the gloves into a dresser drawer and promptly forgot them.

It was not until months later, when he was leaving for a convention in a different city, that his wife suggested he wear the new gloves. When he agreed and started to put them on, he found his finger blocked. Investigating by turning one of the fingers inside out, he discovered a ten dollar bill. That was when his wife took over and her excited examination showed a ten dollar bill in each of the gloves' ten fingers!

Now, the gentleman had one hundred dollars in his possession all of the time, but the money was of no actual use or value to him. As a matter of fact, he did not even know he possessed this wealth. Thus it is, I fear, in the case of many Christians. They have almost no awareness of the wealth which belongs rightfully to them, wrapped up in God's "so great salvation."

Yes, how great is Paul's high calling. . .*and ours*!

Work of the Trinity in Our Redemption

According as he hath chosen us in him before the foundation of the world, that we should be holy and without blame before him in love:

Having predestinated us unto the adoption of children by Jesus Christ to himself, according to the good pleasure of his will,

To the praise of the glory of his grace, wherein he hath made us accepted in the beloved.

In whom we have redemption through his blood, the forgiveness of sins, according to the riches of his grace;

Wherein he hath abounded toward us in all wisdom and prudence;

Having made known unto us the mystery of his will, according to his good pleasure which he hath purposed in himself:

That in the dispensation of the fulness of times he might gather together in one all things in Christ, both which are in heaven, and which are on earth; even in him:

In whom also we have obtained an inheritance, being predestinated according to the purpose of him who worketh all things after the counsel of his own will:

That we should be to the praise of his glory, who first trusted in Christ.

In whom ye also trusted, after that ye heard the word of truth, the gospel of your salvation: in whom also after that ye believed, ye were sealed with that holy Spirit of promise,

Which is the earnest of our inheritance until the redemption of the purchased possession, unto the praise of his glory.—Ephesians 1:4-14.

The doctrine of the Trinity is one of the most vital tenets of the Christian faith. It is a cornerstone apart from which our whole theological system would collapse. How there can be three distinct Persons but only one God has been a deep and dark mystery to multitudes, although it has been aptly illustrated in many ways. A man may have *many* sheep, but only **one** flock. There are *many* bananas in **one** bunch. There are often *several* equal partners in **one** business. We have *fifty* separate states in our **one** great nation. A shell, white and yolk comprise **one** egg.

However, none of these, while illustrating that many can be separate and yet one, exemplifies the trinitarian relationship. It is in the tiny atom that we see it best exemplified. The atom consists of proton, electron and neutron. The proton is a positive charge of electricity; the electron is a negative charge; and the neutron is, as indicated by its name, without charge. Each is a distinct entity. As a matter of fact, the atom is such a perfect trinitarian relationship that the late Dr. V. C. Oltrogge said one could, without irreverence, paraphrase I John 5:7: "For there are three basic particles that manifest themselves in the atom—the electron, the proton, and the neutron; and these three are one—one atom."

In what Paul called "the Godhead" (Col. 2:9) are three separate, distinct persons: Father, Son and Holy Spirit. Paul introduced this Trinity in the opening verses of Ephesians, saying: *"Blessed be the God and Father of our Lord Jesus Christ, who hath blessed us with all spiritual blessings in heavenly places in Christ"* (vs. 3). He spoke of God, that is, the Father; he spoke of the Lord Jesus Christ, that is, the Son and he referred to spiritual blessings—or, as the Amplified alternate reading gives it, "Holy Spirit given" blessings—that is the Holy Spirit.

In our text, Paul is pointing out that the redemption of the child of God is dependent upon no one personality of the Trinity, but on all three. Sometimes happy Christians say, "I am saved. Praise Jesus!" But it is not just "Praise Jesus"; it is equally

"Praise the Father," and, "Praise the Holy Spirit!" The Son's part in our redemption would not be complete without the Father's part and the Holy Spirit's part. The Father's part would not be adequate without the portion provided by the Son and by the Holy Spirit. And the Holy Spirit's part would be insufficient apart from the Father's share and the Son's share. It is the Trinity to whom we are indebted for salvation.

Paul commences this passage with what seems to be a key word, **"according."** He points out that we have spiritual blessings *"according* as he hath chosen us in him" (vs. 4). He tells us that we have divine sonship *"according* to the good pleasure of his will' (vs. 5). He says our redemption is *"according* to the riches of his grace" (vs. 7). He tells us the mystery of God's will is made known *"according* to his good pleasure which he hath purposed in himself" (vs. 9). And he reminds us that we have an inheritance *"according* to the purpose of him who worketh all things after the counsel of his own will" (vs. 11).

The atonement provided by the Trinity is a complete atonement. As Augustus M. Toplady wrote so beautifully:

> From whence this fear and unbelief?
> Hath not the Father put to grief
> > His spotless Son for me?
> And will the Righteous Judge of men
> Condemn me for that debt of sin
> > Which, Lord, was charged on Thee?
>
> Complete atonement Thou hast made,
> And to the utmost farthing paid,
> > Whate'er Thy people owed;
> How then can wrath on me take place,
> If sheltered in Thy righteousness,
> > And sprinkled with Thy blood?
>
> If Thou hast my discharge procured,
> And freely in my room endured
> > The whole of wrath Divine;
> Payment God cannot twice demand—
> First at my bleeding Surety's hand,
> > And then again at mine.
>
> Turn then, my soul, unto thy rest!
> The merits of thy great High Priest
> > Have bought thy liberty;
> Trust in His efficacious blood,

> Nor fear thy banishment from God,
> Since Jesus died for thee.

I. THE WORK OF GOD THE FATHER

This is summed up:

"According as he hath chosen us in him before the foundation of the world, that we should be holy and without blame before him in love: Having predestinated us unto the adoption of children by Jesus Christ to himself, according to the good pleasure of his will, To the praise of the glory of his grace, wherein he hath made us accepted in the beloved."—vss. 4-6.

A. Choosing Us!

Consider this choosing, or selecting, first of all in the negative. Paul did not mean that God selected certain ones to be saved and certain ones to be damned, merely on the basis of His own whims. This choosing was, as Peter tells us, "according to the foreknowledge of God the Father" (I Pet. 1:2). Abundant are the statements assuring all mankind that God longs for each one to be saved.

Peter charged the men of Jerusalem: "Ye denied the Holy One and the Just, and desired a murderer to be granted unto you; And killed the Prince of life. . ." (Acts 3:14,15). Yet they were the very ones over whom the Lord Jesus bared His agonized soul in tears, crying, "O Jerusalem, Jerusalem, thou that killest the prophets, and stonest them which are sent unto thee, how often would I have gathered thy children together, even as a hen gathereth her chickens under her wings, and ye would not" (Matt. 23:37). Obviously, since God is not willing that any should perish, the fact that some are lost and some are saved has a logical basis in the mind and plan of God.

This is indicated in the words "he hath chosen." Intelligent choices are based upon reason. If a man chooses a Ford over a Chevrolet, he has some reason for his choice. Perhaps it is the style, perhaps the type of motor, perhaps it has to do with the price—but there is a reason behind his choice. Yet some would have us think God chose certain ones in redemption without any logical basis for so choosing. This simply is not so. Anyway, Paul is not saying here that He chose anyone *to be saved.* But this choosing is that "we should be holy and without blame before him."

Paul points out also that this selection was made "before the foundation of the world." Just as in the mind of God the Lamb was slain from the foundation of the world (Rev. 13:8; I Pet. 1:20), so the redeemed were chosen in Him at the same time.

Contrary to what some people seem to think about it, God's provision for man's redemption was not a makeshift, emergency plan. Some have the idea that it was something like a chess game where one player makes his move, then the other player tries to outwit the first in his move. Oh, no! This was not a battle of wits between God and Satan, with humans mere pawns on the board. The end was known in eternity past by God who has "from the beginning chosen you to salvation through sanctification of the Spirit and belief of the truth" (II Thess. 2:13).

Plans for this building (see 2:21, 22) were drawn by the Master Architect long in advance. Just as when a giant skyscraper is built in our day, long before the first spadeful of dirt is turned for the foundation the architect has designed and planned every facet of the building, so God, in His infinite wisdom, planned every aspect of redemption.

A story is told concerning the architect who designed the Brooklyn Bridge more than one hundred years ago. Injured and hospitalized during the construction of the span, after it was completed he had friends carry him on a stetcher to examine, the best he could, every detail. Finally, he happily exclaimed, "It is just according to plans!" How much more is this true of God's building.

J. Danson Smith wrote:

> Amazing Grace—that in the past—
> Back in eternities so vast,
> The Father God His Son should slay—
> The sin of unborn man to pay:
> And in that act included me—
> I wonder much—how could it be.

> Amazing Grace—that He the Son,
>   The blessed and Eternal One,
> Should leave at length the hallowed bliss
>   Of Heaven's unsullied righteousness
> And come to earth and take the place
>   Of every man of Adam's race.
>
> Well might angelic hosts have wept
>   When Christ to God His promise kept;
> And heavenly choirs had ceased to sing
>   At sight of Christ's dark suffering.
> 'Tis all, indeed, too deep to trace;
>   We can but say—"Amazing Grace."[1]

Remember that this choosing was so we might "be holy and without blame before him." This, obviously, is something completely impossible in ourselves. Since we are told that any act of rebellion (James 4:17), any act of lawlessness (I John 3:4), any manifestation of unrighteousness (I John 5:17), any lack of faith (Rom. 14:23), and even the plowing of the wicked (Prov. 24:9) is sin, how unholy and full of blame each stands in himself. John reminds us: "If we say that we have no sin, we deceive ourselves, and the truth is not in us. . . .If we say that we have not sinned, we make him a liar and his word is not in us" (I John 1:8,10).

In the light of this, could any claim to be "holy" or "without blame" in himself? Especially is this impossible since it is not "before our neighbors," or other mere mortals, but "before him."

Yet this is our position "in Christ" because of His work on the cross. We are told in II Corinthians 5:21, "For he hath made him to be sin for us, who knew no sin; that we might be made the righteousness of God in him." Hence, as Romans 4:8 tells us, God will not charge any sin to us. Paul quotes David enthusiastically in that verse, "Blessed is the man to whom the Lord will not impute sin."

B. Predestinating Us

Paul expressed it: "Having predestinated us unto the adoption of children by Jesus Christ to himself according to the good

---

[1] From 742 HEART-WARMING POEMS, compiled and edited by John R. Rice. Copyright, 1964, by Sword of the Lord Publishers. Used by permission.

pleasure of his will." This predestination is best understood by adding the closing two words of the previous verse: "...**in love** having predestinated us." Since this is a predestination of love, it in no way contradicts the many "whosoever will" invitations in the Word of God.

One Easter time in California, a Sunday school teacher was explaining to her class that Easter was also an important time in the Jewish religion. Pointing out that it was the Passover to them, she asked, "Does anyone know what that is?"

A little girl piped up: "We have a boy in our family who was born on the twenty-ninth of February, and he gets passed over all the time."

There are some who think that this is the story of predestination; that is, God passed over some and selected some others. *No,* **no!** "In love" the offer is made to all and those who respond are, by God's foreknowledge, elected. As Paul described it in Romans 8:29,30: "For whom he did foreknow, he also did predestinate to be conformed to the image of his Son, that he might be the firstborn among many brethren. Moreover whom he did predestinate, them he also called: and whom he called, them he also justified: and whom he justified, them he also glorified."

This loving predestination was "unto the adoption of children...to himself." The word *adoption* here is "son-placing." It refers to the custom in ancient times wherein a man took to the forum the children he wanted as heirs and had them recognized as legally his. They were his children both by birth and by son-placing. So we are born into the family of God (children by birth), and are legally placed as sons before the courts of Heaven (adopted as children).

The key, of course, is in the words "by Jesus Christ." Galatians 4:4,5 tells us: "But when the fulness of the time was come, God sent forth his Son, made of a woman, made under the law, To redeem them that were under the law, that we might receive the adoption of sons." Or, as Galatians 3:26 expresses it: "For ye are all the children of God by faith in Christ Jesus." There simply is no other way possible to share in the blessings of eternity.

Paul also tells us that this loving predestination is "according to the good pleasure of his will." As he said in Philippians 2:13, "For it is God which worketh in you both to will and to do of his good pleasure." The good pleasure of our will would lead us into trouble and despair, but the good pleasure of His will is always the best. This is one reason why it is so important to pray according to our Lord's example, and to mean sincerely, "Nevertheless not what I will, but what thou wilt" (Mark 14:36).

C. Accepting Us

The work of the Father in our redemption was not only in *choosing* and *predestinating,* but also in *accepting.* Verse 6 says, "To the praise of the glory of his grace, wherein he hath made us accepted in the beloved." This is, literally, "he hath taken us into favor in the beloved."

The only other time this word is found in the Bible is with reference to the Virgin Mary. The angel saluted her, "Hail, thou that art highly favoured. . . ." (Luke 1:28). The moment a sinner is saved, he is "graciously accepted," or "highly favoured," just as was Mary. Incidentally, in this light it would be just as logical for Christians to say prayers to each other, hoping thereby to gain favor with God, as to say prayers to Mary in hopes that she could influence the Lord Jesus in one's behalf.

Paul points out also that this acceptance into the Beloved is that we might learn to praise the glory of His grace. As the psalmist said repeatedly, "Oh, that men would praise the Lord for his goodness, and for his wonderful works to the children of men!" (Ps. 107:8,15,21,31).

II. THE WORK OF GOD THE SON!

The Son's work in our redemption is described in verses 7 through 12:

"In whom we have redemption through his blood, the forgiveness of sins, according to the riches of his grace; Wherein he hath abounded toward us in all wisdom and prudence; Having made known unto us the mystery of his will, according to his good pleasure which he hath purposed in

himself: That in the dispensation of the fulness of times he might gather together in one all things in Christ both which are in heaven, and which are on earth; even in him: In whom also we have obtained an inheritance, being predestinated according to the purpose of him who worketh all things after the counsel of his own will: That we should be to the praise of his glory, who first trusted in Christ."

How much we owe the Son! Sometime ago a roving reporter asked six people in New York City: "What was the most important happening in history?" Five of the replies, coming from two men and three ladies, were: "The invention of the wheel," "The defeat of the Japanese," "The splitting of the atom," "The defeat of the Saracens at Tours," and, "The settlement of Jamestown by the English."

However, the answer given by a fourteen-year-old schoolboy showed more wisdom than the other five combined. He simply replied: "The birth of Jesus Christ." We suppose he meant everything involved in that first coming; that is, all of His work in our redemption.

A. Purchasing Our Souls!

Paul says: "In whom we have redemption through his blood, the forgiveness of sins, according to the riches of his grace; Wherein he hath abounded toward us in all wisdom and prudence" (vss. 7,8). There are three words in our New Testament which are translated "redemption." The one used here means "to be loosed." In Christ we have been loosed from sin, loosed from the curse of the law, and loosed from the wrath and judgment of God our sins deserved.

A couple was saved in Michigan one Sunday morning. As they came out of the inquiry room, the lady gripped the hand of the pastor and said, "The blood of Jesus Christ did today what $6,000 could not do."

Going on, she explained, "I'll tell you what I mean. My husband has been the victim of a sin on which we have spent $6,000 trying to get him released. Today the blood of Christ did what the $6,000 could not do."

Incidentally, notice that Paul's statement is in the present tense. He enthuses, "In whom **we have** redemption. . . ." It is not something to *be* received, perhaps, on some far-off judgment morning. It is a present possession for the child of God.

How could such a glorious redemption be made available to grievous sinners? The price is described as "through his blood." Peter explained it, "Who his own self bare our sins in his own body on the tree. . . ." At an Arbor Day meeting at the University of Maryland, a man from the Bartlett Tree Expert Company, pointing out the value of trees for breaking wind, deadening noises, screening unsightly sights from view, as well as enhancing the beauty of property, estimated that a single shade tree to a home owner might be worth as much as $10,000. But who can estimate the value of the tree on which the Son of God was crucified?

Speaking of crucifixion, this was a most degrading thing and considered shameful beyond words. The great Cicero once said about it: "The very name should be excluded from the thoughts, eyes and ears of a Roman citizen. It is a crime to bind a Roman citizen, but what shall I say about lifting him on a cross. No word can adequately describe such a nefarious thing." Yet the Son of God gladly and joyfully went to the cross. Talking about laying down His life, He said: *"No man taketh it from me, but I lay it down of myself. I have power to lay it down, and I have power to take it again. This commandment have I received of my Father"* (John 10:18).

Can you fathom what Christ did in removing our sin debt through the shedding of His blood?

Back in the early struggling days of the United States, its national debt was almost entirely an amount owed to France. The latter country, in the throes of a costly revolution, demanded the payment, a sum totaling $2,024,899.93. Our government did not have the money. However, an American millionaire by the name of James Swan, who had arrived as a penniless immigrant boy from Scotland at the age of eleven, realizing how good this country had been to him, decided to pay the entire debt himself. He did, writing to Washington on July 9, 1795, to say: "The entire American debt was paid and does not exist anymore." Noble as this was, how insignificant it is when compared to the paying of the debt of sin by the Son of God at the cross of Calvary.

Never lose sight of the fact that this redemption is **by blood.** A bloodless theology is a salvationless theology and leads straight to an eternal Hell. Hebrews 9:22 tells us, "And almost all things are by the law purged with blood; and without the shedding of blood is no remission."

One time a young man was ridiculing salvation by blood to an elderly saint of God. He called it a "slaughterhouse religion," a "gospel of gore," and used other terms of a kindred nature. He said, "I think if one follows Jesus as an example, he will be all right."

The saint replied, "All right, let's take the first step in following Him. The Bible says of Him, 'He did not sin,' He was perfect; He never sinned. He was absolute holiness personified. Son, can you take that step? Can you say, 'I follow Jesus in His perfection?' "

The young man answered honestly, "No, I cannot."

"Then," said the dear saint, "what you need is a Saviour. An example will not do for you."

Those who want to be saved by their good deeds and morality remind me of a preacher who was exhorting his hearers to exercise will power, turn over a new leaf, make a new start and through strength of character live the kind of life pleasing to God. One who listened was a fallen woman who had been in the depths of despair over her failure. She said to him, "Sir, your rope is not long enough for me."

Thank God, the blood of Jesus Christ is a rope long enough to reach any sinner, no matter how far down he has sunk into the depths of depravity. Bob Ripley tells us that a sprig of the Gerpicula Verticillita plant will purify a pail of stagnant water. But the blood of Jesus Christ will wash away every sin of any sinner who ever lived, if he will put his faith and trust in Him.

The late James H. McConkey tells of a missionary in Africa who went into an area where no white men had ever been before. One little lad, older than the other curious children, approached his side, took the missionary's white hand in his own, looked at it steadfastly for a few moments, then exclaimed, "Oh, Sir, won't you please tell me the name of the river where you wash your hands?" For the soul-purified saint, the answer is the "fountain filled with blood, drawn from Immanuel's veins."

This redemption through His blood is further described as "the forgiveness of sins." The psalmist declared: "For as the heaven is high above the earth, so great is his mercy toward them that fear him. As far as the east is from the west, so far hath he removed our transgressions from us" (103:11,12).

The distance from north to south and south to north can be measured, but not east from west. As the poet wrote:

> How far is the East from the West?
> It cannot be measured or proved;
> But farther than this, so the Bible tells me,
> My sins have fore'er been removed.
>
> How high are the heavens above?
> An infinite measureless space;
> But higher than this is the gift of God's love,
> So great is His mercy and grace.
>
> How deep are the depths of the sea?
> A fathomless measure you say;
> But farther than this, so my Saviour tells me,
> My sins are fore'er cast away.
>
> They're gone and forgotten by God,
> And God has removed every doubt;
> For covered by blood are my many transgressions,
> My sins are fore'er blotted out.
>
> "Return unto Me," saith the Lord
> For I have redeemed thee by blood,
> Thy name is engraved in the palms of My hands,
> And pardoned thou art, by thy God.
>
> To Him we would joyfully sing,
> Our praises to Him would ascend;
> Our Saviour, our Shepherd, our Priest and our King,
> Our True and unchangeable Friend.

Paul takes note of the fact that this redemption through His blood, even the forgiveness of sins, is "according to the riches of his grace."

One might go to a Rockefeller for a contribution to a worthy cause and expect a donation amounting to thousands of dollars, yet receive only a token gift of $25 or $50. For a Rockefeller that would be giving "out of" his riches, but not "according to" that wealth. God does not give *out of;* He gives *according to.* As already noted, someone has defined G-R-A-C-E as "**G**od's **R**iches **A**t **C**hrist's **E**xpense."

Pitch Lake, on the island of Trinidad, surely should be included among the wonders of the world. It resembles an inactive volcano and has a radius of one-half mile. The crater area is filled with asphalt hard enough to walk on, although in some places one can see bubbles on the surface where gas is escaping. Two crews of men with sharp picks dig into the asphalt, breaking it into large chunks weighing from 50 to 100 pounds each. These are loaded on trolley cars numbering eight to ten in a train, then hauled to a refinery.

The men do not dig any deeper than five or six feet and within 72 hours the spot where the asphalt has been removed is again filled to its original level, with no indication whatsoever that any asphalt has been removed. There is just as much asphalt in Pitch Lake as when the men began to excavate it three-quarters of a century ago. On one occasion operators drilled a hole in the center of the lake to try to ascertain the depth of the asphalt. When they had drilled 280 feet, there was so much pressure on the drill that the experiment was abandoned.

How illustrative of the grace of God and the blood of Christ made available to sinners! All down through the centuries men have been coming to the fountain filled with blood, finding complete cleansing for their sins, yet the cure is just as effective today as ever. The blood of Christ is an inexhaustible supply.

So much is this so that Paul says in verse 8, "Wherein he hath abounded toward us in all wisdom and prudence." God has **abounded** grace toward us! His abounding grace is manifested in all wisdom. That is His planning: wisely, perfectly, the best way. And He has abounded grace in all prudence. That is the executing of His plan: justly, holy, and with divine justice satisfied. Grace *is not* and *cannot be* the flaunting of the law.

John L. Baker beautifully expressed it in his song, "My Plea":

> Should I at the gates of Heaven appear
> To answer the challenge, "What claim hast thou here?
> What hast thou to offer, yea, what is thy plea?"
> With blessed assurance my answer would be:
>
> Of all earthly treasures nothing I've brought,
> No great deeds of merit have I ever wrought.
> Though vile and unworthy as mortal can be,
> I've nothing to offer, but this is my plea:
>
> My sins, they are many, my virtues are few.
> The blood of my Saviour will carry me through.
> When Christ in my place died on Calvary's tree,
> Hallelujah! That opened God's Heaven for me!
>
> All that I have is Jesus,
> All that I claim is Jesus,
> All that I want, all that I need,
> All that I plead is Jesus.

B. Revealing the Father's Purpose

Paul describes it:

"Having made known unto us the mystery of his will, according to his good pleasure which he hath purposed in himself: That in the dispensation of the fulness of times he might gather together in one all things in Christ, both which are in heaven, and which are on earth; even in him. . . ."—vss. 9,10.

Note that this "mystery of his will" is not something hidden, it is something "made known unto us."

What is that mystery? It is what Paul revealed in verse 10!

A dispensation is an "economy," an ordered condition of things. God has had different dispensations for different periods of time during man's habitation of this earth.

Saint Augustine once said: "Distinguish the ages, and the Scriptures are plain." This is what Paul, in his admonition to young Timothy about studying the Scripture, called "rightly dividing the word of truth" (II Tim. 2:15).

When Paul says "that he might gather together in one," he is not advocating a universal salvation philosophy, for he goes on to add the qualifying phrase: **"in Christ."** In other words, this mystery is the forming of the one body of Christ, which Paul deals with in much greater detail in a later chapter.

C. Providing an Inheritance

In verses 11 and 12, Paul says:

"In whom also we have obtained an inheritance, being predestinated according to the purpose of him who worketh all things after the counsel of his own will: That we should be to the praise of his glory, who first trusted in Christ."

The word "obtained" in verse 11 is literally "allotted." It has a twofold meaning. For one thing, just as in the Authorized Version, it is saying that those redeemed through the blood of Christ have obtained an inheritance. Paul says the same thing in Romans 8:16,17,

"The Spirit itself beareth witness with our spirit, that we are the children of God: And if children, then heirs; heirs of God, and joint-heirs with Christ; if so be that we suffer with him, that we may be also glorified together."

Peter agrees, saying to the sojourners of the dispersion:

"Blessed be the God and Father of our Lord Jesus Christ, which according to his abundant mercy hath begotten us again unto a lively hope by the resurrection of Jesus Christ from the dead,. To an inheritance incorruptible, and undefiled, and that fadeth now away, reserved in heaven for you, Who are kept by the power of God through faith unto salvation ready to be revealed in the last time. . . ."—I Pet. 1:3-5.

But this word *allotted* not only means we have received something, but as the Revised Version expresses it, "We were made a heritage." We not only *receive* something, we *are* something. We are His purchased possession, we are the joy that was set before Him which caused Him to endure the cross, despising the shame (Heb. 12:2). How easily this explains verse

12, "that we should be to the praise of his glory, who first trusted in Christ."

III. THE WORK OF GOD THE HOLY SPIRIT

The part of the Holy Spirit in our redemption is described in verses 13 and 14:

"In whom ye also trusted, after that ye heard the word of truth, the gospel of your salvation: in whom also after ye believed, ye were sealed with that holy Spirit of promise, Which is the earnest of our inheritance until the redemption of the purchased possession, unto the praise of his glory."

A. Opening Our Hearts to the Truth

This is indicated in the words "ye heard the word of truth." Here is the "being born of water" of John 3:5 and a pinpointing of the fact that faith comes only as the Holy Spirit uses the Word of Truth.

Dr. Lee Roberson tells of a church in Ohio which, in olden days, appointed two officers to help the preacher in its services of worship. One was called "Mr. Beaner" and the other "Mr. Pointer."

It was the task of the first officer to sit in a prominent place in the choir loft and scan the congregation during the sermon. Whenever he saw a parishoner about to drop off into the limbo of dreamland, he would lift his bean shooter to his lips and with one blow restore the delinquent to the ranks of the attentive. But it was Mr. Pointer's job, after the preacher emphasized a particularly pertinent point in the message, to single out the hearer whom the matter best suited, point and cry, "You there, John Smith, that applies to you!"

The Holy Spirit is the Mr. Pointer in any gospel service. When a faithful preacher presents the Word of God, the sweet Holy Spirit drives it to the heart and consciousness of the hearer, softly saying, "This applies to you."

B. Sealing Us When We Believed

Paul says, ". . .in whom also after that ye believed, ye were sealed with that holy Spirit of promise." Norman B. Harrison gives a threefold use and significance of this word *seal:* (1) A finished transaction; unchangeable when stamped with a seal. (2) A mark of ownership, such as in branding cattle. (3) A guarantee of safe delivery, as the seal of a package by an express company. All three are true, of course, when a sinner receives Christ as Saviour. His salvation is settled forever, that matter is unchangeable; he belongs to God as God's private property; and he is guaranteed a safe delivery in Heaven. The integrity of Almighty God stands behind the transaction.

Someone has used the illustration of logs being shipped from the timberland down the river to the sawmills. All the companies use the same river and oftentimes the logs are sent at the same time. In spite of this, there is no mixup regarding the ownership of the logs and each arrives at its proper destination.

How?

Every log carries the stamp of the company shipping it down the river and ownership is easily distinguished by those marks which penetrate into the end of the log. Thank God, the child of God has the mark, the brand of the Holy Spirit upon him and there will be no question about his destination or ownership when he leaves this world.

C. Becoming the "Earnest" of Our Inheritance

Paul says, regarding the Holy Spirit, in verse 14: "Which is the earnest of our inheritance until the redemption of the purchased possession, unto the praise of his glory."

This word *earnest* means a pledge, the part payment of a purchase which seals a bargain. It is as one might go into an automobile dealer's showroom, order a new automobile costing $5,000 and give the dealer a check for $1,000, promising him the balance on delivery of the automobile. That check for $1,000 would be the "earnest" in the transaction, the dealer's assurance that the balance will be paid on delivery. The indwelling Holy Spirit is God's pledge to us that eventually we will be fully conformed to the image of His dear Son.

Tom Malone says that when Fridtjof Nansen went to the North Pole, he took a homing pigeon with him. He had no contact whatsoever with the outside world and after two years he released the pigeon. Two thousand miles separated Nansen from his wife—a thousand miles of frozen water and ice, and a thousand miles over frozen wasteland. That little homing pigeon circled Nansen's camp two or three times and then headed south. For 2,000 miles it flew straight as an arrow to the Nansen home. When it arrived, Mrs. Nansen put it in the cage at home and gratefully exclaimed, "My husband is all right!"

When a sinner comes to Christ on the basis of His shed blood, the Heavenly Father sends His Dove of Peace to the heart of the Christian, as a permanent resident. The Holy Spirit dwells within him as a pledge, an earnest of his eventual safe arrival in the Land that is fairer than day. Not only so, but as another has said, "The Holy Spirit is a down payment, a guarantee to the believer that Heaven will bring all the human heart desires."

Paul closes his discussion regarding the Holy Spirit's work in our redemption, saying again, "unto the praise of his glory." God does not want us to ever forget that this is the purpose of His grace in us! So much is this so, He reminds us of it in describing each member of the Trinity's part in our redemption. Of the Father he said: "To the praise of the glory of his grace" (vs. 6). Of the Son he said, "That we should be to the praise of his glory" (vs. 12). And of the Holy Spirit, he said again, "Unto the praise of his glory" (vs. 14).

Conclusion

No wonder the Bible speaks of this salvation as a "so great salvation" (Heb. 2:3). The price God paid to provide it staggers the human imagination.

Not long before Pearl Harbor, the Gideons presented members of the Pacific Fleet with copies of the small, white New Testament they provide for Navy personnel. Inside the cover was stamped, **"To the Pacific Fleet of the United States Navy."**

Not long after the presentation was made, on December 7, 1941 (I am dictating these lines on the anniversary of that infamous day), the Japanese bombed the Pacific Fleet at Pearl Harbor and literally hundreds of young American men lost their lives. It was probably the single most disastrous day in American history.

On one occasion, when the late Dr. Harry Rimmer was talking about the work the Gideons were doing, he reached into his pocket and held high one of those white New Testaments, saying, "This is the kind of New Testament the Gideons are giving our men in the Navy."

After the service was over and others had finished talking with Dr. Rimmer, a man who had been standing in the background stepped up, pulling a white Testament from his pocket like the one Dr. Rimmer held up, but one with the unmistakeable brown stains of blood upon its cover. The man, fondling that small New Testament as if it were his most valuable possession, told Dr. Rimmer how his boy had stood at his post at Pearl Harbor until his body had been riddled with many bullets from the straffing planes. The father had found the Testament among the personal effects the Navy had sent home.

He said, "Dr. Rimmer, this is the most wonderful possession I own. This book is stained with the blood of my son."

Dr. Rimmer, greatly moved, not knowing for a moment what to say, pulled his own Testament from his pocket, held it up, and said, "And this one was stained with the blood of God's Son."

Oh, dear friend, the Word of God is a blood-stained Book. The message it contains has been made available to you at a tremendous price to God the Father, God the Son, and God the Holy Spirit. If you have never yet received Jesus Christ as your Lord and Saviour, do so in gratitude at once.

William Wordsworth wrote:

> Oh, Trinity, in unity! One only God and Persons Three
>   In Whom, through Whom, by Whom we live,
>   In Thee we praise and glory give.

Oh, grant to us to use Thy grace
That we may see Thy glorious face,
And ever with the heavenly host
 Praise Father, Son and Holy Ghost.

"Lord, Open Our Eyes!"

Wherefore I also, after I heard of your faith in the Lord Jesus, and love unto all the saints,

Cease not to give thanks for you, making mention of you in my prayers;

That the God of our Lord Jesus Christ, the Father of glory, may give unto you the spirit of wisdom and revelation in the knowledge of him:

The eyes of your understanding being enlightened; that ye may know what is the hope of his calling, and what the riches of the glory of his inheritance in the saints,

And what is the exceeding greatness of his power to us-ward who believe, according to the working of his mighty power,

Which he wrought in Christ, when he raised him from the dead, and set him at his own right hand in the heavenly places,

Far above all principality, and power, and might and dominion, and every name that is named, not only in this world, but also in that which is to come:

And hath put all things under his feet, and gave him to be the head over all things to the church,

Which is his body, the fulness of him that filleth all in all. — Ephesians 1:15-23.

The First Baptist Church of West Hollywood, Florida, was founded about 1955 by Dr. Elbert Bowers. When I first knew him—and held meetings for him—he was pastoring a little country church in North Florida.

One day he read in the Bible that God is no respecter of persons. Noting what mountains the Almighty moved for men like Abraham, David, Daniel and Paul, he determined to prove

Him by going to West Hollywood and launching a work.

He went to that city, cleaned off a lot and gathered a handful of people about him. They had a ground-breaking service and ordered nearly three thousand dollars' worth of concrete and steel, intending to put up the first small unit of what they hoped would someday be a great testimony. *They didn't have a single dime when they placed the order.*

The following Wednesday the supplier called and said, "Reverend, we've got to have a payment on those materials."

"When do you have to have it?"

"Tomorrow morning."

"How much do you have to have?"

"Eight hundred dollars."

"All right, we'll have it for you."

That night, when about 35 adults gathered for the mid-week service in the store building they were temporarily using for worship, Pastor Bowers read Hebrews 11:1 to his flock. He confessed to his people that he didn't fully understand it, but he was sure if God's people acted by faith, God would honor them.

Then he said, "How many of you believe that God hears and answers prayer?"

Thirty-five hands shot skyward.

"How many of you believe that God could hear and answer **your** prayer **tonight**?"

Again he beheld the picturesque sight of thirty-five upraised palms.

Then he queried, "How many of you believe that God would hear and answer your prayer tonight by giving us $800?"

The response was like the opening of the seventh seal— ". . .there was silence in heaven about the space of half an hour" (Rev. 8:1)—until finally a white-haired saint stood and said, "Pastor, I believe that if we ask God for this $800, He will give it to us."

Shortly, all thirty-five were on their faces, crying to God for the needed funds. After the prayer meeting was over and only a couple of the members were still standing around in came a man to confess, "I've lied to God. I promised Him that if He would allow me to build two homes and sell them for a profit, I would tithe it. He did, but I didn't. Here is my check for $500!"

In a little bit, in came another man with a check, then another, and another. When Dr. Bowers finally turned out the lights in that storefront building and went home, the treasurer was in possession of $818.42 not in hand a few hours before.

When I went to that church for meetings, they were running about 500 in Sunday school. Today Verle Ackerman is the pastor and they have over 2,000 in regular attendance.

God answers prayer!

The Apostle Paul *knew* it; he *believed* it; he *practiced* it. Our text comprises the first of two great Holy Spirit-inspired prayers that sprang from his passionate heart and flowed from his pungent pen in this epistle. The other is in 3:13-21 and both start with the word "wherefore."

A familiar law reminds us that when we run across a "wherefore" we should see *what it's there for!* While the "wherefore" in Paul's second prayer looks back to the church, God's hidden mystery, this "wherefore" looks back to the calling and position "in Christ" of the child of God. Paul is saying that since God has chosen, predestinated, accepted and redeemed them, since He has unfolded His mystery to them, given them an inheritance and sealed them by His Holy Spirit, they ought to have divine wisdom and revelation in order to fully appropriate all the spiritual blessings. As we might express it today, "We've got it! Now let's take advantage of it!"

Just as the second prayer in this epistle is a petition for love, so in this prayer Paul is praying for light. Surely every earnest Christian heart echoes the apostle's prayer and plea: "Lord, open our eyes!" As Clara H. Scott expressed it in song:

> Open my eyes, that I may see
> Glimpses of truth Thou hast for me;
> Place in my hands the wonderful key
> That shall unclasp and set me free.
> Silently now I wait for Thee,
> Ready, my God, Thy will to see;
> Open my eyes—illumine me,
> Spirit divine!

Paul prays especially for eyes to be opened in three areas: our calling, our inheritance and our power.

I. PAUL'S PRAYER

The apostle explains the gist of his prayer for the Ephesians, beginning with verse 15 continuing through the first clause of verse 16. The remainder of the passage is more the result of the prayer than the prayer itself. He said:

"Wherefore I also, after I heard of your faith in the Lord Jesus, and love unto all the saints, Cease not to give thanks for you, making mention of you in my prayers; That the God of our Lord Jesus Christ, the Father of glory may give unto you the spirit of wisdom and revelation in the knowledge of him: The eyes of your understanding being enlightened."

A. Thanksgiving

Paul expressed thankfulness to God for the Ephesian's faith in the Lord Jesus Christ. This was not only *saving* faith, although that was included, it was also *daily* faith. They trusted God about everything. They believed him when He spoke. Whatever He said, they accepted. Statements such as John 14:1, where Jesus said, "Let not your heart be troubled: ye believe in God, believe also in me," was a reality to them, not merely a funeral notation.

The Ephesian saints had untroubled hearts. As a matter of fact, such seemed to be a characteristic of New Testament saints. Paul referred to the faith of the Roman Christians as being "spoken of throughout the whole world" (Rom. 1:8). This is the kind of faith God wants His people today to manifest; yea, they *must* manifest it if they are to live victorious, triumphant lives.

As Paul told the Corinthians, "For we walk by faith, not by sight" (II Cor. 5:7). What our Lord told the two blind men, "According to your faith be it unto you" (Matt. 9:29), is the experience of 20th century Christianity.

Perhaps we need to point out that many people have many

kinds of faith in many things. We are not talking about this. The Christian's faith must be in the right *place,* and in the right *Person,* as Paul said about these Ephesians: "In the Lord Jesus" (vs. 15). While faith is not faith unless it is sincere, sincere faith is *foolish* faith, *futile* faith and *powerless* faith if it is not *right* faith.

However, Paul was not only grateful for their faith in the Lord Jesus, but also for their "love unto all the saints" (vs. 15). This reminds us of I John 3:14,15:

"We know that we have passed from death unto life, because we love the brethren. He that loveth not his brother abideth in death. Whosoever hateth his brother is a murderer: and ye know that no murderer hath eternal life abiding in him."

Nor let us forget I John 4:20,21:

"If a man say, I love God, and hateth his brother, he is a liar: for he that loveth not his brother whom he hath seen, how can he love God whom he hath not seen? And this commandment have we from him, That he who loveth God love his brother also."

No heart is big enough to harbor long both hate and love.

Incidentally, note that this love the Ephesians manifested was unto "all" the saints. Biblical Christianity should never be divided into cliques. While we freely admit that some saints are diamonds in the rough—and plenty rough at that—we are to play no favorites. In fact, some of the saints, by their actions toward us, may be especially difficult to love, but that is not the point.

It is said that on one occasion General Robert E. Lee was praising in the highest terms an officer to President Davis. Later, another officer, who had been greatly amazed at what Lee said, remarked to him, "General, don't you know the man of whom you spoke so highly to the President is one of your bitterest enemies and misses no chance to malign you?"

"Yes, I know," replied the South's great military statesman.

"But the President asked my opinion of him—not his opinion of me."

We think also of the man whose wild son had disgraced him and was told by a friend, "If that were my boy, I'd kick him out of my home." And the grieving father, whose love for his son could not be measured, replied, *"If he were your boy, so would I.* **But he is mine."**

It is such "family love" that children of God are to manifest for one another. If Christ could find anything in us to love, certainly we can find something in the most unlovable saint—*if we try*.

Noting the order might help us here: it is first faith, then love. Just as in Ephesians 1:2 we noted grace always comes before peace, so faith must always precede love. Perhaps this is why there is such a lack of love among the brethren today—*there is so little faith in Christ!* If your own love is weak, the way to correct it is by developing your faith.

Paul's thanksgiving was not an occasional matter, it was continual. He said he did not cease giving thanks. Such uninterrupted praise was what resulted in his earnest intercession.

B. The Supplication

Paul's petition to God was "that the God of our Lord Jesus Christ, the Father of glory, may give unto you the spirit of wisdom and revelation in the knowledge of him: The eyes of your understanding being enlightened. . ." (vss. 17,18, f.c.).

Note the person addressed: "The God of our Lord Jesus Christ." In verse three Paul spoke of "the God and Father of our Lord Jesus Christ." In this prayer he addresses his petition to *the God* of Christ; in the prayer of chapter three he addresses his intercession to *the Father* of Christ.

Why the difference? This prayer has to do with the counsels and purposes of God; the second prayer has to do with family relationships.

Paul here also refers to the God of Christ as "the Father of glory." Just as the Son is the Lord of Glory and the Holy Spirit is the Spirit of Glory, so with the Father. Incidentally, He is the

Father of Glory because He is the glorious Father.

What was the purpose Paul had in mind while praying? It was that wisdom and revelation in the knowledge of Christ might be given by the Holy Spirit. Paul knew that the Ephesian saints could not mature in spiritual knowledge apart from the enlightenment of the Holy Spirit. As he told the saints at Corinth: "For what man knoweth the things of a man, save the spirit of man which is in him? even so the things of God knoweth no man, but the Spirit of God" (I Cor. 2:11).

This is what our Lord told His disciples in John 16:12-14:

"I have yet many things to say unto you, but ye cannot bear them now. Howbeit when he, the Spirit of truth, is come, he will guide you into all truth: for he shall not speak of himself; but whatsoever he shall hear, that shall he speak: and he will shew you things to come. He shall glorify me: for he shall receive of mine, and shall shew it unto you."

All Christians have the indwelling Holy Spirit, of course. However, not all—*yea, few*—let Him teach them.

Dr. H. A. Ironside told an interesting incident which illustrates this point. As a young Christian worker, he had gone home for a visit and found a man of God from the north of Ireland living as a guest in a small tent under some olive trees near his mother's home. This elderly gentleman, Andrew Fraser, was dying of what doctors in that day called "quick consumption."

Although his lungs were so far gone he could barely speak above a whisper, day after day, in the little tent, he unfolded the things of Christ to young Ironside. The latter had never entered into such truths before and, while not realizing it, tears were soon streaming down his face and he pleaded with his teacher, "Where did you get these things? Could you tell me where I could find a book that would open them up? Did you learn them in some seminary or college?"

And the memorable answer was, "My dear young man, I learned these things on my knees on the mud floor of a little sod cottage in the north of Ireland. There, with my Bible open before me, I knelt for hours at a time, asking the Spirit of God to reveal Christ to my soul and open His Word to my heart. He taught me more on my knees on that mud floor than I could have ever learned in all the seminaries and colleges of the world."

This is what Paul wanted for the Ephesians: **enlightenment!** And he was not thinking so much of the eyes of the intellect as he was the eyes of the emotions. The word "understanding" used here is literally "heart." The Amplified New Testament has it, "having the eyes of your heart flooded with light." It is the heart, not the head, which Paul has in view. There is only a little profit in an opened intellect, but, oh, the blessing, the wealth of an opened heart!

Two Christian men can sit side by side in a Sunday service listening to the Word of God being unfolded by a man of God. One has the eyes of his intellect opened and leaves a more informed and intelligent Christian. The other not only has his intellect broadened, but the message moves his heart and he goes away with a life that is changed. It is the latter that Paul desires for the Ephesians.

Every portion of the Word of God has undiscovered riches. It is a spiritual gold mine waiting for the Christian to stake his claim and mine its lode. Let us pray with David, "Open thou mine eyes, that I may behold wondrous things out of thy law" (Ps. 119:18).

For one thing,

II. OPEN OUR EYES TO KNOW THE HOPE OF HIS CALLING!

Paul prayed, "The eyes of your understanding being enlightened; that ye may know what is the hope of your calling . . ." (vs. 18). This has to do with the work of God the Father.

A. "That Ye May KNOW"

This is literally, "Which will make you to realize." How few Christians really *know,* really realize the hope of God's calling.

There is so very much involved in the "so great salvation" which God has provided.

It does not take very much knowledge to be saved. The dying thief, with his limited understanding, was saved on the cross. Little children come to Christ in what some would call amusing simplicity, but later years prove the reality of their decision. Many of us, when we came to Christ, had little knowledge about God or His Word.

Philip, as soon as he came into contact with Christ, immediately set out to win his friend, Nathaniel, although he knew nothing about such theological matters as the virgin birth (John 1:43-46).

While this is wonderfully and blessedly true, how pathetic it is not to *grow* in grace and knowledge *after* salvation. Paul's prayer was for growth and maturing in spiritual matters.

The Irish poet, Thomas Moore, enthused:

> Since first Thy Word awaked my heart,
>   Like new life dawning o'er me,
> Where e're I turn mine eyes, Thou art
>   All light and love before me.
> Nought else I feel or hear or see;
>   All bonds of earth I sever;
> Thee, O God, and only Thee,
>   I live for, now and ever!
>
> Like him whose fetters dropped away
>   When light shone o'er his prison,
> My spirit, touched by mercy's ray,
>   Hath from her chains arisen.
> And shall a soul thou bidd'st be free
>   Return to bondage? Never!
> Thee, O God, and only Thee,
>   I live for, now and ever.

And, as something every Christian ought to know, Paul especially mentions

B. "What Is the Hope of His Calling"

Paul wrote to the Romans, "For we are saved by hope: but hope that is seen is not hope: for what a man seeth, why doth he yet hope for?" (8:24).

He said to the saints at Colosse,

"For the hope which is laid up for you in heaven, whereof ye heard before in the word of the truth of the gospel. . . .To whom God would make known what is the riches of the glory of this mystery among the Gentiles; which is Christ in you, the hope of glory."—Col 1:5,27.

Peter enthused, while writing to the sojourners of the dispersion, "Blessed be the God and Father of our Lord Jesus Christ, which according to his abundant mercy hath begotten us again unto a lively hope by the resurrection of Jesus Christ from the dead" (I Pet. 1:3).

And John referred to this hope, saying,

"Beloved, now are we the sons of God, and it doth not yet appear what we shall be; but we know that, when he shall appear we shall be like him: for we shall see him as he is. And every man that hath this hope in him purifieth himself, even as he is pure."—I John 3:2,3.

This is a hope that is within every child of God! It is one that transforms his life and, the more the eyes of his heart are enlightened, it revolutionizes his service. It is a calling to sonship, a calling to service, and a calling that will eventually include the transformation of our bodies and the partaking of heavenly joys and glories.

Thank God, it is also a calling which will be completed, finished, fully carried out. Men often start projects that they do not or cannot bring to a conclusion. Our Lord spoke of this human frailty in Luke 14:28-33, regarding building towers and going to war.

God never does this! In Philippians 1:6 we are told, "Being confident of this very thing, that he which hath begun a good work in you will perform it until the day of Jesus Christ." Even Balaam, with the Spirit of the Lord upon him, testified: "God is not a man, that he should lie; neither the son of man, that he should repent: hath he said, and shall he not do it? or hath he spoken, and shall he not make it good?" (Num. 23:19).

The writer of the Book of Hebrews had the same to say about this hope, declaring:

"Wherein God, willing more abundantly to shew unto the heirs of promise the immutability of his counsel, confirmed it by an oath: That by two immutable things, in which it was impossible for God to lie, we might have a strong consolation, who have fled for refuge to lay hold upon the hope set before us: Which hope we have as an anchor of the soul, both sure and stedfast, and which entereth into that within the veil; Whither the forerunner is for us entered, even Jesus, made an high priest for ever after the order of Melchisedec."—Heb. 6:17-20.

Why did Paul want the Christians to have their eyes enlightened about their calling? So, as he points out later in the epistle, that they might "walk worthy of the vocation wherewith ye are called" (4:1).

Next,

III. OPEN OUR EYES TO KNOW THE RICHES OF THE GLORY OF HIS INHERITANCE IN THE SAINTS

Paul prayed, "The eyes of your understanding being enlightened; that ye may know what is. . .the riches of the glory of his inheritance in the saints" (vs. 18). This concerns the work of God the Son.

Is Christ whom He claimed to be? In the final analysis, there are only three possible views about the Person of Christ: (1) He was bad; (2) He was mad; or (3) He was exactly what He claimed to be, God manifest in the flesh. What Paul speaks of here is possible only if the latter be true.

A. "The Riches of the Glory"

This phrase is literally "the glorious wealth" and speaks of what is wrapped up in the believer's inheritance in Christ. So immeasurable is this wealth that Paul told the suffering saints at Rome, "For I reckon that the sufferings of this present time are not worthy to be compared with the glory which shall be revealed in us" (Rom. 8:18). And he assured the badgered and beleaguered saints at Corinth, "For our light affliction, which is but for a moment, worketh for us a far more exceeding and eternal weight of glory" (II Cor. 4:17).

These riches are emphasized repeatedly in Ephesians. Paul speaks of the "the riches of his grace" (1:7); "The riches of the glory of his inheritance" (1:18); God being "rich in mercy" (2:4); "The exceeding riches of his grace" (2:7); "the unsearchable riches of Christ" (3:8); and, "the riches of his glory" (3:16).

These riches are available to the undeserving and are based entirely upon the limitless love and matchless mercy of God.

James H. McConkey tells of being in the home of a Christian lady when a tramp knocked on the door and asked for food. Explaining that she had nothing else to give him, she buttered some bread and handed it to him. McConkey and the lady watched the tramp walk off the porch, down the steps and out the gate, throwing the bread into the gutter when he reached the sidewalk. In disgust the lady turned from the window and exclaimed, "That is the last tramp I will ever feed!"

But God's riches are neither limited, as were hers, nor are they tempered for one because of abuse by another. His actions are more like the late Mr. William Jay Gaynor, a former mayor of New York City. When one who had reached the lowest levels made an appeal to him for aid, Mayor Gaynor granted his request. A lawyer friend remonstrated, saying, "That man is no good and he has been receiving the fortunes of his just desserts. With his yellow streak—."

"Wait a minute," the mayor interrupted, "that may be true." Then he told of the mother who pleaded with Napoleon for the life of her condemned son. The emperor explained that her boy had committed the same serious offense on two separate occasions and justice demanded that his life be taken. The mother responded, "But, Sir, I am not here to plead for justice, but for mercy." And so God deals with His children on the basis of mercy, making available to them all of His glorious riches.

B. "Of His Inheritance in the Saints"

Here is an amazing thing: Paul speaks of Christ's inheritance "in the saints." While the average Christian understands that Christ is his inheritance, how few understand that we are His! Our riches are in God; God's riches are in His saints.

This is the same thought as noted previously in verse eleven. We have "obtained" an inheritance, as the Authorized Version expresses it. And we have been "made a heritage," as the Revised Version puts it. Both are true.

Next,

IV. OPEN OUR EYES TO KNOW THE EXCEEDING GREATNESS OF HIS POWER TO US-WARD WHO BELIEVE

Here Paul prays that the eyes of their hearts might be enlightened to know

". . .what is the exceeding greatness of his power to us-ward who believe, according to the working of his mighty power, Which he wrought in Christ when he raised him from the dead, and set him at his own right hand in the heavenly places, Far above all principality, and power, and might, and dominion, and every name that is named, not only in this world, but also in that which is to come: And hath put all things under his feet, and gave him to be the head over all things to the church, Which is his body, the fulness of him that filleth all in all."—Vss. 19-23.

This pertains to the work of God the Holy Spirit.

A. "Exceeding Greatness"

This means "surpassing or transcendent witness" and it is "of his power." The word for power is *dunamis,* meaning "inherent power." It is power capable of reproducing itself. Our English words "dynamo" and "dynamic" come from this and are indicative of the power of God available to saints.

The kind of power in us who believe is further described later in the epistle when Paul says, "Now unto him that is able to do exceeding abundantly above all that we ask or think, according to the power that worketh in us" (3:20).

B. The Power Manifested in the Resurrection of Christ

As further indication of this power, Paul describes it as "the working of his mighty power, Which he wrought in Christ when he raised him from the dead." What is called here "his mighty power" is literally, "the strength of his might." That mighty strength was manifested when,

> Death could not keep his prey
> Jesus, my Savior!
> He tore the bars away
> Jesus, my Lord!

No wonder Paul prayed for himself, "That I may know him, and the power of his resurrection. . ." (Phil. 3:10).

C. The Power Manifested in the Ascension of Christ

Paul said, "According to the working of his mighty power, Which he wrought in Christ, when he. . .set him at his own right hand in the heavenly places" (vss. 19,20).

This, you will recall, is where Stephen saw Him. Just before the wild, angry mob at Jerusalem stoned him to death, Acts 7:55,56, says, "But he, being full of the Holy Ghost, looked up steadfastly into heaven, and saw the glory of God, and Jesus standing on the right hand of God, And said, Behold, I see the heavens opened, and the Son of man standing on the right hand of God."

Actually, this is our position also in Him. As we saw in verse 3, He has "blessed us with all spiritual blessings in the heavenlies in Christ." In Colossians 3:1, it says, "If ye then be risen with Christ, seek those things which are above, where Christ sitteth on the right hand of God."

D. The Power Manifested in the Exaltation of Christ

This is twofold: (1) putting all things under His feet (vss. 21,22 f.c.); and, (2) giving Him to be head over all things to the church (vss. 22, f.c., 23).

Regarding the Headship of Christ, note that Paul describes it with a sevenfold (number of perfection) description. His Headship is far above (1) all principalities; (2) all powers; (3) all might; (4) all dominion; (5) every man; (6) all things; and (7) the church.

E. Power for Believers!

We remind you that this "working of his mighty power" manifested in the resurrection of Christ, the ascension of Christ and the exaltation of Christ is available to every Christian. Paul called it "the exceeding greatness of his power to us-ward who believe" (vs. 19). Here is power for victory in the daily life. It is power that makes reality of the poetry we sing:

> I want to live above the world,
> Tho' Satan's darts at me are hurled;
> For faith has caught the joyful sound,
> The song of saints on higher ground.

We are not talking about sinless perfection. Some teachers hold such a condition out for believers in this life, but it is a doctrine fraught with repeated frustration and despair, to say nothing of hypocrisy.

A psychiatrist friend of mine told me of counseling with a man who had unsuccessfully been trying to get "entire sanctification," sometimes referred to as the "second blessing." After three counseling sessions, the man called my friend at two in the morning to cancel his next appointment, saying he simply could not get victory over several sins which he named. Then, as my friend pleaded with him on the telephone, he put a gun to his temple and blew out his brains.

No, *no!* That is not what we are talking about. Charles Spurgeon said of a certain man of his acquaintance, "I always thought he was sinless until he said he was."

Actually, the more Christlike a child of God becomes, the less he is aware of his holiness. But this in no way depreciates the truth of Colossians 3:1-3, beseeching us:

"If ye then be risen with Christ, seek those things which are above, where Christ sitteth on the right hand of God. Set your affection on things above, not on things on the earth. For ye are dead, and your life is hid with Christ in God."

Do you grasp it? The power manifested in Christ is the power God seeks to manifest in you. May God help us, as Paul prayed, to "know" that power. When we do, there is no battle, no victory that we cannot win.

As a poet, unknown to me, expressed it:

> Head of the Church, Thy Body,
> O Christ, the great Salvation!
>   Sweet to the saints
>   It is to think
> Of all Thine Exaltation.
> All power's to Thee committed—
>   To Thee a Name
>   Of widest fame
> Above all glory's given.
>
> With Thee, believers, raised,
> In Thee on High are seated;
>   All guilty once,
>   But cleared by Thee;
> Redemption toil's completed.
> And when Thou, Lord and Saviour,
> Shalt come again in glory,
>   There, by Thy side,
>   Thy spotless bride
> Shall crown the wondrous story.
>
> At length—the final Kingdom!
> No bound, no end possessing!
>   When Heaven and Earth,
>   God—all in all—
> Shall fill with largest blessing.
> All root of evil banished,
> No breath of sin to wither;
>   On Earth—on High—
>   Naught else but joy,
> And blissful peace for ever!

*From Depths of
Depravity to
Summits of
Grace*

And you hath he quickened, who were dead in trespasses and sins:

Wherein in time past ye walked according to the course of this world, according to the prince of the power of the air, the spirit that now worketh in the children of disobedience:

Among whom also we all had our conversation in times past in the lusts of our flesh, fulfilling the desires of the flesh and of the mind; and were by nature the children of wrath, even as others.

But God, who is rich in mercy, for his great love wherewith he loved us,

Even when we were dead in sins, hath quickened us together with Christ, (by grace ye are saved;)

And hath raised us up together, and made us sit together in heavenly places in Christ Jesus:

That in the ages to come he might shew the exceeding riches of his grace in his kindness toward us through Christ Jesus.— Ephesians 2:1-7.

It may be of interest to point out that the *Pulpit Commentary* calls attention to how this passage, along with the verses immediately following (vss. 8-10), corresponds to Genesis 1: *the history of creation!* First, the chaos is pictured in the opening three verses. Next, the dawn—the Spirit of God moving upon the face of the waters—is indicated in the first half of verse four. Then, commencing with the second half of verse four and continuing through verse ten, is the work of creation in its successive stages.

One thing is truly obvious: the passage before us emphasizes beautifully the greatness of the grace of God. Here are the **MATERIALS** with which grace works (vss. 1-3). Here are the **MOTIVES** through which grace works (vss. 4,7). And here are the **MIRACLES** which grace produces (vss. 5,6).

Before grace can be truly appreciated, depravity's depths must be plumbed. Only as we are brought face to face with our true condition in sin can we evaluate the real worth of God's marvelous grace in redemption. So Paul makes us face first,

I. THE DEPTHS OF DEPRAVITY!
Vss. 1-3

Here is the pitiful biography of every one of us, without a single exception:

"And you hath he quickened, who were dead in trespasses and sins: Wherein in time past ye walked according to the course of this world, according to the prince of the power of the air, the spirit that now worketh in the children of disobedience: Among whom also we all had our conversation in times past in the lusts of our flesh, fulfilling the desires of the flesh and of the mind; and were by nature the children of wrath, even as others."

A. What Do We Mean by Depravity

Our English word *depravity* is defined by the authorities as "the quality or state of being depraved" (Webster's Seventh New Collegiate Dictionary). The same source then defines *depraved* as "marked by corruption or evil."

The late Dr. Henry C. Thiessen, in his *Lectures in Systematic Theology*, declared: "By depravity we mean man's want of original righteousness and of holy affections toward God, and also the corruption of his moral nature and his bias toward evil."

How true it is that man has a natural tendency—yea, *a bias, if you please*—toward sin, rebellion and wrongdoing. It affects every phase of his being: his will, his intellect, his emotions, his heart, his all!

Admittedly, this thought of depravity is repugnant and repulsive to the natural mind. Thoughts of abhorrence, however, do not make truth any less a reality. The horrors of war are repugnant and repulsive, but they are true. The same could be said of such diseases as leprosy and cancer, such social ills as poverty and starvation, and such political abuses as graft and corruption. If unattractive truth were no longer reality, what a wonderful earthly paradise this world would suddenly become.

Yet how clear is the scriptural teaching of man's utter and total depravity! Consider, by way of example, the revelation in Jeremiah 17:9: "The heart is deceitful above all things and desperately wicked: who can know it?"

Earlier, Jeremiah had given a birth-to-death biography of all mankind, saying, "We lie down in our shame, and our confusion covereth us: for we have sinned against the Lord our God, we and our fathers, from our youth even unto this day, and have not obeyed the voice of the Lord our God" (3:25).

Solomon added the grudging acknowledgment of the natural man, viewing things "under the sun" and admitting, "For there is not a just man upon earth, that doeth good, and sinneth not" (Eccles. 7:20). As Paul told his more youthful but fellow preacher, Titus: "We ourselves also were sometimes foolish, disobedient, deceived, serving divers lusts and pleasures, living in malice and envy, hateful, and hating one another" (Titus 3:3).

Speaking of Paul, elsewhere in this Ephesian epistle he pinpointed depravity: "Having the understanding darkened, being alienated from the life of God through the ignorance that is in them, because of the blindness of their heart: Who being past feeling have given themselves over unto lasciviousness, to work all uncleanness with greediness" (4:18,19).

And to the Romans he wrote, confessing the depravity of his own fleshly nature: ". . .I am carnal, sold under sin. For that which I do I allow not: for what I would, that do I not; but what I hate, that do I" (7:14,15).

But perhaps the strongest declaration of man's depravity in

the Word of God is found in Paul's fourteenfold indictment of Romans 3:9-19. There he charged:

"What then? are we better than they? No, in no wise: for we have before proved both Jews and Gentiles, that they are all under sin; As it is written, There is none righteous, no, not one: There is none that understandeth, there is none that seeketh after God. They are all gone out of the way, they are together become unprofitable; there is none that doeth good, no, not one. Their throat is an open sepulchre; with their tongues they have used deceit; the poison of asps is under their lips: Whose mouth is full of cursing and bitterness: Their feet are swift to shed blood: Destruction and misery are in their ways: And the way of peace have they not known: There is no fear of God before their eyes. Now we know that what things soever the law saith, it saith to them who are under the law: that every mouth may be stopped, and all the world may become guilty before God."

And he added in verses 22 and 23,

". . .for there is no difference: For all have sinned, and come short of the glory of God."

The depravity of man was illustrated by the poet who, when he could not think of anything darker to illustrate the degree of blackness he was trying to describe, wrote:

> Black, oh, so black!
> Black as the starless night's dark track,
> Black as the unclean raven's wing,
> Black as man's sin—earth's blackest thing!

One of the best loved Lincoln stories was told by a neighbor who heard a loud commotion one day which sounded like children screaming in terror. Rushing to his front door, he saw the great emancipator striding along, dragging a small boy in each hand.

He called out, "Why, Mr. Lincoln, what is the matter with the boys?"

"The same thing," muttered Lincoln without looking back,

"that's the matter with the whole world. I've got three walnuts and each boy wants two."

There is in every man a nature that wants the extra walnut, the largest dish of ice cream, the fastest car, the biggest house—and we do not especially care how we attain our goal, as long as we get them. As Thiessen said, we have a "bias toward evil."

B. Paul's Sixfold Description of Depravity

The apostle deals with depravity in other portions of his writings, but nowhere does he do it as pungently as in this passage. Here are the characteristics of depraved human nature, just as the Holy Spirit impelled him to describe them.

1. Dead!

He begins, in verse 1: "and you hath he quickened, who were dead in trespasses and sins." What is meant by death? In the Word of God, death always indicates separation. Lehman Strauss quotes H. S. Miller as calling it "the separation of a person from the purpose or use for which he was intended."

Why is man dead? Because of his "trespasses and sins." In Vine's *Expository Dictionary of New Testament Words*, he defines *trespass* as "primarily a false step, a blunder. . .lit., 'a fall beside,' used ethically, denotes a trespass, a deviation from uprightness and truth."

The word *sin* simply means "to miss the mark." It is a failure to meet the standards of holiness set by God, a missing of the mark which He demands of His creatures. Hence the Amplified New Testament expresses it: "You were dead [slain] by [your] trespasses and sins."

We hasten to point out that this spiritual death is the state of *all* outside of Jesus Christ. While all have not sinned to the same extent, and those degrees of difference are quite obvious to other men, the fact of death for all is nonetheless a grim reality. Dr. Louis T. Talbot illustrates it beautifully in his commentary as follows:

> Sometime ago, I was called upon to conduct two funerals in one day. The first was held in the morning and was that of a young man who had died in France and had been placed into one of those hastily-constructed graves. At the close of the war, the United States government removed his body to this country. The casket was not opened for his loved ones to see because the body was in a state of putrefaction. Had that casket been opened, no one would have raised the question as to whether or not he was dead, for the evidence would have been abundant.
>
> In the afternoon, however, I conducted the funeral of a young woman who had died suddenly at the age of twenty-one. I stood by the side of the casket in which her body lay. There was light playing upon her features and she looked so life-like that it was difficult to believe that she was dead. Putrefaction had not set in; her features were just as they were in life, and she looked as though she were just sleeping or resting.
>
> Standing by the casket, I thought of the funeral in the morning, making a contrast between the two bodies. When I did so, I remembered that there was a parallel as well as a contrast. They were parallel in that the girl was as dead as the man whom we had buried in the morning. And after the service, we went to the cemetery where her body was lowered as deeply into the earth as was the man's. The application is this: It is true that we see a difference in people morally; however, that difference passes away in the spiritual realm. If a man is without Christ, though he be circumstantially good, he is just as 'dead' as those whose lives are outwardly corrupt, and absolutely void of virtues.

It should be obvious that this is one of the reasons why an individual must experience salvation before he can live the kind of a life God intended. No dead person can *live* the Christian life; he must receive "life" first.

2. Dedicated!

This is brought out in the first phrase of verse two: "Wherein in time past ye walked according to the course of this world . . . ." I have used our English word *dedicated* to describe this aspect of depravity, even though it admittedly means "to devote to the worship of a divine being" (Webster's Seventh New Collegiate Dictionary), because it also means "to set apart to a definite use," and "to become committed to." And that is how depravity is described here: dedicated, committed entirely, sold out completely to sin!

The Amplified New Testament ties this into the "trespasses and sins" of verse one by saying, "In which at one time you walked habitually." That is, it was the natural, easy thing to do.

Man, in his natural state, is set apart to sin. He is committed to a plan and program of rebellion against God, against His Word, against His will, against His Son. Man is dedicated to a life of following the course and fashion of this present world system in its admitted defiance to Almighty God.

3. Devilish!

Not only does the natural man walk according to the course of this world, but "according to the prince of the power of the air." He is obedient to Satan; he is under his control.

To my mind comes the newspaper account of a fifteen-year-old girl in Irving, Texas, who made about fifty anonymous telephone calls, announcing to each lady who answered the phone that her husband had just been killed in an automobile accident. Methodist Hospital in Dallas got more than fifty frantic calls. Relatives rushed to the hospital for more information. One woman, ready to give birth to a child, went into a coma. Others had to be placed under the care of a physician. One of the policemen, Lt. Paul Barger, said: "I have never heard of anything so sickening. Some of the wives nearly had a heart attack."

After the culprit was apprehended, pressed for a cause for her actions, she simply said, "The old Devil made me do it." *And he surely had!*

This is the thought of II Timothy 2:26: "And that they may recover themselves out of the snare of the devil, WHO ARE TAKEN CAPTIVE BY HIM AT HIS WILL." He says *"Frog!"* and they jump.

Thank God, deliverance here is part of the "so great" salvation God offers sinners. Paul described it to the saints at Colosse:

"Who hath delivered us from the power of darkness, and hath translated us into the kingdom of his dear Son: In whom we have redemption through his blood, even the forgiveness of sins."—Col. 1:13,14.

What a startling thought is this "devilish" phase of depravity!

He, whose name is associated with the fall of Adam, the murder of Abel, the treachery of Judas and the seduction of Jezebel, is also LORD and LEADER of every person outside of Jesus Christ. Worse still, it is by the *personal choice* of the sinner!

We must point out also that Paul says he "now worketh" in those who are lost. If you are still outside of Christ, Satan is *right now* performing his devilish work in *you!* You are clay in his hands and he is molding your life into the shape and pattern of his own desire. That does not mean that he is necessarily preparing you for murder, adultery or some of the other so-called baser sins. It simply means he is making you the most effective tool possible according to his purpose for your life.

4. Disobedient!

The fourth phase of man's depravity, as Paul outlines it in this passage, is summed up in the last part of verse two: ". . .the spirit that now worketh in the children of disobedience." The phrase *children of disobedience* is literally "sons of disobedience."

This disobedience to God may be either of two things: (1) an immoral, filthy, wretched, perverse, wicked life; or, (2) a moral, refined, even religious life apart from Christ. One who refuses to be saved is a child of disobedience whether he is a down-and-out sinner or an up-and-out sinner. Disobedience is rejecting God's way and choosing one's own way. As Isaiah 53:6 expresses it: "All we like sheep have gone astray; we have turned every one to his own way. . . ."

Why is man disobedient? What is the cause? It lies in his lack of love for God. As Jesus said in John 14:24: "He that loveth me not keepeth not my sayings: and the word which ye hear is not mine, but the Father's which sent me."

5. Defiled!

Paul, still talking about the devilish control of the lost individual's life by Satan, goes on to charge: "Among whom also we all had our conversation in times past in the lust of our flesh, fulfilling the desires of the flesh and of the mind. . . ." He is pointing out that man is defiled *in his manner of life.* He first desires and then fulfills the appetites of the flesh and the mind. What starts out as a longing ends up as a partaking.

What about defilement in the flesh? Paul said in Romans 7:18, "For I know that in me (that is, in my flesh) dwelleth no good thing. . . ."

What about the mind? Proverbs 23:7 declares: "For as he thinketh in his heart, so is he. . . ." And wicked minds are the fruit of wicked hearts, as Jesus pointed out in Matthew 15:18-20:

"But those things which proceed out of the mouth come forth from the heart; and they defile the man. For out of the heart proceed evil thoughts, murders, adulteries, fornications, thefts, false witness, blasphemies: These are the things which defile a man: but to eat with unwashen hands defileth not a man."

Perhaps we should call attention to the fact that this lusting and living in appetites of flesh and mind is not the failing of some, it is the condition of all. Paul said: "Among whom also **WE ALL** had our conversation. . . ."

But not only is man defiled in his manner of life, he is defiled *in his very nature.* This is not just a matter of defiled habits and defiled customs, it is a defiled being. What a strong, positive answer the Word of God gives here to today's foolish theory: "We are all by nature the children of God." Nothing could be farther from the truth! As Jesus told the lost of His day, even the unconverted religious leaders:

"Ye are of your father the devil, and the lusts of your father ye will do. He was a murderer from the beginning, and abode not in the truth, because there is no truth in him. When he speaketh a lie, he speaketh of his own: for he is a liar, and the father of it."—John 8:44.

Once again, in the Ephesian passage, Paul includes everyone by saying: *"even as others."* There is a tendency today to think that such matters as education and culture make people different, but they do not.

I noted recently that a security consultant, Lincoln M. Zonn, a former counterintelligence officer and a professional psychologist, said that an executive who earns $15,000 to $40,000 a year is just as prone to steal from his employer as a $45-a-week clerk. Zonn explained:

> In fact, the higher the salary, the bigger a dishonest employee's appetite for larceny is—he steals merchandise by the truckload or cash in big chunks, whereas the clerk pilfers $5 items or postage stamps.

He went on to say:

> We have caught so many executives engaged in stealing that we are convinced that pay levels don't have too much to do with pilferage. We have found dishonest employees in all brackets from $40 a week to $40,000 a year. The plain truth is that there is more pilferage of merchandise and money from business firms today than at any time in history.

Zonn described the known loss from such thievery as "well over one billion dollars a year in the United States alone."

But coming back to Paul, he not only describes man as dead, dedicated, devilish, disobedient and defiled, he also evaluates his condition as

6. Damned!

He points out, in the latter part of verse three, ". . .and were by nature the children of wrath, even as others." That is literally "Children doomed to wrath." The Amplified New Testament expresses it: "Children of [God's] wrath and heirs of [His] indignation."

How prevalent is this teaching in the Word of God! Romans 1:18 says: "For the wrath of God is revealed from heaven against all ungodliness and unrighteousness of men, who hold the truth in unrighteousness."

John 3:18 says: ". . .he that believeth not is condemned already, because he hath not believed in the name of the only begotten Son of God." And John 3:36 adds, ". . .he that believeth not the Son shall not see life; but the wrath of God abideth on him."

Ephesians 5:6 says: "For this ye know, that no whoremonger nor unclean person, nor covetous man, who is an idolator, hath any inheritance in the kingdom of God and of Christ." And Colossians 3:6 says: "For which things sake the wrath of God cometh on the children of disobedience."

This is the end of the rebel trail: damnation and Hell. How foolish to continue on in sin when there is only "a certain fearful looking for of judgment and fiery indignation, which shall devour the adversaries" (Heb. 10:27).

Dr. John R. Rice compares this folly of the sinner to the manner in which monkeys are caught in Africa. He says they put nuts in the bottom of earthenware jars having long, narrow necks. When the monkey arrives on the scene, the smell of the fresh nuts kisses his nostrils, causing him to excitedly shove his paw down into the jar and grab a handful of nuts. But with his fist closed, the monkey cannot pull the paw out of the jar. He jumps up and down and screams, he dances and pulls and jabbers—*but he won't turn loose of the nuts.* Then the trappers slip up and place a sack over his head and another "entertainer" is ready for a far-off zoo. How much better it would be for the monkey to turn loose of the nuts!

And how much better it would be for a sinner to let go of his sin and turn to Christ for salvation, than to hold on to any fancied earthly pleasure. But so much for the depth of depravity.

Consider next,

II. THE SUMMITS OF GRACE!
Vss. 4-7

Here is the amazing record:

"But God, who is rich in mercy, for his great love wherewith he loved us, Even when we were dead in sins, hath quickened us together, with Christ, (by grace ye are saved;) And hath raised us up together, and made us sit together in heavenly places in Christ Jesus: That in the ages to come he might shew the exceeding riches of his grace in his kindness toward us through Christ Jesus."

Paul well introduces this section of grace with the words: **"BUT GOD!"** Norman B. Harrison appropriately says: "These two words mark the turning point of human destiny." And so they do. You have the same idea in Romans 5:8, where we are told: "BUT GOD commendeth his love toward us, in that, while we were yet sinners, Christ died for us."

Here were those dead, dedicated to sin, devilish, disobedient, defiled and doomed to wrath. . .*but God!*

The only possible explanation of what happens in salvation is summed up in this word: **"Grace!"** It appears more than 150 times in the New Testament, and well it might. In this Ephesians passage grace is explained as "his kindness toward us through Christ Jesus" (vs. 7).

A. The "Motives" of Grace!

Since the word *motive* means "that which moves or excites to action," verse four well describes it: "But God, who is rich in mercy, for his great love wherewith he loved us."

1. Riches of His Mercy

The first of grace's motives is the riches of His mercy. The One who is rich in grace (1:7) and rich in glory (1:18) is also rich in mercy. Second Corinthians 1:3 describes Him as the "Father of mercies."

The resources of His mercies are unlimited; the wealth of His mercy is boundless. Jeremiah described them: "It is of the Lord's mercies that we are not consumed, because his compassions fail not. They are new every morning: great is thy faithfulness" (Lam. 3:22,23). David declared:

"The Lord is merciful and gracious, slow to anger, and plenteous in mercy. . . .For as the heaven is high above the earth, so great is his mercy toward them that fear him. . . .The mercy of the Lord is from everlasting to everlasting upon them that fear him, and his righteousness unto children's children."—Ps. 103:8,11,17.

2. Abundance of His Love

The second motive of grace which Paul pinpoints is the abundance of His love, the "great love wherewith he loved us." This is reminiscent of John 3:16: "For God so loved the world, that he gave his only begotten Son, that whosoever believeth in him should not perish, but have everlasting life."

John elsewhere described it:

"He that loveth not knoweth not God; for God is love. In this was manifested the love of God toward us, because that God sent his only begotten Son into the world, that we might live through him. Herein is love, not that we loved God, but that he loved us, and sent his Son to be the propitiation for our sins."— I John 4:8-10.

This is "Calvary" love!

Philip P. Bliss was an associate of D. L. Moody. A gracious, greatly gifted and talented young man, he gave the Christian world such songs as "The Light of the World Is Jesus," "Let the Lower Lights Be Burning," "Hold the Fort," "Wonderful Words of Life," and the invitation lament, "Almost Persuaded." Yet when he was only 30 years of age, traveling with his wife back to Chicago from the Christmas holidays, the train in which they were riding had a tragic accident near Astabula, Ohio. Bliss was thrown free, but his wife was pinned in the wreckage. As fire raced through the wooden coaches, the young musician crawled back to where she was, held her in his arms and refused to leave her.

But Philip Bliss only died *with* his wife, not *for* her. He sacrificed his life in a tremendous manifestation of love, it is true, but he was unable to accomplish anything in saving the life of that one he loved. Thank God the love of Christ was not merely a dying *with,* it was a dying *for!*

Note, as Paul points out in verse five, he loved us **"EVEN WHEN"**! He loved us when we were still in the far country, when we were unlovely and unlovable. His love was manifested when we were dead, dedicated, devilish, disobedient, defiled and doomed.

Some years back, when we made our evangelistic headquarters in Texas, we lived on the same side of Dallas as the famed Buckner Orphanage. This social institution of the Southern Baptists was founded years ago by Dr. Buckner. And, as with most faith organization when they are launched, the shortage of money caused him to be on the road much of the time seeking help from churches, businesses and individuals.

As would be expected, the children dearly loved this kindly man who had proven so surely his love for them. It was always a big day in the life of the orphanage when Dr. Buckner was scheduled to arrive home from a trip. The children would scurry around to the fields and woods gathering flowers to present him as tokens of their affection. Then they would crowd around him as soon as he arrived on the grounds to present their gifts in person.

One of the little girls was not normal. In her retarded mental condition, she was not able to distinguish between the precious and the profane. So while other children would gather pretty flowers, she would, as likely as not, gather weeds and broken sticks. But when Dr. Buckner arrived home and the children pressed around him to be the first to kiss him and present their offerings, the kindly minister would look over the crowd for the little retarded lady. Then he would push the other children aside and go to her, wrap his big arms around her, kiss her tenderly, take her bouquet of trash and speak sweet words of endearment into her little ears.

How poorly, yet how sweetly, the actions of Dr. Buckner imitated the Saviour's action toward fallen, totally depraved sinners.

The poet has tried to describe it:

> Behold your King! Though the moonlight steals
>   Through the silvery sprays of the olive tree,
> No star-gemmed sceptre or crown it reveals,
>   In the solemn shade of Gethsemane.
> Only a form of prostrate grief,
> Fallen, crushed, like a broken leaf!

> Oh, think of His sorrow, that we may know
> The depth of love in the depth of woe!
> Behold your King, with His sorrow crowned,
> Alone, alone in the valley is He!
> The shadows of death are gathering round,
> And the cross must follow Gethsemane.
> Darker and darker the gloom must fall,
> Filled is the cup, He must drink it all!
> Oh, think of His sorrow, that we may know
> His wondrous love and His wondrous woe!

Yes, how rich is His mercy and how great is His love!

B. The "Togetherness" of Grace!

This is described in verses 5 and 6:

"Even when we were dead in sins, hath quickened us together with Christ, (by grace ye are saved;) And hath raised us up together, and made us sit together in heavenly places in Christ Jesus."

1. "Made Alive" Together

This togetherness is threefold: first of all, we are "quickened" together. We were dead in sins, but we have been made alive and united to Christ. This is the truth of Colossians 2:13: "And you, being dead in your sins and the uncircumcision of your flesh, hath he quickened together with him, having forgiven you all trespasses." It is what Jesus referred to in John 5:24, when He said: "Verily, verily, I say unto you, He that heareth my word, and believeth on him that sent me, hath everlasting life, and shall not come into condemnation; but is passed from death unto life."

And, as He said to Martha: "I am the resurrection, and the life: he that believeth in me, though he were dead, yet shall he live: And whosoever liveth and believeth in me shall never die. Believest thou this?" (John 11:25,26).

It is because of this fellowship, this union and life that Paul was able to triumphantly declare, "For ye are dead and your life is hid with Christ in God. When Christ, who is our life, shall appear, then shall ye also appear with him in glory" (Col. 3:3,4).

2. "Raised" Together

But not only are the redeemed made alive together, they are "raised" together. This pertains to our practice, our walk: *a newness of life!* As Colossians 3:1,2 says:

"If ye then be risen with Christ, seek those things which are above, where Christ sitteth on the right hand of God. Set your affection on things above, not on things on the earth."

Romans 6:4 describes it:

"Therefore we are buried with him by baptism into death: that like as Christ was raised up from the dead by the glory of the Father, even so we also should walk in newness of life."

This is part of what Paul means in Philippians 3:10,11:

"That I may know him, and the power of his resurrection, and the fellowship of his sufferings, being made conformable unto his death; If by any means I might attain unto the resurrection of the dead."

What a blessed change results from salvation! There is a change *in the individual's position.* Colossians 1:21,22 describes it: "And you, that were sometime alienated and enemies in your mind by wicked works, yet now hath he reconciled In the body of his flesh through death, to present you holy and unblameable and unreproveable in his sight."

There is a change *in the individual's practice.* As II Corinthians 5:17 triumphantly exclaims: "Therefore if any man be in Christ, he is a new creature: old things are passed away; behold, all things are become new."

3. "Seated" Together

However, not only are the redeemed "quickened" and "raised up" together, they are also "seated" together. Think of it! Enthroned with Christ! As the Amplified New Testament puts it: "Giving us joint seating with Him."

This is the believer's position *right now.* As Colossians 3:3, already quoted, describes it: ". . .your life is hid with Christ in

God." No other religion even *dares* make such a claim for the present.

Incidentally, perhaps this being made to "sit together" could be helpfully illustrated from the only other place in the New Testament where the Greek term is used. It pertains to Peter's fall when he followed the Lord afar off and sat down with his Saviour's enemies. Luke 22:55 describes it: "And when they had kindled a fire in the midst of the hall, and were set down together, Peter sat down among them."

Unlike those of us in the West—who build a big fire and the heat drives us from it—the Easterner kindles a small fire and those desiring warmth huddle closely together about the blaze. It was in this compact kind of a little circle that Peter *sat down together* with the Lord's enemies. And the use of it in Ephesians 2:6 is indicative of the intimateness of the believer's relationship with Christ after redemption.

As the olden hymnwriter expressed it:

> Near, so very near to God,
> Nearer I could not be;
> For in the Person of His Son,
> I'm just as near as He.

C. An Indication of Grace's Greatness

Look at verse 7: "That in the ages to come he might shew the exceeding riches of his grace and his kindness toward us through Christ Jesus."

The expression "in the ages to come" is literally: "unto the ages of the ages." This ought to make every reader ask himself the question: "Where will I be during the eternities of the eternities?" Your never-dying immortal soul *must* be somewhere.

The same description of the ages to come is used in Revelation 14:11, relative to souls in Hell. It says: "And the smoke of their torment ascended up for ever and ever. . . ."

Here is kindness that lasts through "the ages to come," and here is torment which lasts unto "the ages to come." Which will it be for you: endless ages of torment or endless ages of kindness? It all depends upon your answer to the question: "What shall I do then with Jesus which is called Christ?" (Matt. 27:22).

During the ages to come, He is going to "shew the exceeding riches of his grace." They are truly inexhaustible. Surely this is indicated by the fact that it is going to take our Saviour unto the ages of the ages just to show them to us.

Ponder well Titus 3:4-7:

"But after that the kindness and love of God our Saviour toward man appeared, Not by works of righteousness which we have done, but according to his mercy he saved us, by the washing of regeneration, and renewing of the Holy Ghost; Which he shed on us abundantly through Jesus Christ our Saviour; That being justified by his grace, we should be made heirs according to the hope of eternal life."

Conclusion

Being brought from the depths of depravity to the summits of grace is made possible by Jesus Christ—*in and through Him alone!* How strongly the apostle emphasized this truth in this passage. It is "with" Christ (vs. 5), "in" Christ (vs. 6), and "through" Christ (vs. 7). Acts 4:12 tells us: "Neither is there salvation in any other: for there is none other name under heaven given among men, whereby we must be saved."

And Jesus Himself insisted: "I am the way, the truth, and the life: no man cometh unto the Father, but by me" (John 14:6).

Before we close, let me remind you that one of the most glorious, blessed words in the human language is found in verse 5. I refer to the word "saved." Paul simply states, in parenthesis: "by grace ye are saved."

Are *you* saved? If not, happily acknowledge that Romans 10:13 declares: "For whosoever shall call upon the name of the Lord shall be saved." If you will call, you will be saved. Acts 16:30,31, puts it this way: "Sirs, what must I do to be saved? And they said, Believe on the Lord Jesus Christ, and thou shalt be saved, and thy house."

Decision for Christ

You have read the message and studied the Scripture; now settle for eternity this vital matter of your soul's salvation. Make the following decision the sentiment of your heart, then send a copy to us as an indication of your earnestness and seriousness.

Evangelist Robert L. Sumner
P. O. Box 157
Brownsburg, Indiana 46112

Dear Brother Sumner:

I have read the sermon, *"From the Depths of Depravity to the Summits of Grace."* I readily acknowledge that I am a sinner, just as outlined in the message. My condition, as far as anything I am able to do, is hopeless and helpless. However, I rejoice to learn from the Word of God that Jesus Christ offers to give me His so great salvation. I want to take Him at His Word that He will deliver me from Hell and take me to Heaven. So, right now, the best I know how, I ask Him to forgive my many sins and give me His salvation.

The first opportunity I have, I will make my decision known to others and will seek a Bible-preaching, Bible-teaching church where I can be baptized and serve the Saviour. Please send me a letter of counsel, instruction and encouragement.

(Signed) _____

Address _____

*Saved by Grace. . .
for Service!*

For by grace are ye saved through faith; and that not of yourselves: it is the gift of God:
Not of works, lest any man should boast.
For we are his workmanship, created in Christ Jesus unto good works, which God hath before ordained that we should walk in them.—Ephesians 2:8-10.

God saves sinners *without* works *unto* works!

There is a foolish and evil tendency among moderns: either they emphasize works to the exclusion of faith, or they emphasize faith to the exclusion of works. Sometimes shallow-thinking individuals have imagined a contradiction between what Paul taught and what James wrote in his epistle. But Paul, in our text, is saying exactly what James insisted. There is a simple order of *first* faith, *then* works. True faith produces true works. James pointed out that if you do not have true works, you do not have true faith.

Our text contains one of the best definitions of the *way of* salvation and the *purpose in* salvation in all the Bible. Let us examine the negative aspect first, noting,

I. HOW IT IS IMPOSSIBLE TO BE SAVED!

It is so easy to be wrong! A number of years ago someone wrote a song, the title of which has been quoted repeatedly, "Fifty Million Frenchmen Can't Be Wrong." However, they not only can be, the writer of the song himself was wrong. There are not fifty million Frenchmen.

In 1967, the French National Institute of Statistics informed President Charles De Gaulle that the fifty millionth Frenchman had been born: *a little girl named Sybille Lemoine.* The happy general was overjoyed and offered to be the godfather. Sybille received gifts from individuals and from firms, there were celebrations and receptions, and daughter and parents appeared on television.

However, the institute later rechecked its figures and discovered, to its utter dismay, that Sybille was really only the 49,400,000th Frenchman. Sybille kept her presents and De Gaulle remained her godfather, but the sincerity of the nation in thinking she was the fifty millionth was obviously misplaced.

Sometimes misplaced sincerity leads to tragedy. At a hospital in New York, a tank of carbon dioxide was mislabeled oxygen and the poison was administered to a patient during a minor operation. He died almost instantly. At a hospital in Regina, Canada, a jug of boric acid, mislabeled distilled water, was used in mixing bottle formulas in the nursery. Ten babies got the wrong mixture which proved fatal to five of them. In Binghamton, New York, salt got into the sugar jar and was used in mixing the formula for the babies in the nursery. Seven babies died before the problem was discovered. No one doubted the sincerity of any of the people on any of these hospital staffs, but sincerity is powerless to help when wrong.

The Boxer uprising in China years ago was helped along through the strange belief of the Boxers regarding their invincibility. Because of the incantations and rites they performed, they sincerely felt they were invulnerable to enemy bullets. When a Chinese officer suggested they prove their sincerity by allowing his soldiers to shoot at them, the foolish rebels immediately lined up and faced the firing squad. When the officer shouted "Fire!" and the guns blazed, the Boxers were instantly killed, of course. Being sincere in their wrongness did not make them any less dead.

It is the same regarding the way to Heaven. Thousands upon thousands of misguided souls are sincerely headed toward eternal damnation, confident all of the time that they are bound for

Heaven. Paul pinpoints the most popular of these misconceptions.

A. "Not of Ourselves"

Oh, that it were possible in some way or ways for people in the twentieth century to realize this vital biblical truth. Hardly a funeral is ever conducted but what some one comments, "Well, if any man is in Heaven, he is; he was such a good man." But goodness has *nothing* to do with one's salvation.

A preacher friend of mine in Maryland tells about a man in his church who is employed as a truck dispatcher. One of the drivers was involved in an accident and this Christian, feeling it would be a good time to witness for Christ, asked him: "Sam, suppose you had been killed? Would you have gone to Heaven?"

And the driver's amazing answer was: "Yes, Sir. I am *sure* I would have gone to Heaven because that wreck wasn't my fault."

Actually, we have nothing of merit in ourselves with which to seek or obtain God's favor. While we may look good in our own eyes, perhaps, it is not according to our standards that Heaven is obtained. As Paul told the Corinthians, "For not he that commendeth himself is approved, but whom the Lord commendeth" (II Cor. 10:18). Earlier he had told them:

"For we dare not make ourselves of the number, or compare ourselves with some that commend themselves: but they measuring themselves by themselves, and comparing themselves among themselves, are not wise."—Vs. 12.

Some people remind me of the little boy in Kansas. He ran into the house and proudly announced to his mother that he was nine feet and four inches tall. Told by his mother that he was not, he insisted that he was.

He said, "I measured myself!"

Since she was still unconvinced, he insisted that his mother come and see for herself. He took her by the hand and led her outside and, sure enough, he had found a stick, on the top of which he had written "nine feet, four inches." And he had cut the stick off at just his height. He was nine feet, four inches tall—

and he had a measuring stick to prove it!

Most people are like that. They have made their own measuring stick and when they measure themselves by their own standards, of course, they measure up. So they feel that if anyone ought to go to Heaven, they should.

Isaiah wrote the biography of every living individual when he declared: "But we are all as an unclean thing, and all our righteousnesses are as filthy rags; and we all do fade as a leaf; and our iniquities, like the wind, have taken us away" (Isa. 64:6). Our filthy rags are not proper apparel in which to appear before a holy God. We must have the righteousness of Christ.

The psalmist was describing our hopeless situation when he wrote:

"The Lord looked down from heaven upon the children of men, to see if there were any that did understand, and seek God. They are all gone aside, they are all together become filthy: there is none that doeth good, no, not one."—14:2,3.

Yet we are always trying to tell ourselves we aren't so bad. We are like the young soldier who heard the chaplain preach a powerful message on the Ten Commandments. The young private left in a sober mood, but suddenly he brightened up. "Anyway," he said, "I have never made a graven image!"

People console themselves that they have "never murdered," or that they have never "robbed any banks," or they have "never run off with anyone else's mate." The Apostle Paul repeated what the psalmist said when, writing to the Romans, he declared:

"As it is written, There is none righteous, no, not one: There is none that understandeth, there is none that seeketh after God. They are all gone out of the way, they are together become unprofitable; there is none that doeth good, no, not one."—Rom. 3:10-12.

The famous Scottish preacher, Dr. Alexander Whyte, was preaching one time on the rich young ruler who assured Jesus that he had kept the commandments from his youth. He described the heinous laughing of the demons in Hell when the rich young ruler arrived. He described them as roaring, "Kept the commandments, *and you're here!* Kept the commandments, *and you're here!"*

Even by being highly religious, it is not possible to save ourselves. I think of John Wesley, who, when he was a missionary, pitifully lamented, "But who shall save me?" A preacher friend of mine in Georgia held a crusade in which every deacon of the church was saved in the opening service, except one—and he wasn't present.

Lance B. Latham tells of a Bible teacher who used Luke 14:26, "If any man come to me, and hate not his father, and mother . . .he cannot be my disciple," as a condition of salvation. The futility of this was pinpointed moments later when the professed teacher added, "Just how far God will hold us to this I do not know." But the righteousness that takes us to Heaven must be *perfect* righteousness. There cannot be even the slightest blemish.

Did you know that one-sixth of a vote kept General Francis Marion Cockrell out of the governor's chair in Missouri? Back in 1874, at the time of the election in question, each county in Missouri was represented by one delegate, providing it had a population of at least 500. Counties with less than that number were represented on a pro-rated status. In those days of sparsely populated areas, some counties had less than 100 inhabitants and were entitled to only one-sixth of one vote. Charles H. Hardin defeated General Cockrell by exactly such a margin: *one-sixth of one vote!*

In much the same manner, a fraction of imperfection would keep a soul out of Heaven. To enter that land which is fairer than day it is necessary to be clothed in perfect righteousness. And, thank God, the availability of that righteousness is described by Paul in II Corinthians 5:21: "For he hath made him to be sin for us, who knew no sin; that we might be made the righteousness of God in him."

It is impossible to be saved of ourselves.

B. "Not of Works"

Gopal, a Hindu fakir near Karachi, Pakistan, was so conscious of the sins he had committed with his hands that he wore tight metal bracelets on his arms. It cut off the circulation, of course, and made his hands useless. *But that did not atone for his sins!* Nor does it help to climb the twenty-eight steps of the holy stairs in Rome, even though Roman Catholic authorities claim it gives the penitent a nine-year indulgence for Purgatory. It was while climbing these stairs on his knees that the great reformer, Martin Luther, rose to his feet and exclaimed, **"The just shall live by faith."**

There is absolutely nothing of human endeavor that will fix one up for Heaven. Oswald Smith described it:

> Weeping will not save you—
> Though your face were bathed in tears—
> That could not allay your fears—
> Could not wash the sins of years—
>   Weeping will not save you.
>
> Working will not save you—
> Purest deeds that you can do—
> Holiest thoughts and feelings, too,
> Cannot form your soul anew—
>   Working will not save you.
>
> Waiting will not save you—
> Helpless, guilty, lost you lie;
> In your ears is mercy's cry;
> If you wait you'll surely die—
>   Waiting will not save you.
>
> Faith in Christ will save you;
> Sinner, trust God's risen Son;
> Trust the work that He has done;
> To His arms now quickly run;
>   Faith in Christ will save you.
>
> Jesus wept and died for thee;
> Jesus suffered on the tree;
> Jesus waits to make thee free;
>   He alone can save thee.

Dr. Robert E. Neighbour tells of asking a man if he were a Christian. The good gentleman replied, "I am doing the best I know."

When Neighbour asked him what he was doing, he said, "I try to live right. I pay my debts when I can. I fulfill the golden rule, 'Do unto others as you would have them do unto you.' "

Neighbour asked, "Is that all?"

He replied, "No, that isn't all."

"Well," Neighbour insisted, "what else?"

"I go to church. I am a member. I give money to help pay your salary every week. I go to prayer meeting sometimes."

Neighbour persisted, "Is that all?"

Angrily, the gentleman replied, "What more do you think a man ought to do?"

"Why," Neighbour said, "he ought to believe in the Lord Jesus Christ and receive Him as his personal Lord and Saviour."

If salvation is of grace—and it is—it **cannot** be by works. Romans 4:4 insists: "Now to him that worketh is the reward not reckoned of grace, but of debt." *We* can do *nothing!* Oh, that men might learn this truth and accept God's salvation by grace through faith.

> 'Twas not my works that saved my soul,
> Nor yet my zeal, my prayers, my tears.
> 'Twas Jesus Christ, the Son of God,
> He bore my sins, He calmed my fears.

C. The Reason It Is Not of Ourselves, Not of Works

God is not going to share His glory with another. If we merited salvation, we would have reason to glory. So our text tells us it must be "Not of works, *lest any man should boast.*"

How plain is the Scripture to this effect. **Romans 4:2 says:** "For if Abraham were justified by works, he hath whereof to glory; but not before God." If Abraham got to Heaven by the merit of his deeds, he would have reason to boast. But he did not; he was justified by grace through faith.

Paul, in reminding the Corinthians how they were called of God and saved, explained it: "That no flesh should glory in his presence" (I Cor. 1:29). And he went on: "But of him are ye in Christ Jesus, who of God is made unto us wisdom, and righteousness, and sanctification, and redemption: That, according as it is written, He that glorieth, let him glory in the Lord" (I Cor. 1:30,31).

The apostle goes into the matter quite thoroughly in the third chapter of Romans, summing it up:

"Where is boasting then? It is excluded. By what law? of works? Nay: but by the law of faith. Therefore we conclude that a man is justified by faith without the deeds of the law."—vss. 27,28.

One of the early Wesleyan ministers was talking to a very self-righteous man one day who insisted that he did not need Christ. He said, "My life is all I need. I am satisfied that when I face God and He sees how good I have been, He will not be hard on me."

And this earnest preacher—who had lived a rather profane life before his own conversion—excitedly exclaimed: "Listen! God couldn't let you into Heaven. You would bring discord. Heaven will be filled with saved sinners singing, 'Glory to the Lamb who was slain and has washed us from our sins in His own blood.' You would be singing, 'Glory to me because of my morality, my good life and my consistent living. I prepared myself for Heaven.' If the angels caught you doing that, they would take you by the nape of your neck and throw you over the wall." And so they would. All the bragging in Heaven is going to be on Jesus.

> You will never go to Heaven just because you join the church,
>   For religion cannot save your guilty soul;
> You will have to be converted, just as anybody else,
>   And accept the One who died to make you whole.
>
> You will never go to Heaven just because you do your best,
>   Even though you turn away from every sin;
> You are lost and need a Savior, you must have eternal life,
>   Jesus Christ will have to come and dwell within.
>
> You will never go to Heaven just because you work and pray,
>   For your efforts, God has said, are all in vain;
> Jesus purchased your redemption, "It is finished," was His cry,
>   Now He bids you trust Him and be born again.

II. HOW IT IS POSSIBLE TO "BE SAVED!"

Now that we have considered how it is impossible to be saved, let us answer positively by the Word of God life's greatest question: *"What must I do to be saved?"*

A. By Grace!

We are faced point-blank in the text with the humbling fact: **no one deserves to be saved!** Salvation is—from start to finish, beginning to end, first and last—a matter of grace.

This answers the question, "Is God just in sending heathen who never heard of Christ to Hell?" He would be just in sending *everyone* to Hell without offering salvation to *anyone.* He never offered salvation to angels who sinned, and II Peter 2:4 tells us: "God spared not the angels that sinned but cast them down to hell, and delivered them into chains of darkness, to be reserved unto judgment." He was under no more obligation to offer man redemption than He was angels.

Are you saved? *Then give God the glory!*

We might also point out that salvation is *all* of grace, not just the starting point. It is amazing how many want to use Christ and the finished work of the cross as a launching point for salvation—to sort of qualify them for a salvation of their own merit. Instead of singing, "Only a sinner, saved by grace," they want to sing, "Only a sinner, saved by grace—*plus my labors and works and faithfulness and holding out to the end!"*

Alas, such is not possible.

The grace that saves is described as "the exceeding riches of his grace in his kindness toward us through Christ Jesus" (Eph. 2:7). It is also described, "In whom we have redemption through his blood, the forgiveness of sins, according to the riches of his grace" (Eph. 1:7).

Did you hear of the Lancashire factory worker who went on an excursion and witnessed the Irish Sea for the first time? When she saw that mighty blue expanse and the seeming limitlessness of the ocean rolling in, she gasped and exclaimed: "At last, here comes something there is enough of!"

That is the way it is with the grace of God. Isaiah 1:18 says, "Come now, and let us reason together, saith the Lord: though your sins be as scarlet, they shall be as white as snow; though they be red like crimson, they shall be as wool."

Moody expressed it quaintly: "Jesus is able to save the Devil's castaways!"

It is important to note that Paul, in describing it to the Ephesians, dogmatically said, "By grace are ye saved." Or, literally, **"ye ARE saved,"** as verse 5 expresses it. What a truth! What a glorious realization! Those who would come to Christ are saved right here and now. It is not a matter of someday, some time, some where being saved—*it is a present possession!* First John 5:12 insists, "He that hath the Son hath life; and he that hath not the Son of God hath not life."

It is as simple as that! It is not as that almost sacrilegious hymn expresses it:

> "Nothing left but Heav'n and prayer,
> Wond'ring if our names were there. . . ."

No, *no!* This is a know-so salvation, not a wondering-so proposition. It is like the gospel chorus by Everek R. Storms the children used to sing:

> Some think so, they hope so, they trust so, they guess so,
> But I know, I know I am saved.
> Some hope they'll reach Heaven, reach Heaven at last,
> But I know, I know I am saved.
> For I've opened my heart's door and Christ has come in,
> And I know that He saves me and keeps me from sin;
> And the Spirit Himself beareth witness within,
> And I know, I know I am saved.

The only way we could ever know is through a salvation of grace. Assurance could never be ours if eternal life depended upon us and what we did. We would never know whether we were good enough, whether we were going to hold out, or whether our works would be acceptable to Him.

B. Through Faith!

It is amazing how difficult the religions of the world make salvation.

In *The Sword of the Lord* some years ago an unnamed writer pointed out how world religions answer the Philippian jailor's cry, "What must I do to be saved?" He wrote:

> The Mohammedan replies: "Repeat the words, There is no God but Allah and Mohamet is his prophet"; pray five times daily; give alms to beggars; keep the fasts; read the Koran and make a pilgrimage to Mecca."
>
> The Hindu priest replies: "Observe the rules of the caste; worship the monkey and the cow; crawl through the dust like a measuring worm to some sacred temple; bathe in the waters of the Ganges; erect a temple to one of the million divinities. You may then escape rebirth as a reptile or a beast or a woman and become absorbed in the deity."
>
> The Buddhist replies: "Forget that you have a body; become indifferent to pleasure and pain and you may attain to Nirvana—the state of the extinguished flame."
>
> The Confucius scholar replies: "Study the sacred classics and learn the rules of righteousness. Confucius shows the path of duty but cannot help you to follow it. You must save yourself."
>
> Contrast these with the simple, all-sufficient answer of Paul: "Believe on the Lord Jesus Christ, and thou shalt be saved." No need to understand the deep questions of theology or to perform impossible tasks. You cannot save yourself. Entrust yourself to Christ and He will save you.

In our modern day we are able to pick up the telephone and direct dial to just about anywhere. But if you were able to place a direct-dial call to Heaven and ask, "What must I do to be saved?" you would not get any other answer than, "Believe on the Lord Jesus Christ, and thou shalt be saved, and thy house." It is by grace, *through faith.*

Do you remember blind Bartimaeus? Jesus said to him, in Mark 10:52, "Go thy way; THY FAITH HATH MADE THEE WHOLE." Do you recall the sinful woman who anointed Jesus' feet? He told her, "Thy sins are forgiven." And then He added, "THY FAITH HATH SAVED THEE: go in peace" (Luke 7:48,50).

As a matter of fact, Paul shocks a self-righteous world hoping to go to Heaven on merit, by saying: "But to him that worketh not, but believeth on him that justifieth the ungodly, his faith is counted for righteousness" (Rom. 4:5).

When John G. Paton, the noted missionary to the New Hebrides, was translating the Gospel of John, he had a problem about a native word for believe. He could not find a word or phrase that expressed the New Testament idea and no matter how or where he inquired, he could not come up with a solution to his problem.

Not long after making it an urgent matter of prayer, a native came into the hut where he was translating and threw himself into a chair, commenting as he did so, "I am casting all my weight upon this chair."

Paton exclaimed, "That's the phrase I want: *casting all your weight upon!*"

And that is what salvation is. When you put your trust in Jesus Christ, you are casting all your weight upon Him to save you from sin and take you to Heaven.

Salvation is by grace through faith. Grace is the fountain, the reservoir; faith is the channel, the pipeline. Be careful, however, that you do not make faith your saviour. Jesus is the Saviour, not faith. As Paul said in II Timothy 1:12, ". . .I know whom I have believed, and am persuaded that he is able to keep that which I have committed unto him against that day." It was not *what* or *how* he believed, but *whom* he believed.

Oh, how simple is salvation by faith. Anyone can be saved who *desires* to be saved.

C. It Is a Gift of God!

John 3:16 says: "For God so loved the world, that he gave his only begotten Son, that whosoever believeth in him should not perish, but have everlasting life." And Romans 6:23 adds, ". . .but the gift of God is eternal life through Jesus Christ our Lord."

You cannot pay for a gift. If you obtain the whole world for a penny, it would not be a gift. It would be a mighty good bargain—there is no doubt about that—but it would not be a gift.

When the Dutch obtained Manhattan Island from the Indians

for the equivalent of $24, they received a tremendous bargain, but they did not receive a gift.

If you paid anything for salvation, it would not be a gift. You cannot make a payment of baptism, or a payment of confirmation, or a payment of living by the golden rule, or a payment of commandment keeping, or any other kind of a payment. *It is a gift.*

When Colonel Teddy Roosevelt was commanding a regiment of Rough Riders in Cuba, during the Spanish War, a number of his men fell sick. The future President learned that Miss Clara Barton—the founder and first president of the American Red Cross—had recently received a supply of delicacies for the wounded whom she was nursing, so he went to her and asked her to sell some of them for the sick in his regiment.

She refused.

Roosevelt was very upset and offered to pay any amount for the supplies out of his own pocket, if he could only have them for his men. In desperation he said, "I must have proper food for my sick men. How can I get them?"

Smilingly, the lovely lady said: *"Just ask for them, Colonel."*

"Oh," exclaimed the now beaming Roosevelt, "That's the way, is it? Then I do ask for them at once." And they were immediately given.

How many, like Roosevelt, have the idea that the needed salvation can be obtained through the payment of some price. No, *no;* a thousand times no! It is absolutely free; the price has already been paid by Almighty God and now He offers it by grace through faith plus nothing.

> Nothing to pay? No, not a whit;
>   Nothing to do? No, not a bit:
>   All that was needed to do or to pay
>   Jesus has done it His own blessed way.
>
> Nothing to do? No, not a stroke;
>   Gone is the captor, gone is the yoke:
>   Jesus at Calvary severed the chain,
>   And none can imprison His free-man again!
>
> Nothing to fear? No, not a jot;
>   Nothing within? No, not a spot:

> Christ is my peace, and I've nothing at stake,
> Satan can that neither harass nor shake.
>
> Nothing to settle? All has been paid,
> Nothing to worry, peace has been made;
> Jesus alone is the sinner's resource,
> Peace He has made by the blood of His cross.
>
> What about judgment? I'm thankful to say,
> Jesus has met it and borne it away;
> Drank it all up when He hung on the Tree,
> Leaving a cup full of blessing for me.

III. WHY DOES GOD SAVE SINNERS?

Just why does a holy God want to save those who are dead, disobedient, defiled and doomed? The apostle explains: "For we are his workmanship, created in Christ Jesus unto good works, which God hath before ordained that we should walk in them."

A. To Bear His Trademark

Fly-by-night operations do not put their trademark on anything they produce, but great corporations boast of their handicraft.

I think, by way of example, of the *"Body by Fisher"* symbol and the desire of this great corporation to let everyone know that it produces the beautiful body of each General Motors automobile. In one of its advertisements, Fisher boasted: "One of the nicest satisfactions of traveling in a car with a body by Fisher is the calm satisfaction you have of being approved on arrival. You are ready for admiration." Fisher is justifiably proud of the automobile bodies which bear its trademark.

Well, the Christian bears God's trademark. He is His "workmanship." How about it? Does the world see His trademark in you?

Every saved soul is the special work of God. There are no self-made or self-created Christians. And remember the material with which He has to work:

"And you hath he quickened, who were dead in trespasses and sins: Wherein in time past ye walked according to the course of this world, according to the prince of the power of

the air, the spirit that now worketh in the children of disobedience: Among whom also we all had our conversation in times past in the lusts of our flesh, fulfilling the desires of the flesh and of the mind; and were by nature the children of wrath, even as others."—Eph. 2:1-3.

What wonders God creates with such worthless material! It is somewhat like the artist who took an ordinary handkerchief on which a blot of ink had been spilled, and used that spot as a basis for a fine design in India ink, making the ordinary handkerchief a thing of unusual value and beauty.

Our wonderful Lord takes blotted, spotted, worthless lives and transforms them into things of beauty and usefulness.

History records the delightful background of Michelangelo Buonarroti's famous statue of David. He was passing a newly or nearly finished cathedral when he spotted, among other refuse, a large piece of marble. Although it was a costly stone from the famous Carrara quaries, it had an imperfection that caused its rejection by the builders.

On an impulse, Michelangelo had the stone brought to his studio and, on September 11, 1501, he began his work. *What a masterpiece he created!* The finished product portrayed the young shepherd, sling in hand, ready to throw the stone that terminated the life of the giant Goliath. Placed on the terrace of the Palazzo Vecchio, the public square of Michelangelo's city, Florence, along the bank of the Arno, it was removed in 1882 to take its place in the city's Academy of Fine Arts.

Here was a supposedly worthless stone, rejected by the experts, turned into a thing of wonder, beauty and pricelessness by a master hand. Thus it is with God's creative power in redemption.

B. Walk in Good Works?

God does not merely save sinners to be a thing of beauty, He saves them to do a job. Paul's expression is: "Created in Christ Jesus unto good works." This is a theme Paul often emphasized. In Ephesians 4:24 he declared: ". . .put on the new man, which after God is created in righteousness and true holiness." In I Thessalonians 4:7 he insisted: "For God hath not called us unto uncleanness, but unto holiness." And to the young preacher, Titus, he offered the reminder: "Who gave himself for us, that he might redeem us from all iniquity, and purify unto himself a peculiar people, zealous of good works" (Titus 2:14).

However, note carefully God's order: first, the salvation; then, the works.

The famous evangelist, D. L. Moody, tells of leaving home as a boy and going to Boston. The first few weeks, when he was without employment, were times of loneliness and homesickness. He would go to the post office several times a day and ask for mail. Eventually a letter came from his younger sister and he opened it eagerly to get news from home. Instead, however, the entire letter was filled with admonitions to watch out for pickpockets, a class of people his sister had heard were common in the big city. Moody said he thought he had better get some money in his pocket first, then worry about the pickpockets!

It is the same with salvation. You get the salvation *first,* then you walk in good works. Paul told the Thessalonians that their reputation was being spread far and wide, "How ye turned to God from idols to serve the living and true God" (I Thess. 1:9). That is the order. First you turn to God from sin, then you are qualified to serve the living and true God.

Paul expressed it to Titus:

"This is a faithful saying, and these things I will that thou affirm constantly, that they which have believed in God might be careful to maintain good works. These things are good and profitable unto men."—Titus 3:8.

Once again the apostle is pointing out that "believing in God" comes before one is qualified "to maintain good works." As a matter of fact, he insists that this is a faithful teaching and one to be "affirmed constantly."

> I dare not work, my soul to save;
> That work my Lord hath done;
> But I will work like any slave
> For love of God's dear Son.

In thinking about good works, remember that God has said we should *walk* in them. This means to advance, to go forward, to make progress. Henry Drummond once said:

> God does not make the mountain tops to be inhabited; they are not for the homes of men. We ascend the height to catch a broader vision of our earthly surroundings, but we do not tarry there. We descend to our farms, our shops, our studies, our household tasks. This need not be a downfall. Let life hold its true meaning and all duty becomes sacred.

God expects us to *do* something. Salvation is no WPA project, it is a life of committal to the One who redeemed us. We are saved to work.

Conclusion

The Bible salvation is by *grace*. . .through *faith*. . .plus *nothing*. But once we have been saved, our life belongs to our Redeemer and should be used for His glory in whatever way He directs. The all-important question is: **Are you saved?**

If not, *now* is the time to get it settled. John 1:12 assures us: "But as many as received him, to them gave he power to become the sons of God, even to them that believe on his name."

If you would receive Him right now—and *receiving* is explained as *believing*—you would immediately become a child of God. Why not ask Him to save you this very moment? If you will, clip or copy the following decision—or write it in your own words—and send it to us that we may rejoice with you and write you some helpful words of counsel.

Dr. Robert L. Sumner
P. O. Box 157
Brownsburg, Indiana 46112

Dear Brother Sumner:

I have just read your message, *Saved by Grace. . .for Service,* and I realize that I need to be saved. It is true that there is no work I could do to merit salvation and I confess that even religious rites would not help. Salvation is, indeed, a matter of grace to be received by faith. I do believe that Jesus Christ died for my sins and that He is willing to save me. Right here and now I sincerely ask Him to do so.

I also acknowledge that my life will no longer be my own, it will belong to Him. The best I know how, I will follow Him, love Him, serve Him and do whatever He wants me to do. Please send me a letter of counsel, instruction and encouragement.

(Signed)_____

Address_____

_____

*Things Are Different
Now:
We've Got It "Made"!*

Wherefore remember, that ye being in time past Gentiles in the flesh, who are called Uncircumcision by that which is called the Circumcision in the flesh made by hands;

That at that time ye were without Christ, being aliens from the commonwealth of Israel, and strangers from the covenants of promise, having no hope, and without God in the world:

But now in Christ Jesus ye who sometimes were far off are made nigh by the blood of Christ.

For he is our peace, who hath made both one, and hath broken down the middle wall of partition between us;

Having abolished in his flesh the enmity, even the law of commandments contained in ordinances; for to make in himself of twain one new man, so making peace;

And that he might reconcile both unto God in one body by the cross, having slain the enmity thereby:

And came and preached peace to you which were afar off, and to them that were nigh.

For through him we both have access by one Spirit unto the Father.

Now therefore ye are no more strangers and foreigners, but fellow-citizens with the saints, and of the household of God;

And are built upon the foundation of the apostles and prophets, Jesus Christ himself being the chief corner stone;

In whom all the building fitly framed together groweth unto an holy temple in the Lord:

In whom ye also are builded together for an habitation of God through the Spirit.—Ephesians 2:11-22.

Sometime ago, in San Jose, California, Superior Court Judge William F. James received a lengthy 32-page letter from an inmate awaiting trial on forgery charges. The man involved, whose police record dated all the way back to 1943 and who had had three wives by which he fathered eight children, listed his "life's troubles" in the letter to Judge James.

The accused frankly confessed his guilt in forging and cashing one $1,200 check and six $200 ones, then threw himself on the mercy of the court, vowing his forgery days were behind him forever. Then he wrote these startling lines: "I know you won't believe a thief like me, but to show that I'm sincere, I'm going to cut off my writing finger. . . .When you receive this, the finger will be off."

Quickly checking with jail authorities, His Honor learned that the inmate had, indeed, walked into the kitchen of the jail, picked up a meat cleaver and whacked off the index finger on his right hand at the first joint. Authorities had rushed him to the county hospital for treatment, then returned him to his cell.

Yet, surely, no one is so naive as to expect that the forger's problem was in his finger! One might have both hands cut off and learn to forge signatures with a pen held by his teeth. It is a *heart* problem, not a *finger* problem.

For things to be really different, an individual must be remade. Signing pledges, vows of reformation, turning over a new leaf, or chopping off fingers simply will not do the job. Thank God, however, while all such measures inevitably result in total failure, complete success is found when an individual turns to Jesus Christ. As the gospel chorus by Stanton W. Gavitt describes it,

> Things are diff'rent, now, something happened to me
>   When I gave my heart to Jesus.
> Things are diff'rent now; I was changed it must be,
>   When I gave my heart to Him.
> Things I loved before have passed away,
>   Things I love far more have come to stay.
> Things are diff'rent now; something happened that day
>   When I gave my heart to Him.

There is an illustration hoary with age—obviously, since it

talks about *gold* coins—pointing out how Longfellow could take a worthless sheet of paper, write a poem on it, and make it worth $6,000. Or Rockefeller could take a piece of paper and sign his name to it, making it worth millions. Uncle Sam could take a piece of gold, stamp the image of an eagle on it, and make it worth twenty dollars. A mechanic could take some raw material worth five dollars, and make an article worth fifty dollars. Or an artist might take a fifty-cent piece of canvas, paint a picture on it, and make it worth thousands of dollars. Yet these are trifles compared to a life's change in value when Jesus Christ takes over. Second Corinthians 5:17 describes it: "Thereore if any man be in Christ, he is a new creature: old things are passed away; behold, all things are become new."

Paul, in this passage before us, is dealing with the *difference* the new creation makes. For one thing, he assures his readers,

I. THINGS ARE DIFFERENT NOW: WE ARE MADE NIGH!

He writes:

"Wherefore remember, that ye being in time past Gentiles in the flesh, who are called Uncircumcision by that which is called the Circumcision in the flesh made by hands; That at that time ye were without Christ, being aliens from the commonwealth of Israel, and strangers from the covenants of promise, having no hope, and without God in the world: But now in Christ Jesus ye who sometimes were far off are made nigh by the blood of Christ."—Vss. 11-13.

A. What We Were!

He begins this portion with the appeal, "Wherefore *remember*. . . ." Most people do not like to face reality when it is ugly, but it is a vital thing in spiritual experience.

They say that the Great Commoner, Oliver Cromwell, had a blemish on his nose. On one occasion he sat for a noted artist to paint his portrait. The latter, probably because of Cromwell's exalted position in the government, left the facial disfigurement out of the portrait. However, when Cromwell discovered the omission, he angrily demanded that the artist paint in the blemish, saying, "I want to be painted just as I am."

That is what the Divine Artist, the Holy Spirit, using the Apostle Paul as his brush, does in this passage. He, without omitting any of the blemishes, gives a true picture of the unconverted. He commences by reminding the Ephesians that they were,

1. "Gentiles in the Flesh"

For God's X-Ray picture of the Gentiles, the reader is invited to study Romans 1:18-32. Without quoting all of that sordid story here, consider, as a sample, verses 21-23:

"Because that, when they knew God, they glorified him not as God, neither were thankful; but became vain in their imaginations, and their foolish heart was darkened. Professing themselves to be wise, they became fools, And changed the glory of the uncorruptible God into an image made like to corruptible man, and to birds, and fourfooted beasts, and creeping things."

While Paul was talking about himself in Romans 7:18, it still summarizes the true condition of the flesh, no matter whether Jew or Gentile: "For I know that in me (that is in my flesh,) dwelleth no good thing: for to will is present with me; but how to perform that which is good I find not."

2. "Who Are Called Uncircumcision"

When this description was used of unconverted Gentiles, it was a term of contempt and hatred. So real was the enmity between Jews and Gentiles that the latter were called "dogs" by the former. The Syrophenician woman was referring to this custom when, in begging the Lord to heal her "previously vexed with a devil" daughter, and replying to His statement, "It is not meet to take the children's bread, and cast it to dogs," she said, "Truth, Lord: yet the dogs eat of the crumbs which fall from their master's table" (Matt. 15:26,27).

This enmity was so real the early Christians had trouble realizing God actually loved those Gentile "dogs" and wanted them to be saved. Peter, in his experience regarding Cornelius and his reluctance about the "unclean," is a good illustration. In fact, after the Lord convinced him that Cornelius and other Gentiles could be saved, he, in turn, had trouble persuading the other disciples. In fact, when "the apostles and brethren that were in Judaea heard that the Gentiles had also received the word of God," as soon as Peter had returned to Jerusalem, they faced him with the charge: "Thou wentest in to men uncircumcised, and didst eat with them" (Acts 11:1-3).

Peter, in his defense, "rehearsed the matter from the beginning," summing it up: "Forasmuch then as God gave them the like gift as he did unto us, who believed on the Lord Jesus Christ; what was I, that I could withstand God?" (vs. 17). And the next verse tells us that the rebellious apostles submitted to the inevitable will of God, declaring: "When they heard these things, they held their peace, and glorified God, saying, Then hath God also to the Gentiles granted repentance unto life."

3. "Without Christ"

This is literally, "separated from Christ," and is intended to picture a state of *absolute* separation. The position of the unconverted is one of no union, no connection of any kind. Christians are portrayed as branches of the Vine, but not so unbelievers.

It is a pathetic picture. The words "without Christ" are words of despair, of doom and of damnation. "Without Christ" life is hopeless, Hell is sure and Heaven an utter impossibility. The individual "without Christ" has no one to represent him before Almighty God, since I Timothy 2:5 says: "For there is one God, and one mediator between God and men, the man Christ Jesus."

4. "Aliens From the Commonwealth of Israel"

Being alienated means that the individual has no right, no

place among God's people. Spiritually he is a vagrant, a homeless wanderer, a vagabond, truly a man without a country.

We read one time of a man picked up by the police in Florida who, dressed in tattered rags, was sleeping in a Florida bus station. Thinking they would lock him up on a charge of vagrancy, they asked him to empty his pockets. When he did so, the shocked and startled police discovered he had over $187,000 on his person.

Investigation proved that the money rightfully belonged to him, yet he was getting no value from his possession, no benefit or enjoyment.

So with the spiritual vagabonds of today. Although they may wear expensive clothing, live in fashionable homes, drive high-powered automobiles and otherwise manifest the outward display of luxury, yet there is no joy, no peace, no real enjoyment from these things.

5. "Strangers From the Covenants of Promise"

The unconverted are not included in God's holy covenants which He made with Abraham, with Isaac, with Jacob, with Moses, and with David. The Gentiles were not included in the promises made to the Israelites, "to whom pertaineth the adoption, and the glory, and the covenants, and the giving of the law, and the service of God, and the promises" (Romans 9:4). These alienated, uncircumcised Gentiles had no share in the promises.

6. "Having No Hope"

That is, they had no *ground* for hope, nothing on which to *base* hope. It was to Christians who had lost loved ones in death—and only Christians—to whom Paul comfortingly wrote: "But I would not have you to be ignorant, brethren, concerning them which are asleep, that ye sorrow not, even as others which have no hope" (I Thessalonians 4:13).

7. "Without God in the World"

That is, literally, "Without *the* God." They had *their* gods—as Paul said in I Corinthians 8:5, "there be gods many, and lords many"—but none that could offer hope.

How despairing, how forlorn are those words: "Without God." It is far better to be without money, without friends, without food, without water, without shelter, without clothing, without anything and everything, than to be without God. Yet most people put Him last on their lists of priorities.

What a despairing and discouraging picture the artist has painted of the lost in this passage. He has described them as Gentiles in the flesh, without Christ, aliens, strangers, without hope and without God. Yet such a bleak picture only makes more glorious the change when an individual is "made nigh."

B. What We Are!

After the frightening picture of the past, Paul introduces his portrayal of the present with the contrasting opening: **"But now."** This is a reminder of the "But God" after the dead, disobedient, defiled description in the opening three verses of this chapter. And once again Paul is introducing his readers to the grace of God.

John Newton, who gave the world the blessed gospel song, "Amazing Grace," was an infidel, a slave trader, a rumrunner and the vilest of the vile before his conversion. In fact, during one period he was himself a slave to a Negro woman. What God can do in the miracle of redemption is described in the tablet on the north wall of the chapel at Woolnoth, which says:

> JOHN NEWTON, CLERK,
> Once an infidel and libertine,
> A servant of slaves in Africa,
> Was, by the rich mercy of our Lord and Saviour, JESUS CHRIST,
> Preserved, restored, pardoned, and
> Appointed to preach the Faith he
> Had long labored to destroy.

Yes, this is what God can do when He remakes a life through His new creation. Well might we all join heartily and gratefully in singing with William R. Newell,

> Oh the love that drew salvation's plan,
> Oh the grace that brought it down to man,
> Oh the mighty gulf that God did span,
> At Calvary!

1. "In Christ Jesus"

This is the triumphant theme of the epistle. This is the hope of the believer. Herein lies the manifestation of His wondrous grace. What we could not do in resisting the pull of the world, the flesh and the Devil, Christ does for us in the new creation.

In the old Greek myth of women who lured sailors from their course to their doom as they passed their island, singing their siren songs, so the pull of the world and its sinful pleasures proves to be an irresistible fascination for men, women and young people "in the flesh."

In the story of the Greeks, Ulysses, to get by the island, tied his men in their seats at their oars. He, to steer the boat, plugged his ears so that he could not hear the songs. But Orpheus sailed by the island in a far superior manner. He sang so sweetly as to drown out and overpower the songs of the evil women. This is what happens when one comes to Christ. The beauty of redemption is so much greater than the fruits of the flesh, the latter loses its charm. Someone expressed it:

> I tried the broken cisterns, Lord,
> But, ah! the waters failed!
> Even as I stopped to drink, they fled,
> And mocked me as I wailed.
> Now none but Christ can satisfy,
> None other name for me;
> There's love and life and lasting joy,
> Lord Jesus, found in Thee.

2. "Made Nigh"

The word *nigh* describes more than mere contact—*it is vital union!* One might hang a sheet on a branch and the sheet could certainly be said to have "contact" with the tree, but it would not be "union." When one comes to Christ in salvation, it is union he receives, not mere contact. This union is one made by grafting, as Romans 11:13-25 explains. We were "cut out of the olive tree which is wild by nature, and wert grafted contrary to nature into a good olive tree" (vs. 24).

No wonder, being made a part of Christ in such a union, peace and satisfaction are the inevitable result. Years ago we copied the words of a now-unknown poet, describing this experience in sentiments akin to ours:

I once was as fond of the world as you; I was a stranger to Jesus!
But life has become entirely new; since I trusted Jesus.
I was a stranger but He took me in, naked He clothed me and saved me from sin;
Oh! what a treasure I have found in Him: I am satisfied with Jesus.

I searched for pleasure and joy everywhere; I was a stranger to Jesus!
But many a time my heart was sore; until I trusted Jesus!
The pleasures of sin they flee so fast; for God's Word tells us they cannot last,
And, oh, what a sting when the pleasure's past; I am glad I am trusting Jesus!

The world it can never satisfy; if you're a stranger to Jesus,
There is something for which your soul will cry; man, do you know 'tis Jesus?
The Devil for years has blinded your eyes; he says when you are saved all your pleasure dies,
But, glory to God, I know that's all lies, I am happy trusting Jesus.

I am satisfied with Jesus, He's all the world to me;
I never, never had a friend, half as kind as He,
I came to Him the slave of sin, His power has made me free;
I know He'll do the same for you, as what He's done for me!

And, remember, all of this is made possible,

3. "By the Blood of Christ"

The precious blood of Jesus Christ paved the highway into the presence of God. Hebrews 10:19-22 describes it like this:

"Having therefore, brethren, boldness to enter into the holiest by the blood of Jesus, By a new and living way, which he hath consecrated for us, through the veil, that is to say, his flesh; And having an high priest over the house of God; Let us draw near with a true heart in full assurance of faith, having our hearts sprinkled from an evil conscience, and our bodies washed with pure water."

Thank God,

> There is a fountain filled with blood,
> Drawn from Immanuel's veins;
> And sinners plunged beneath that flood,
> Lose all their guilty stains.

But being made nigh is not all in this so great salvation. Paul goes on to exult,

II. THINGS ARE DIFFERENT NOW: WE ARE MADE ONE!

He describes it:

"For he is our peace, who hath made both one, and hath broken down the middle wall of partition between us; Having abolished in his flesh the enmity, even the law of commandments contained in ordinances; for to make in himself of twain one new man, so making peace; And that he might reconcile both unto God in one body by the cross, having slain the enmity thereby; And came and preached peace to you which were afar off, and to them that were nigh. For through him we both have access by one Spirit unto the Father."

A. Position of Jews, Gentiles in Times Past

Paul uses such expressions as "middle wall of partition" and "enmity" to describe this relationship on the other side of Calvary. It is an ugly scene of Gentile hating Jew and Jew hating Gentile. It is a portrayal of confrontation with the Gentile calling the Jew *swine* and the Jew calling the Gentile *dog*. Unfortunately, this same enmity goes on today with reference to the *unconverted* Jews and Gentiles. Witness the crisis in the Middle East, or, closer to home, behold the growing anti-Semitism in our own country.

B. Position of Redeemed: Christ "Made Peace"

For the believer, Christ made peace because "He is our peace" (vs. 14). Romans 5:1 says: "Therefore being justified by faith, we have peace with God through our Lord Jesus Christ." Christ and Christ alone is the true source of peace. Apart from this Prince of

Peace, there is no real peace; yea, there can be none.

Sometime back we read that, in light of the disastrous and bloody wars against each other which France and Germany have experienced, money was being raised to build a giant "cross of peace" at the border of the two nations. It was to tower fifty feet into the sky, weigh fifteen tons, and be erected near Buhl, at the border provinces of Alsace and Baden. Whether or not that "cross of peace" was ever erected, we can state with positive assurance that the cross of Christ destroys enmity and makes peace for all who surrender to Him. As the poet wrote:

> I hear the words of love,
> I gaze upon the blood;
> I see the mighty sacrifice
> And I have peace with God.
>
> 'Tis everlasting peace,
> Sure as Jehovah's name,
> 'Tis stable as His steadfast throne,
> Forever more the same.

1. "Hath Made Both One"; "Hath Broken Down the Middle Wall"

This reference by the apostle was to the wall between the Temple's outer court where the Gentiles were permitted to enter, and the inner court where only Jews could go. This victory was accomplished by "abolishing" and "slaying" the enmity, "the law of commandments contained in ordinances."

We read in Romans 10:4, "For Christ is the end of the law for righteousness to every one that believeth." Jesus Christ fulfilled perfectly the law for us and we are complete in Him.

Colossians 2:14 describes it: "Blotting out the handwriting of ordinances that was against us, which was contrary to us, and took it out of the way, nailing it to his cross." Now Christ and Christ alone is the basis of our acceptance with God. Whether one is a Jew or a Gentile matters little, coming on the basis of the blood of Jesus Christ, each has equal access into the very presence of God, into the holy of holies.

Note that Paul uses the word "abolished"! This enmity is completely removed; it is annihilated!

2. His Purpose? "To Make IN HIMSELF of Twain One New Man"

Jesus Christ was not interested in reforming or patching up the old creation. His purpose was to make a *new creature*. He, Paul told his readers, set out to "reconcile both unto God in one body." Because of this, there is now no division, no distinction between Jew or Gentile. Galatians 3:28 says: "There is neither Jew nor Greek, there is neither bond nor free, there is neither male nor female: for ye are all one in Christ Jesus." And Colossians 3:11 makes it even stronger: "Where there is neither Greek nor Jew, circumcision nor uncircumcision, Barbarian, Scythian, bond nor free: but Christ is all, and in all."

God's purpose was *unity* between the Jew and the Gentile. Yet this is a unity seen today only "in Christ." Outside of Christ, Jew will continue to battle Egyptian, Syrian will continue to battle Jew, and the enmity inspired by Satan will manifest itself in a thousand and one different ways.

3. Made One How? "By the Cross"

The poet said,

> "The very spear that pierced His side
> Drew forth the blood to save."

It is interesting to note that it was when "certain Greeks," that is, Gentiles, came to say, "We would see Jesus," that our Lord made His declaration: "I, if I be lifted up from the earth, will draw *all men* unto me" (John 12:32). This drawing was one for "all men," Jews and Gentiles alike.

And, just as Paul told the Ephesians, it was accomplished "by the cross." So the Holy Spirit interpreted the words of Jesus, "This he said, signifying what death he should die" (John 12:33). Peace for all men alike is ever, only and always "by the cross."

4. "Making Peace"; "Preached Peace"

It is important to note here the "making peace" is something that is exclusively the work of Christ. This is not *anything* we can do. But a "made" peace ought to be a "preached" peace. This blessed and wonderful story needs to be proclaimed to one and all.

> Peace with God is Christ in glory,
> God is life and God is love;
> Jesus died to tell the story,
> Those to bring to God above.

5. Trinity Emphasized in Oneness

Just as Paul repeatedly, in the earlier portion of the epistle, emphasized biblical redemption as being sponsored by each person in the Trinity, so he closes this portion, saying about being made one, "For through him we both have access by one Spirit unto the Father" (vs. 18). *"For through him"*—that is the Son. *"We both have access by one Spirit"*—this is the Holy Spirit. *"Unto the Father"*—this is the third person in the Trinity. Note again his use of the expression: "we both." This oneness and access is for Jew and Gentile alike.

But not only are we *made nigh* and *made one* in Christ, Paul goes on to describe this new creation further,

III. THINGS ARE DIFFERENT NOW: WE ARE MADE HOLY!

He says:

"Now therefore ye are no more strangers and foreigners, but fellowcitizens with the saints, and of the household of God; And are built upon the foundation of the apostles and prophets, Jesus Christ himself being the chief corner stone; In whom all the building fitly framed together groweth unto an holy temple in the Lord: In whom ye also are builded together for an habitation of God through the Spirit."—vss. 19-22.

A. A Holy People

The individual in Christ is no longer a stranger or a foreigner, in terms of the past, as described in verse 12. No longer is he a vagabond without a home, a foreigner without protection, a child with no rights or privileges, a sojourner with no personal interests. Instead, he is a fellowcitizen of the household of God. He has all the rights of citizenship; plus, which is even greater, all the rights of sonship.

The believer, Paul says, is included with "the saints." He is now, truly, a holy one who manifests purity in his daily life.

He is like the truck driver who, asked to describe some specific way in which Christ had changed his life, confessed, "Well, when I find someone tailgating my truck, I no longer drive on the shoulder of the road to kick stones on him."

Christ *does* make a difference!

B. A Holy Foundation

No greater foundation is possible since Jesus Christ Himself is the chief cornerstone. Here is a reminder of that classic passage in Matthew 16:13-18, where we are told:

"When Jesus came into the coasts of Caesarea Philippi, he asked his disciples, saying, Whom do men say that I the Son of man am? And they said, Some say that thou art John the Baptist: some, Elias; and others, Jeremias, or one of the prophets. He saith unto them, But whom say ye that I am? And Simon Peter answered and said, Thou art the Christ, the Son of the living God. And Jesus answered and said unto him, Blessed art thou, Simon Bar-jona: for flesh and blood hath not revealed it unto thee, but my Father which is in heaven. And I say unto thee, That thou art Peter, and upon this rock I will build my church; and the gates of hell shall not prevail against it."

> View the vast building, see it rise!
> The work how great, the plan how wise!
> Nor can that faith be overthrown
> That rests upon the Living Stone.

We are reminded that "Jesus saith unto them, Did ye never read in the scriptures, The stone which the builders rejected, the same is become the head of the corner: this is the Lord's doing, and it is marvelous in our eyes?" (Matt. 21:42).

Yet we need to also remember that He went on to say, "And whosoever shall fall on this stone shall be broken: but on whomsoever it shall fall, it will grind him to powder" (Matt. 21:44).

While Christ is the chief cornerstone, Paul describes the apostles and prophets as "the foundation." Or, rather, he says believers are built upon "the foundation of the apostles and the prophets," probably referring to the foundation they laid. This is what Paul said to those whom he had won to Christ at Corinth:

"According to the grace of God which is given unto me, as a wise masterbuilder, I have laid the foundation, and another buildeth thereon. But let every man take heed how he buildeth thereupon. For other foundation can no man lay than that is laid, which is Jesus Christ."—I Cor. 3:10,11.

C. A Holy Temple

Now that the wall of partition and enmity has been broken down, all believers, both Jews and Gentiles, make up one building, one holy temple. Each believer is a stone in this building. Peter said: "Ye also, as lively stones, are built up a spiritual house, an holy priesthood, to offer up spiritual sacrifices, acceptable to God by Jesus Christ" (I Pet. 2:5).

How nearly complete is this building? At any time the last stone could be placed into the holy temple, making the building complete. When this happens, Jesus Christ will return to receive His own unto Himself.

The purpose of the building? Paul describes it: "For an habitation of God." He explains this further as being "through the Spirit." This is true of each individual in Christ, since Paul says, "What? know ye not that your body is the temple of the Holy Ghost which is in you, which ye have of God, and ye are not your own?" (I Cor. 6:19).

It is also true of the body of Christ as a whole.

Conclusion

We can sum this up best to believers by quoting Peter's words in I Peter 2:9-11:

"But ye are a chosen generation, a royal priesthood, an holy nation, a peculiar people; that ye should shew forth the praises of him who hath called you out of darkness into his marvellous light: Which in time past were not a people, but are now the people of God: which had not obtained mercy, but now have obtained mercy. Dearly beloved, I beseech you as strangers and pilgrims, abstain from fleshly lusts, which war against the soul."

How our exalted position in Jesus Christ behooves us to live holy lives and fight earnestly the good fight of faith!

To those outside of Christ, we merely inquire: *Wouldn't you like to be made a new creation in Christ Jesus?* You could have it "made," even as we. Jesus Christ stands ready and willing to make you *nigh,* to make you *one,* and to make you *holy.* John 1:11,12 says: "He came unto his own, and his own received him not. But as many as received him, to them gave he power to become the sons of God, even to them that believe on his name."

Will you receive Him today?

The True Church, God's Hidden Mystery

For this cause I Paul, the prisoner of Jesus Christ for you Gentiles,

If ye have heard of the dispensation of the grace of God which is given to you-ward:

How that by revelation he made known unto me the mystery; (as I wrote afore in few words,

Whereby, when ye read, ye may understand my knowledge in the mystery of Christ)

Which in other ages was not made known unto the sons of men, as it is now revealed unto his holy apostles and prophets by the Spirit;

That the Gentiles should be fellowheirs, and of the same body, and partakers of his promise in Christ by the gospel:

Whereof I was made a minister, according to the gift of the grace of God given unto me by the effectual working of his power.

Unto me, who am less than the least of all saints, is this grace given, that I should preach among the Gentiles the unsearchable riches of Christ;

And to make all men see what is the fellowship of the mystery, which from the beginning of the world hath been hid in God, who created all things by Jesus Christ:

To the intent that now unto the principalities and powers in heavenly places might be known by the church the manifold wisdom of God,

According to the eternal purpose which he purposed in Christ Jesus our Lord:

In whom we have boldness and access with confidence by

the faith of him.—Ephesians 3:1-12.

A fruit vendor was pushing his cart along a side street in one of our nation's largest metropolises, hawking his wares. Unaware at the time it happened, he dropped a little black appointment book on the pavement. Some hours later a lady spotted it lying in the gutter, picked it up, opened it, and curiously started reading the notations which were written at various dates.

One entry, beside one date, was marked: "Take groceries to Mrs. So-and-so. Destitute widow lady who has no money." Then, at the bottom, was the comment: *"For His body's sake."*

Beside another date was the entry: "Visit the little crippled girl and take her some fruit." At the bottom was the same notation: *"For His body's sake."*

The language of the fruit merchant is the language of the Apostle Paul in our text. He is discussing the "body of Christ," which is the true church.

What is the true church? It is not an organization, a denomination, a council. In fact, it is not even a fundamental, evangelical local church in some community. The true church consists of all the born-again individuals who make up His body.

We once heard a preacher in Texas take an hour to ridicule the idea of an *invisible* church, contrasting such a thought with the advantages of a visible wife over an invisible one. He went to great lengths explaining why he wanted something visible to make love to; in fact, some of his message, we felt, bordered on vulgarity. However, any argument against an invisible *church* could just as truly be used to argue against an invisible *Lord*. Yet we know of no one today, even though redeemed, who fails to fit the category of Peter's words about Jesus Christ: *"Whom having not seen,* ye love; in whom, *though now ye see him not,* yet believing, ye rejoice with joy unspeakable and full of glory" (I Pet. 1:8).

On the other hand, we would not deny or minimize for a moment the fact that, in this church age, the church which receives far and away the most prominence in the pages of the New Testament is the *local* church, not the church which is His body.

The word for church is the Greek *ecclesia,* meaning "called out." In this dispensation our Lord is "calling out" a church which Paul identifies as the body, the bride, the true church.

There are several important Bible distinctives of this true church. For one thing, Christ, in Heaven, is the Head. As we saw in Ephesians 1:22, referring to what the Heavenly Father has done for His Son, *"And hath put all things under his feet, and gave him to be the head over all things to the church."*

Second, this true church is described as Christ's body. Some who do not believe in what they call an "invisible" church, consisting of **all** the redeemed **everywhere**, nonetheless acknowledge that all who are saved make up His one body. Yet Ephesians 1:23, which continues in the same sentence with the verse just quoted—in fact, we will repeat the latter part of the previous verse to enhance the continuity—says: ". . .gave him to be the head over all things to the church, Which is his body, the fulness of him that filleth all in all." *The true church and His body are one and the same!*

Third, while there are sound, biblical local churches by the tens of thousands, there is only *one* true church. The church which is His body is described as *singular,* not plural; it is *one,* not many. Ephesians 4:4-6 says: "There is one body, and one Spirit, even as ye are called in one hope of your calling; One Lord, one faith, one baptism, One God and Father of all, who is above all, and through all, and in you all."

Fourth, it is important to remember that while local churches may fold up, disband, depart from the faith, or otherwise cease to be New Testament churches, the one true church can never be destroyed. As our Lord Himself told Peter in Matthew 16:17,18: "Blessed art thou, Simon Bar-jona: for flesh and blood hath not revealed it unto thee, but my Father which is in heaven. And I say also unto thee, That thou art Peter, and upon this rock I will build my church; and the gates of hell shall not prevail against it."

In the passage before us, Paul is revealing a mystery which had been hidden for many years. Unravelling mysteries is a noble occupation and many have done so in the name of research and science, dedicating their lives to these ends. The amazing George Washington Carver, whose investigations into the depths of the lowly peanut and the soybean brought such fantastic results, is a case in point. He often explained his quest:

"When I was young, I said to God, 'God, tell me the mystery of the universe.'

"But God answered, 'That knowledge is reserved for Me alone.'

So I said, 'God, tell me the mystery of the peanut.'

"Then God said, 'Well, George, that's more nearly your size.' And He told me."

However, in a far greater and nobler manner the Heavenly Father revealed the mystery of the one true church, Christ's body, to the Apostle Paul and he, in turn, has revealed it to the rest of us. Thus he starts the passage with,

I. THE REVELATION OF THE MYSTERY

He says:

"For this cause I Paul, the prisoner of Jesus Christ for you Gentiles, If ye have heard of the dispensation of the grace of God which is given me to you-ward: How that by revelation he made known unto me the mystery (as I wrote afore in few words, Whereby, when ye read, ye may understand my knowledge in the mystery of Christ) Which in other ages was not made known unto the sons of men, as it is now revealed unto his holy apostles and prophets by the Spirit."—Vss. 1-5.

A. Paul's Imprisonment Due to This Mystery

Writing from a Roman dungeon, Paul reminded his readers that it was "for this cause" he was suffering as the Lord's prisoner. The *cause* to which he referred was the one described in the verses immediately preceding, in the last four verses of chapter two. There he had emphasized that the true church is a building with Christ as the chief cornerstone, the apostles and prophets laid the foundation, and all the redeemed—Jews and

Gentiles, strangers and foreigners—have become fellowcitizens and, "together," an habitation of God through the Holy Spirit. This *cause* is "the mystery of Christ," also referred to in Colossians 4:3, where he again declared it was because of this "I am also in bonds."

How matter-of-factly Paul states he is "the prisoner of Jesus Christ." He did not consider himself a prisoner of the Roman government, nor the prisoner of this world-system. *No,* **no!** He was the prisoner of Jesus Christ because he was in the will of God and that will had taken him to a dungeon. An attitude like this explains how he, along with Silas, could sing praises unto God and have a glorious prayer meeting at midnight in a Philippian dungeon, after having been unjustly beaten and imprisoned with "feet fast in the stocks"—all because they had delivered from bondage a demon-possessed girl.

After all, this was part of his commission as an apostle of Jesus Christ. The Resurrected Redeemer had sent his servant Ananias to tell Paul, immediately following his conversion, "He is a chosen vessel unto me, to bear my name before the Gentiles, and kings, and the children of Israel: For I will show him how great things he must suffer for my name's sake" (Acts 9:15,16).

Another has written:

> There might have been a difference in opinion as who could claim Paul as a prisoner. Rome could have said, "He is my prisoner, my soldiers are guarding him, his life is in my hands"; the Jews might have said, "He is my prisoner for had it not been for that tactless invitation given by Paul to Trophimus to enter our temple, Paul never would have been arrested and now in Rome he awaits for judgment"; the Gentiles might have said, "No, he is our prisoner; if he had been content to remain a Jew and to preach Christ as Saviour of the Jews; if he had left us alone, he would still be free; his willingness to go to the far ends of the world to bring the story of Christ and labor that we might receive the gift of God's Spirit is the cause of his imprisonment; it was a self-sacrificing service in our behalf." But to all these suggestions Paul says, "No, you are all wrong; I may be a Jew and a Roman soldier may be chained to me in a Roman prison, and I may have preached to the Gentiles, but I am a prisoner of Christ; He has put me in chains, He owns me, I belong to Him and I have no desire to acknowledge allegiance to anyone else. I am His property; all my services for His sake, my bonds are in Christ."

And so it was.

All down through the ages there has been a shame, a stigma, a sense of reproach and dishonor associated with being in jail. The terms "convict," "ex-con," "jailbird," and kindred expressions have a sinister smirch attached to them. Yet Paul felt his imprisonment, since it was for the cause of Christ, was certainly nothing of which he nor his friends should be ashamed. In fact, he wrote from that Roman prison to the young preacher Timothy, saying: "Be not thou therefore ashamed of the testimony of our Lord, NOR OF ME HIS PRISONER: but be thou partaker of the afflictions of the gospel according to the power of God" (II Tim. 1:8). Paul told Timothy not to be embarrassed because his apostolic friend was imprisoned; in fact, he invited him to take the kind of stand which would cause him to lose his liberty as well!

When one stops to meditate upon it, some of the world's greatest benefits have come through the imprisonment of God's saints. The immortal John Bunyan comes immediately to mind as a case in point. He, from the gloomy, dirty, damp cell of his English Bedford jail, gave us *Pilgrim's Progress, Grace Abounding,* and the *Holy War.* John Huss, imprisoned on the Rhine, used the time to write some of his best works. The most noted, perhaps, of all the reformers, Martin Luther, translated the Sacred Scripture into the native tongue of his fellow Germans while imprisoned. Not the least was Paul, who from his prison dungeon sent forth to the world Ephesians, Philippians, Colossians, Philemon and II Timothy. Truly he was, indeed, "the prisoner of Jesus Christ."

Not only so, but he reminded the Ephesian believers that he was Christ's prisoner in a Roman dungeon *on their behalf.* "For you Gentiles" is the way he described it. He was suffering as he was, experiencing the curses of the cruel imprisonment, in order that the Gentiles might hear the Gospel and have an opportunity to be saved.

Some years ago I read the story of how Denmark's King Christian, at the age of eighty-five, was standing on a street corner waiting for a trolley to pass. Two tiny girls, about four or five years old, playing in an attitude of oblivion characteristic of their age, darted out into the street, unaware of the car bearing down upon them. As they were about to be hit, the elderly king leaped from his position on the curb, grasped each child by an arm, and jerked them from the path of the speeding vehicle.

For the rest of their lives, we suppose, they told everyone who would listen how they had been saved from certain death by the king himself. Yet their testimony was no greater or more thrilling than a single one of these Ephesians, who could witness that the Apostle Paul had paid such a tremendous price in order that he might hear the glorious Gospel of Christ and be saved.

B. Dispensation of God's Grace

Paul described God's plan of governing His household as "the dispensation of the grace of God." Since dispensation means "management of the house"—*domestic economy*—its use here deals with the household of God. It was especially to Paul that "this grace" (vs. 8) had been given, and he was to act as a steward, or manager, of its household. Yet there is a sense in which today's Christian shares in this same responsibility. First Peter 4:10 tells us: "As every man hath received the gift, even so minister the same one to another, as good stewards of the manifold grace of God."

Paul received his dispensation "by a revelation." In his case, it was not through studying the Old Testament, nor was it by searching the writings of the prophets. He had received it directly from Heaven! Galatians 1:11,12 pursues this thought further when it says: "But I certify you, brethren, that the gospel which was preached of me is not after man. For I neither received it of man, neither was I taught it but by the revelation of Jesus Christ."

We, too, can say we have the message by revelation, that we received it directly from Heaven. Unlike Paul, however, our revelation received directly from Heaven is in written form; it is contained in the pages of our New Testament. In fact, part of it is in the passage before us.

C. "The Mystery"

Paul said, ". . .he made known unto me *the mystery*" (vs. 3); and again, ". . .my knowledge in *the mystery* of Christ" (vs. 4). God has many secrets which have been hidden in eternity past and will continue to remain hidden until eternity future. They belong to God, as Deuteronomy 29:29 reminds us.

The late Thomas DeWitt Talmage revealed how he pestered his seminary professor with questions about various Bible mysteries until the latter finally said, with some heat and agitation: "Mr. Talmage, you will have to let God know some things you don't." Thus it is partly God's glory that He have unrevealed secrets (Prov. 25:2).

However, that is not even remotely the thought in this passage. "The mystery" to which Paul refers is not anything mysterious at all; it is something *previously hidden* from men, but *now revealed* by God. Verse 5 describes it as that "which IN OTHER AGES was not made known unto the sons of men," but *is* known in *our* age. Paul, talking about the same thing to the saints at Colosse, wrote: "Whereof I am made a minister, according to the dispensation of God which is given to me for you, to fulfil the word of God; Even the mystery which hath been hid from ages and from generations, but now is made manifest to his saints" (Col. 1:25,26). This had been a mystery only in the sense that it waited the fullness of God's time for unveiling.

Paul immediately emphasizes this in our text, going on to say in verse 5, "It is **now revealed** unto the holy apostles and prophets by the Spirit." The idea of *holy* here simply means "set apart for the service of God," and the *prophets* are, of course, the New Testament prophets. Romans 16:25-27 gives further evidence that this mystery is something **now revealed,** saying:

"Now to him that is of power to stablish you according to my gospel, and the preaching of Jesus Christ, according to the revelation of the mystery, which was kept secret since the world began, But now is made manifest, and by the scriptures of the prophets, according to the commandment of the everlasting God, made known to all nations for the obedience

of faith: To God only wise, be glory through Jesus Christ for ever. Amen."

How is a revelation made? Paul tells us "by the Spirit" (vs. 5). He is the Author of *all* truth and what Paul is saying here—about the unveiling of the mystery concerning the true church, the body of Christ—is a partial fulfillment of John 16:12-15:

"I have yet many things to say unto you, but ye cannot bear them now. Howbeit when he, the Spirit of truth, is come, he will guide you into all truth: for he shall shew you things to come. He shall glorify me: for he shall receive of mine, and shall shew it unto you. All things that the Father hath are mine: therefore said I, that he shall take of mine, and shall shew it unto you."

II. THE MYSTERY DEFINED

Paul wrote: *"That the Gentiles should be fellow heirs, and of the same body, and partakers of his promise in Christ by the gospel"* (vs. 6).

The mystery was not that Gentiles would be saved. The Old Testament repeatedly foretold this truth and it should have been—even though it was not—apparent to all. For example, Psalm 117:1 declares: "O praise the Lord, all ye nations: praise him, all ye people." People from all nations would sing the praises of God, the psalmist prophesied.

In Isaiah 42:6,7, we are told: "I the Lord have called thee in righteousness, and will hold thine hand, and will keep thee, and give thee for a covenant of the people, for a light of the Gentiles; To open the blind eyes, to bring out the prisoners from the prison, and them that sit in darkness out of the prison house." The Servant of Jehovah would be a light to the Gentiles, opening their blind eyes and bringing them out of prison, it was revealed.

In the song of Moses, he had the people singing, "Rejoice, O ye nations, with his people: for he will avenge the blood of his servants, and will render vengeance to his adversaries, and will be merciful unto his land, and to his people" (Deut. 32:43). All the nations, along with the redeemed Jews, would rejoice in the vengeance of God.

The Apostle Paul had previously written to the churches of Galatia about this, pointing out Old Testament teaching regarding the salvation of non-Jews, declaring: "And the scripture, foreseeing that God would justify the heathen through faith, preached before the gospel unto Abraham, saying, In thee shall all nations be blessed. So then they which be of faith are blessed with faithful Abraham" (Gal. 3:8,9).

No, this mystery about which Paul wrote to the Ephesians was not merely that Gentiles would be saved. It was a radical, revolutionary change in the new order he was discussing. Dr. Robert G. Lee wrote:

> Sometimes I think of the wonders which chemistry brings to pass. I think how people can drop mercury into naphthalene and change it into phthalic acid. I think how people can take one and one-half grams of that new chemical that has been invented, or "gotten born," as someone expressed it, and disinfect two and a half billion gallons of water, a lake a mile long, two thousand feet wide, and thirty feet deep, for five years! That is a change that man can bring in foul water by using one and one-half grams of a certain chemical.[1]

Yet the change Paul described was one far greater than chemistry can produce, since it involved making one the Jews and Gentiles, who abhorred each other with a purple passion!

What was this revolutionary change?

A. Gentiles and Jews Co-Heirs of His Possessions

Paul said: *"That the Gentiles should be fellowheirs. . . ."* Gentiles were to have equal rights as members of God's family, right along with the Jews. This was God's equal opportunity act; He would be an "equal opportunity employer."

The situation now is described in Romans 8:14-17:

"For as many as are led by the Spirit of God, they are the sons

---

[1] From BREAD FROM BELLEVUE OVEN by Robert G. Lee, Copyright, 1947, by Sword of the Lord Publishers. Used by permission.

of God. For ye have not received the spirit of bondage again to fear; but ye have received the Spirit of adoption, whereby we cry Abba, Father. The Spirit itself beareth witness with our spirit, that we are the children of God: And if children, then heirs; heirs of God and joint-heirs with Christ; if so be that we suffer with him, that we may be also glorified together."

Note the expression: *"for as many."* It matters nothing whether they are Jews *or* Gentiles, if they have been led by the Spirit they are the sons of God—with all the rights and privileges of God's children, including being heirs of God and joint-heirs with Jesus Christ.

> What a prospect, child of glory,
>   Does the future hold in store!
> By the wildest flights of fancy
>   Thou couldst never ask for more.
> Heir of God, joint-heir forever,
>   With His own beloved Son!
> God could not to you have promised
>   More of bliss than He has done.

B. Gentiles and Jews Co-Members of His Body

It is also said: *"That the Gentiles should be. . .of the same body. . . ."* Each of the redeemed, in this economy, is of equal value in the body, whether Jew or Gentile. None is above the other. Paul describes it in I Corinthians 12:12-22:

"For as the body is one, and hath many members, and all the members of that one body, being many, are one body: so also is Christ. For by one Spirit are we all baptized into one body, whether we be Jews or Gentiles, whether we be bond or free; and have been all made to drink into one Spirit. For the body is not one member, but many. If the foot shall say, Because I am not the hand, I am not of the body; is it therefore not of the body? And if the ear shall say, Because I am not the eye, I am not of the body; is it therefore not of the body? If the whole body were an eye, where were the hearing? If the whole were hearing, where were the smelling? But now hath God set the

members every one of them in the body, as it hath pleased him. And if they were all one member, where were the body? But now are they many members, yet but one body. And the eye cannot say unto the hand, I have no need of thee: nor again the head to the feet, I have no need of you. Nay, much more those members of the body, which seem to be more feeble, are necessary."

In this new dispensation there is but *one* fold and *one* Shepherd for *all* the sheep. Our Lord said, in John 10:14, "I am the good shepherd, and know my sheep, and am known of mine." Then He went on to say, "And other sheep I have which are not of this fold: them also I must bring, and they shall hear my voice; and there shall be one fold, and one shepherd" (vs. 16). Paul is describing the fulfillment of this prophecy.

C. Gentiles and Jews Co-Partakers of His Promises

Paul also said: *"That the Gentiles should be. . .partakers of his promises in Christ by the gospel."* The amillennialist has a bad habit of taking all of the promises which belong to Israel and applying them to the church, but leaving all of Israel's curses for the Jew! There is to be no such division in this new economy of God's. Gentiles are to share and share alike with Jews, and Jews must share alike with Gentiles.

Admittedly, the promises of God had formerly been of primary concern to the Jew. Romans 9:4 describes it: ". . .Israelites; to whom pertaineth the adoption, and the glory, and the covenants, and the giving of the law, and the service of God, AND THE PROMISES." Now all the promises are to be shared equally with redeemed Gentiles.

Perhaps we should point out that promises *must be claimed* to be of value. Those of us who are redeemed Gentiles must possess the possessions that are ours to possess. Hyman Appelman tells of an Irish woman whose son, Jack, was not much account. One day, while drunk, he was shanghaied aboard a ship sailing to Australia. After arriving, he jumped ship and made his way into the interior, discovered a gold mine, and became fabulously wealthy.

In spite of Jack's intemperate habits, he loved his mother and wrote her devotedly, about once every two weeks. He would describe his wealth, his wife, his children, his various possessions.

In the meantime, his mother had become old and infirm, unable to longer work. One day, when a priest of her parish went to discuss moving her to a poorhouse, the two got into a discussion about her son. She, in motherly fashion, bragged on his successes, possibly even overstating the case, as mothers are prone to do.

The confused priest inquired, "You mean that your son is wealthy, writes to you regularly, yet has never inquired about your condition, or asked if you needed financial aid?"

"No," the mother replied. "And I didn't want to worry him about it."

However, further discussion revealed that in each letter "a little greenish-blue slip of paper" had been enclosed. The mother boasted that they were so pretty she had used them to decorate her bedroom.

Asking to see them, the clergyman went into the room and found, neatly pasted over each wall, the ceiling, and even the floor, Australian money orders totalling thousands of dollars. The poor woman did not know what they were, but since they were pretty and were mementos from her son, she had plastered the room with them!

In like manner, many a Christian—both Jew and Gentile—has failed to cash in on the promises of God available to him. In the case of the Irish mother, ignorance was her excuse. We cannot plead that. We know what God has promised and still, beggars and paupers that we are, we fail to claim our possessions.

Incidentally, Paul stresses the fact that Jews and Gentiles are co-heirs, co-members and co-partakers *only* "in Christ by the gospel."

"In Christ!" The whole story of salvation, deliverance from Hell and a home in Heaven hinges on these words. It is to *His* person, *His* work, *His* sacrifice that we owe our position. To remove Him would mean no sonship, no unity, no sharing. For both Jews and Gentiles, it is a matter of union with Him. No substitute will suffice.

Several years ago the Associated Press, with a Manila dateline, told of a 35-year-old Filipino bootblack being nailed to a cross, at his own request. Eusebio Libes, of Pampanga Province, about 65 miles north of Manila, described his Good Friday crucifixion as an act of thanksgiving to God for recovery after a long illness. He called it "the only way I can repay the good Lord for all the graces He has given me."

About four hundred residents witnessed as Libes' hands were nailed to a 12-foot wooden cross, ether was administered to him by friends, and then the cross was hoisted to an upright position. Relatives knelt and prayed as he hung unconscious for several minutes, wearing his white loincloth and a crown of thorns. Then he was hurriedly removed from the cross and rushed home for medical treatment.

Ah, but such an act of crucifixion is completely without benefit, either to the crucified one or anyone else. It is only in the crucifixion and resurrection of the Lord Jesus Christ that our inheritance becomes a reality.

Paul also explained it: *"by the gospel."* Christ is the *Giver;* the Gospel is the *channel.* As Paul told the Corinthians, ". . .in Christ Jesus I have begotten you through the gospel" (I Cor. 4:15).

It is because of this that believers join him in triumphantly shouting: "I am not ashamed of the gospel of Christ: for it is the power of God unto salvation to every one that believeth; to the Jew first, and also to the Greek" (Rom. 1:16).

III. MINISTERS OF THE MYSTERY

In describing the ministers of this now-revealed mystery, among whom he was one, Paul wrote:

"Whereof I was made a minister, according to the gift of the grace of God given unto me by the effectual working of his power. Unto me, who am less than the least of all saints, is this

grace given, that I should preach among the Gentiles the unsearchable riches of Christ; And to make all men see what is the fellowship of the mystery, which from the beginning of the world hath been hid in God, who created all things by Jesus Christ."—Vss. 7-9.

A. Ministers "According to the Gift of the Grace of God"

Only Heaven can qualify a man for this work. Paul readily conceded that his position was a gift; *"given unto me,"* is the way he described it. He acknowledged the gift of this ministry also to the Colossian Christians, saying: "Who now rejoice in my flesh for his body's sake, which is the church: Whereof I am made a minister, according to the dispensation of God which is given to me for you, to fulfill the word of God; Even the mystery which hath been hid from ages and from generations, but now is made manifest to his saints" (Col. 1:24-26).

Paul pointed out that this gift came about through *"the effectual working [energy] of his power."* This is another way of saying that Christ was working in him. As he told the Colossians, "Whereunto I also labour, striving according to his working, which worketh in me mightily" (Col. 1:29).

You will find much of this emphasis in Paul's writings. His philosophy was summed up in the words: "I can do all things through Christ which strengtheneth me" (Phil. 4:13). In fact, he told these same Philippians: "For it is God which worketh in you both to will and to do of his good pleasure" (Phil. 2:13).

There was an absolute and burning conviction raging in Paul's breast that merit had nothing to do with his ministry. He said in our text, "Unto me, who am less than the least of all saints, is this grace given. . ." (vs. 8). This same humility is seen elsewhere in his description of himself as the chief of sinners (I Tim. 1:15) and "the least of the apostles, not meet to be called an apostle" (I Cor. 15:9). In fact, he went on to say, in the next verse, "But by the grace of God I am what I am: and his grace which was bestowed upon me was not in vain; but I laboured more abundantly than they all: yet not I, but the grace of God which was with me."

Perhaps herein lies the reason why more men are not used in our day as was Paul in his. We do not have many who say with Abraham, while seeking to lay hold upon the Almighty, "I. . . am but dust and ashes" (Gen. 18:27). Who, in our midst, sincerely joins Jacob in confessing to the God of Abraham and Isaac, "I am not worthy of the least of all the mercies, and of all the truth, which thou hast shewed unto thy servant" (Gen. 32:10)? Most of us have not descended to the position of Job, acknowledging, "I abhor myself, and repent in dust and ashes" (Job 42:6).

How many of us, when God has a job for us to do, face the commission as an Isaiah, crying, "Woe is me! for I am undone; because I am a man of unclean lips, and I dwell in the midst of a people of unclean lips" (Isa. 6:5)? We have not experienced Peter's falling on his face before Jesus, exclaiming, "I am a sinful man, O Lord" (Luke 5:8). Instead, we rush into our ministries with a confidence that belies John the Baptist's sense of unworthiness even to stoop down and unloose the Lord's shoe latchet (Mark 1:7). Yet Paul considered himself beneath the poorest saint in existence, marveling that God would choose such an unworthy instrument to reveal His mystery and preach His Word. He went on to say that he "should preach among the Gentiles the unsearchable riches of Christ."

When the late Aga Khan was reigning over the Ismaili Moslem sect, on his 25th anniversary his followers gave him his weight in silver. On the 50th anniversary he was presented with his weight in gold. On another anniversary, in Bombay, he got his weight in diamonds. Since he weighed 243½ pounds at the time, it was a $2,500,000 bonanza. His followers in East Africa repeated the diamond weighing with kindred results. On his seventy-fifth birthday, still tipping the scales at 240 pounds, he received his weight in platinum—a windfall of approximately $3 million.

Yet, how paltry are these sums compared with the "unsearchable riches of Christ." The word "unsearchable" is literally "untrackable," "untraceable." These riches are beyond tracing out, they are impossible to fully discover or totally comprehend. One may plunge deeper, *deeper* and **deeper** into the riches of Christ and never touch bottom. This is one pool where the diver need never fear cracking his head on a rock.

B. A Ministry of Opening Blind Eyes

Paul described it in verse 9: *"To make all men see what is the fellowship of the mystery, which from the beginning of the world hath been hid in God, who created all things by Jesus Christ."*

In other words, this is a fulfillment of the prophecy in Isaiah 42:6,7:

"I the Lord have called thee in righteousness, and will hold thine hand, and will keep thee, and give thee for a covenant of the people, for a light of the Gentiles; To open the blind eyes, to bring out the prisoners from the prison, and them that sit in darkness out of the prison house."

Note that, in Paul's understanding of the matter, it was a ministry "to make **ALL MEN** see." This was not a ministry limited to a certain select group of people; *it was for all!* Paul was commissioned by Christ to do what he could to open *every* spiritually blinded man's eyes. We are to do the same today.

He emphasized again that it was a ministry of revealing a mystery which had been "hid in God" from "the beginning of the world." It was not merely a truth hidden in the Old Testament; it was something which could never have been discovered by man apart from a revelation in God's time.

IV. GOD'S ETERNAL PURPOSE IN THE MYSTERY

Paul explains it:

"To the intent that now unto the principalities and powers in heavenly places might be known by the church the manifold wisdom of God, According to the eternal purpose which he purposed in Christ Jesus our Lord: In whom we have boldness and access with confidence by the faith of him."—Vss. 10-12.

A. Reveal God's Manifold Wisdom to Principalities, Powers

Did you know that not even the angels knew of God's plan for the body of Christ, the church? How truly this mystery had been "hid in God." Now the principalities and powers are witnessing God's manifold wisdom in His dealings with His church. It was in this light that someone called the church "God's University for Angels!" And so it is.

You will remember that Paul, writing to the Corinthians and instructing women about their head covering, said, "For this cause ought the woman to have power on her head because of the angels" (I Cor. 11:10). And Peter, discussing our so great salvation, said:

"Of which salvation the prophets have inquired and searched diligently, who prophesied of the grace that should come unto you: Searching what, or what manner of time the Spirit of Christ which was in them did signify, when it testified beforehand the sufferings of Christ, and the glory that should follow. Unto whom it was revealed, that not unto themselves, but unto us they did minister the things, which are now reported unto you by them that have preached the gospel unto you with the Holy Ghost sent down from heaven; which things the angels desire to look into."—I Pet. 1:10-12.

The latter phrase has been translated literally, "the angels passionately desired to bend low and look into."

Ah, the angels never saw the love, the grace, the humility, the self-sacrifice of God until they witnessed it manifested through His wisdom and dealings in the church.

B. This Eternal Design "Purposed in Christ Jesus Our Lord"

We are reminded again of Ephesians 1:22,23: "And hath put all things under his feet, and gave him to be the head over all things to the church, Which is his body, the fulness of him that filleth all in all." It is all *in* and *through* and *by* Jesus Christ. Yet, in the passage before us, Paul is emphasizing the part that it is *"in* whom" (vs. 12), not merely *"through* whom."

It is *in Christ* that we have "boldness." We do not fear God's wrath or doubt God's love when we are "in him." And it is *in Christ* that we have "access with confidence," Paul tells us. It is described in Hebrews 10:19, "Having therefore, brethren, boldness to enter into the holiest by the blood of Jesus." So, "Let us therefore come boldly unto the throne of grace, that we may obtain mercy, and find grace to help in time of need" (Heb. 4:16).

All of this "boldness" and "access with confidence" is, Paul reminds us, "by the faith of him." There can be no boldness or confidence in approaching God apart from Jesus Christ.

Conclusion

What a wonderful mystery, hid in God since the beginning of the world, but now revealed: **that anyone and everyone can become a co-heir, a co-member, and a co-partaker of the redemption God offers!**

Dear friend, do you belong to the *true* church? While you might be a member of any number of local churches, such membership will not guarantee Heaven to you. There is absolutely no salvation whatever apart from membership in the true church, which is Christ's body.

We close with the words of an unknown author, penned in reference to the phrase in our text, *"the unsearchable riches of Christ."* He wrote:

>In the heart of London city,
>   'Mid the dwellings of the poor,
>These bright golden words were uttered,
>   "I HAVE CHRIST! What want I more?"
>
>Spoken by a lonely woman,
>   Dying on a garret floor;
>Having not one earthly comfort—
>   "I HAVE CHRIST! What want I more?"
>
>He who heard them ran to fetch her
>   Something from the world's great store;

It was needless—died she, saying,
  "I HAVE CHRIST! What want I more?"

But her words will live forever;
  I repeat them o'er and o'er.
God delights to hear me saying,
  "I HAVE CHRIST! What want I more?"

Oh, thou careless one, unheeding
  Coming wrath and fire in store,
Dark indeed thy doom before thee,
  YOU NEED CHRIST! Your need is sore.

Haste thee, hide thee, death awaits thee,
  Naught but wrath doth lie before,
Unless thou art sweetly boasting,
  "I HAVE CHRIST! What want I more?"

You have much gold and grandeur,
  Yet by God be reckoned poor;
He alone has riches truly
  WHO HAS CHRIST! though nothing more.

Look away from earth's attractions,
  All earth's joys will soon be o'er;
Rest not, till thy heart exclaimeth—
  "I HAVE CHRIST! What want I more?"

"Lord, Open Our Hearts!"

Wherefore I desire that ye faint not at my tribulations for you, which is your glory.

For this cause I bow my knees unto the Father of our Lord Jesus Christ,

Of whom the whole family in heaven and earth is named,

That he would grant you, according to the riches of his glory, to be strengthened with might by his Spirit in the inner man;

That Christ may dwell in your hearts by faith; that ye, being rooted and grounded in love,

May be able to comprehend with all saints what is the breadth, and length, and depth, and height;

And to know the love of Christ, which passeth knowledge, that ye might be filled with all the fulness of God.

Now unto him that is able to do exceeding abundantly above all that we ask or think, according to the power that worketh in us,

Unto him be glory in the church by Jesus Christ throughout all ages, world without end. Amen.—Ephesians 3:13-21.

Love causes people to do amazing things, as the late devotee of the unique and unusual, Bob Ripley, was fond of pointing out. He told, for example, of a French sea captain, Christophe, Chevalier de Freminville (1787-1848) who, after his beloved Caroline died, abandoned male clothing and attired himself in a gauzy white dress with a sash of green silk and green slippers, the costume his beloved was wearing when he last saw her, quitting the sea and devoting the rest of his life to perpetuating her memory.

Yet how insignificant is *any* human love when compared to the marvellous, magnificent love of the Almighty. Thomas C. Upham wrote:

> Go, count the sands that form the earth,
>   The drops that make the mighty sea;
> Go, count the stars of heavenly birth,
>   And tell me what their numbers be;
>   And thou shalt know Love's mystery.
>
> No measurement hath yet been found,
>   No lines or numbers that can keep
> The sum of its eternal round,
>   The plummet of its endless deep,
>   Or heights to which its glories sweep.
>
> Yes, measure Love, when thou canst tell
>   The lands where seraphs have not trod,
> The heights of Heaven, the depths of Hell,
>   And lay thy finite measuring-rod
>   On the Infinitude of God!

Our text comprises Paul's second great prayer in this epistle. The other, in Ephesians 1:15-23, we called, "Lord, Open Our Eyes!" The first prayer had to do with *light;* the second has to do with *love.* The first had to do with *the intellect;* the second has to do with *the emotions.* The first had to do with *knowledge;* the second has to do with *experience.* The first had to do with *our position in* Christ; the second has to do with *our fellowship with* Christ. The first prayer was *doctrinal;* this prayer is *practical.*

As we examine this second prayer, we join Charles H. Scott in singing,

> Open my mouth, and let me bear
>   Gladly the warm truth ev'rywhere;
> Open my heart, and let me prepare
>   Love with Thy children thus to share.
> Silently now I wait for Thee,
>   Ready, my God, Thy will to see;
> Open my heart, illumine me, Spirit divine!

I. PAUL'S PERSONAL PLEA!

Paul expressed himself:

"Wherefore I desire that ye faint not at my tribulations for you, which is your glory. For this cause I bow my knees unto the Father of our Lord Jesus Christ, Of whom the whole family in

heaven and earth is named."—Vss. 13-15.

A. Don't Be Discouraged!

Paul did not want his Ephesian converts to be discouraged over his tribulation. He began his plea with the word "wherefore," pointing back to verse 12 and the believer's assurance in our Lord Jesus Christ: "In whom we have boldness and access with confidence by the faith of him." **God knows what He is doing!**

The urgency of this plea is summed up in the words, "I desire." Paul was saying, "I *beg* you, I *entreat* you." All the love of the apostle *for* them was behind this plea, and also involved was all the love the apostle could command *from* them.

"That ye faint not." While this is literally, "that ye be not dispirited," it carries the still deeper meaning: "to behave badly, and, to give in to evil." It is a picture of discouragement leading to sin. Paul knew how easy it would be for Satan to get the Ephesian saints to lower their standards if they became discouraged. It is still true today.

Someone has described discouragement as Satan's greatest tool, and well it may be. We need ever to keep in mind that "with God nothing shall be impossible" (Luke 1:37). The word *impossible* commences with an "imp"—and Satan surely is behind all discouragement.

J. Allen Blair tells of a soldier being court-martialed because he was always complaining; everything was "sour grapes" to him and his attitude was undermining the morale of the others in his company. How contagious is discouragement and how quickly one rotten apple ruins the whole bushel in this matter.

Our Lord offered His antidote in Luke 18:1, where we find: "And he spake a parable unto them to this end, that men ought always to pray, and not to faint." A saint who stays prayed up will not get discouraged.

One such person was the elderly widow who lived in a humble cottage, raised a few chickens and vegetables, yet in cash received only a few hundred dollars a year for her support.

Reading the newspaper one day, she suddenly broke out into loud and almost uncontrollable laughter. Looking up, she commented to a friend, "This is so funny. According to the government statistics here on incomes, I am classified an *underprivileged* person! Oh, my! That *is* silly!"

She had learned the lesson of Hebrews 13:5, commanding her to be "content with such things as ye have." One who does will not be plagued with discouragement.

In Paul's case, however, he was not concerned with the Ephesians becoming discouraged over their own problems, but with his. His desire was that they "faint not at *my* tribulations." His tribulations were something which never troubled Paul himself. He had written in Philippians 4:4, "Rejoice in the Lord alway: and again I say, Rejoice," and he practiced what he preached.

He had long before learned that tribulations are stepping stones to greater spiritual victories, writing in Romans 5:3-5: "And not only so, but we glory in tribulations also: knowing that tribulation worketh patience; And patience, experience; and experience, hope." He could say with Christ, "Not my will, but thine, be done" (Luke 22:40).

Paul knew that Christians are something like persimmons. This strange fruit, in the Fall, is possibly the bitterest fruit one could ever sink his teeth into. It causes the mouth to pucker and the entire body shudders with the bitterness of its flavor. Yet with the coming of frost and cold weather it begins to mellow. The more snow that falls and the lower the freezing temperature drops, the sweeter and the more delectable becomes the persimmon.

In a comparable manner, the snow and freezing weather of tribulations mellow and sweeten the child of God.

So Paul's triumphant attitude was, "For I reckon that the sufferings of this present time are not worthy to be compared with the glory which shall be revealed in us" (Rom. 8:18). *Setbacks* are not necessarily *defeats,* and the loss of a trench is not the loss of a battle. Even the loss of a city is not the loss of a nation, or of a war. Quite the contrary; losses can become educational experiences which will eventually turn the tide of the war.

Why should Paul fear that the Ephesians would become discouraged over *his own* tribulations? Quite simply, because they were caused **because of them.** He spoke of "my tribulations for you"; literally, "in your behalf." Remember that he had described himself earlier in the chapter as "the prisoner. . .for you Gentiles" (vs. 1). His was suffering brought about as a consequence of his efforts to win them to Christ and to build them up in the most holy faith. Paul did not want any guilt complexes following his tribulations in their behalf.

How eloquently those tribulations spoke of Paul's love for the Ephesians.

Are you familiar with the story behind the popular "praying hands" which adorn walls, books, cuff links, tie tacks and all the rest? Late in the fifteenth century two young artists, Franz Knigstein and Albrecht Durer, decided that neither would ever be a success in his field if compelled to work for a living while trying to study art. They drew straws to see who would work and support the other, then the educated one would support the other while he got his education.

Durer went off to school first and Knigstein struggled to support him. When Durer became a success, he returned to keep his end of the bargain and allow his friend to go off to school.

But, alas and alack, the hard manual labor Knigstein had been compelled to do had ruined for life his slender, sensitive hands. Instead of being bitter, Knigstein rejoiced in his friend's success.

One day Durer walked into the room and found his friend on his knees in prayer, his gnarled hands clasped in prayer. Hurriedly getting his brushes and easel, Albrecht Durer sketched the hands of his faithful friend, later completing the masterpiece the world knows as "The Praying Hands."

Just as Franz Knigstein suffered for Albrecht Durer, so Paul had suffered for the Ephesians. And, like Durer, Paul wanted them to realize that his sufferings could still be summed up, "which is your glory." As he elsewhere told the saints at Philippi, "But I would ye should understand, brethren, that the things which happened unto me have fallen out rather unto the furtherance of the gospel" (Phil. 1:12).

Most of our tribulations are not so bad after all, and when we compare them with our Lord's suffering, how minute and insignificant they become. The unknown poet expressed it for us:

> LORD, when I am weary with toiling,
> And burdensome seem Thy commands,
> If my load should lead to complaining,
> LORD, SHOW ME THY HANDS,
> Thy nail-pierced hands,
> Thy cross-torn hands,
> My Savior, show me Thy hands.
>
> CHRIST, if ever my footsteps should falter,
> And I be prepared for retreat;
> If desert and thorn cause lamenting,
> LORD, SHOW ME THY FEET,
> Thy bleeding feet,
> Thy nail-scarred feet,
> My Jesus, show me Thy feet.
>
> LORD, when I am sorely wounded
> With battle and toil of the day,
> And I complain of my suffering,
> LORD, LET ME HEAR THEE SAY,
> "Behold My side,
> My spear-pierced side,
> MY GOD, DARE I SHOW THEE
> MY HANDS AND MY FEET?

B. The Apostle's Explanation

Why did Paul not want them to be discouraged about his tribulations? Why was he willing to suffer in such fashion, perhaps more so than any other man who ever lived? He said, "For this cause I bow my knees unto the Father of our Lord Jesus Christ, Of whom the whole family in heaven and earth is named" (vss. 14,15).

This cause—their "glory" (vs. 13)—not only made Paul willing to suffer in their behalf, but also induced him to "bow my knees"; that is, it caused him to throw himself prostrate before the Lord in praise of His wonderful plan of redemption.

The reference to bowing his knees explains that it was prayer in definite earnest; it was the deepest intercession and supplication of the soul. This was not just a hurried sentence prayer as he walked or rode along the highway or sat on the edge of his bunk in a prison cell. Here was one who prostrated himself before God in contriteness and soul-searching agony.

Before whom did he fall on his face? It was "unto the *Father* of our Lord Jesus Christ." In his previous prayer it was to the *"God* of our Lord Jesus Christ" (1:17).

Ah, but that prayer had to do with God's counsels and purposes, so he rightly addressed the "God" of our Lord Jesus Christ. This prayer has to do with family relationships, so he cries out to "the Father"! You can depend upon the Holy Spirit to always lead one in submission to Him in choosing exactly the *right* word.

Notice that He is not only the Father of our Lord Jesus Christ, but also of "the whole family in heaven and earth." Right here is a death blow to the diabolical doctrine of soul sleeping. According to the inspired apostle, part of the family was not **on** the earth and part **in** the earth. No, no. Part of the family was on the earth and part of the family was already, in Paul's day, in Heaven.

If he had believed in soul sleep, he would have said, in verse 15, "Of whom the whole family in the grave and on earth is named." Thank God, for the believer, "to be absent from the body" is "to be present with the Lord" (II Cor. 5:8).

Notice also that Paul, speaking of this spiritual family in Heaven and earth, points out that it "is named" of the Father. Believers carry the name of God, the name Christian.

While direct descendants of George Washington, Abraham Lincoln and other great men may be justly proud of their heritage, how much more should be the child of God, who carries the name of God. How earnestly we should seek—how carefully we should endeavor—to *do* nothing, to *say* nothing, to *write* nothing which would bring reproach upon our family name.

II. PAUL'S PASSIONATE PRAYER!

After throwing himself upon his face before the Heavenly Father, Paul's actual intercession in behalf of the Ephesians is recorded in verses 16 through 19.

Years ago we ran across Dr. H. A. Ironside's seven-word outline describing this prayer and we would like to "borrow" it here. In fact, if we recall correctly, Dr. Ironside acknowledged he had received it from someone else. The seven words summing up this passionate prayer are endowment, enduement, enthronement, establishment, enlightenment, enlargement, and enrichment.

A. Our Endowment

First, Paul prayed that the Father "would grant you, according to the riches of his glory." That is, literally, "out of the glorious richness of His resources." Oh, the wealth of our inexhaustible inheritance in Jesus Christ!

His resources, His riches are not limited, although they are often unseen. Hagar, the water spent from the bottle for her young child, sat down and wept, praying that she might not see the death of her precious son. Yet, when "God opened her eyes," she saw "a well of water; and she went, and filled the bottle with water, and gave the lad drink" (Gen. 21:19).

Our limited vision often keeps us from seeing God's resources, yet they are there nonetheless.

When Ben-hadad's Syrian warriors compassed Dothan, planning to capture and no doubt kill Elisha, the prophet's servant was distressed, crying out, "Alas, my master! how shall we do?" (II Kings 6:15). He was certain that the cause was lost and death was imminent. But, you will recall, Elisha prayed, saying, "Lord, I pray thee, open his eyes, that he may see. And the Lord opened the eyes of the young man; and he saw: and, behold, the mountain was full of horses and chariots of fire round about Elisha" (vs. 17).

Yes, the resources are there even though they may not be seen until the glasses of faith are appropriated.

Notice also that, once again, Paul says our endowment is "*according* to the riches" of God, not "out of" those riches. This is how he described it in Ephesians 1:7, discussing salvation: "In whom we have redemption through his blood, the forgiveness of sins, *according to the riches of his grace."* Now, in the Christian life just as in redemption, needed grace is "according" to the Father's riches.

Thank God, we can sing along with Harriet E. Buell,

> My Father is rich in houses and lands,
> He holdeth the wealth of the world in His hands!
> Of rubies and diamonds, of silver and gold,
> His coffers are full, He has riches untold.
> I'm a child of the King, A child of the King!
> With Jesus, my Saviour, I'm a child of the King!

B. Our Enduement

Paul prayed that the Ephesians might "be strengthened with might by his Spirit in the inner man." The great apostle desired, and God intended, every Christian be strong spiritually. In the plan and program of God, there is no place for spiritual weaklings. Later in this epistle the apostle is found pleading: "Finally, my brethren, be strong in the Lord, and in the power of his might. Put on the whole armour of God, that ye may be able to stand against the wiles of the devil" (Eph. 6:10,11). When he wrote to the Corinthians, he exhorted, "Watch ye, stand fast in the Lord, quit you like men, be strong" (I Cor. 16:13).

What kind of strength is this enduement? It is to be "with might by his Spirit." Once again we are reminded of Isaiah 40:28-31:

"Hast thou not known? hast thou not heard that the everlasting God, the Lord, the Creator of the ends of the earth, fainteth not, neither is weary? there is no searching of his understanding. He giveth power to the faint; and to them that have no might he increaseth strength. Even the youths shall faint and be weary, and the young men shall utterly fall: But they that wait upon the Lord shall renew their strength; they shall mount up with wings as eagles; they shall run, and not be weary; and they shall walk, and not faint."

Christ's last promise to His disciples, before ascending back to His rightful place at the right hand of the Majesty on High, concerned this enduement of the Spirit.

Luke described the departing twice, once in his Gospel, where he wrote: "Behold, I send the promise of my Father upon you: but tarry ye in the city of Jerusalem, until ye be endued with power from on high."

Then, again, in the Book of Acts, Luke recorded the Saviour's words: "But ye shall receive power, after that the Holy Ghost is come upon you: and ye shall be witnesses unto me, both in Jerusalem, and in all Judaea, and in Samaria, and unto the uttermost part of the earth."

Actually, one of the designations for this member of the Trinity is "the Spirit of. . .power" (II Tim. 1:7).

Where is this enduement needed? Paul said, "in the inner man." Someone has suggested that this might be translated: "That he would enable you. . .to know the strength of the Spirit's inner re-enforcement." He wants to make us strong to suffer, strong to serve, strong to battle, strong to witness.

King Croesus had a son whose vocal chords were muted from birth, but during the siege of Sardis the lad saw a warrior rush to thrust a sword through his father. Then, for the first time in his life, the burst of anguish the lad felt in his soul broke the impediment and he cried in a loud voice, "Man, kill not Croesus!"

Thus it is with the enduement of the Holy Spirit in the inner man. Christians who have been muted from their spiritual birth, unable to boldly witness for Christ, find their tongues loosed and, with passionate voices, cry out the message of God's redemption to the slaves of sin and Satan, beseeching them to turn to Christ and find pardon.

The secret for witnessing with boldness is wrapped up in this enduement of strength—yea, of "might"—in the inner man.

C. Our Enthronement

Paul describes it, "That Christ may dwell in your hearts by faith." Kenneth S. Wuest, long professor of Greek at the Moody Bible Institute, said of this:

> The word "dwell" is from a Greek word made up of two words, one meaning "to live in a home" and the other, literally meaning "down." Paul prays that our Lord might live in our hearts as His home. He is

already in us, therefore Paul's thought must be that He feel at home in our hearts. The tense speaks of finality, the word for "down" speaking of permanency. The full translation is, "That Christ may finally settle down and feel completely at home in your hearts."

It is one thing to be in a person's home, another thing to feel completely at home there. Our Lord condescends to live in the heart of the sinner saved by grace. What an honor to have such a guest in our hearts. Do we make Him feel at home? Does He have free access to all parts of our heart life, or is He shut out from this thing or that? Is He our constant companion or are we occupied at times with persons or things that we feel are not consistent with our fellowship with Him. Is He Lord of our lives, the invited guest to occupy the throne room of our hearts?[1]

This is in contrast to what Zophar, in his first discourse to Job, called letting "wickedness dwell in thy tabernacles" (Job 11:14). How much better for Christ to settle down and feel at home in our hearts than for wickedness to sit upon the throne.

If Christ is not reigning in your life, it would be beneficial to heed the injunction: "Examine yourselves, whether ye be in the faith; prove your own selves. Know ye not your own selves, how that Jesus Christ is in you, except ye be reprobates?" (II Cor. 13:5).

Paul wanted Christ to be preeminent in the lives of all believers; he desired Christ *reigning* upon the heart-throne of every child of God. As someone has expressed it,

> "If Christ is not Lord of all,
> He is not Lord at all."

Note, too, this enthronement is to be "by faith," or, "through faith." This is not merely a matter of feeling, although feeling there may well be.

D. Our Establishment

Paul went on to pray, "that ye, being rooted and grounded in love." He wanted the believers *rooted,* as a tree; he wanted them *grounded,* as a building. In other words, he thought they should

---

[1] From GOLDEN NUGGETS FROM THE GREEK NEW TESTAMENT by Kenneth S. Wuest. Copyright, 1940, by the author. Wm. B. Eerdmans Publishing Company. Used by permission.

be as stable as an oak and as firm, as solid as a gigantic skyscraper.

If you have ever tried to pull up a plant or a tree with long roots, you will understand the "rooted" symbol. And when you investigate the kind of foundation a building such as the Empire State Building has, with a solid rock foundation, you will understand better what Paul is saying about being "grounded." As the poet prayed,

> "Thou, my Life, O let me be
> Rooted, grafted, built in Thee!"

Paul pleads with believers not to be like those whom he later described as "children, tossed to and fro, and carried about with every wind of doctrine, by the sleight of men, and cunning craftiness, whereby they lie in wait to deceive" (4:14).

Note, also, that this rooting and grounding is to be "in love." We feel nothing but pity for the woman—one of the best-known ladies in America—who announced to the press, "I have resolved never to love again." We think she made this statement because she confused love with passion; no one who had ever experienced *real love* would want to lose it, or, if having lost it, would never want it back.

The love Paul spoke of was, of course, the love of God. First John 4:18 tells us, "There is no fear in love; but perfect love casteth out fear: because fear hath torment. He that feareth is not made perfect in love."

In other words, if the soil the Christian tree is *rooted in* and *feeds upon* is the love of God, there will be confidence and fearlessness in both life and service. Oh, to be built up in the love of God!

E. Our Enlightenment

Paul's passionate prayer reached a crescendo when he said of God's love: "That ye. . .may be able to comprehend with all saints what is the breadth, and length, and depth, and height."

With some love stories, the less known about them the better. By way of example, for hundreds of years one of history's greatest love stories related to the Taj Mahal. We were told that the Shah Jahan, fifth dynasty Mogul Emperor of Delhi, India, built the Taj Mahal as a memorial to his beautiful and lovely wife, Mumtaz Mahal. She was his favorite wife and, when she died in 1629, he started this magnificent mausoleum, completing it in 1645.

Now some historians are telling us that the whole thing is one big fake. They say the Taj Mahal was never built as a mausoleum, but as a palace. They say it was not built by Shah Jahan, nor for Mumtaz Mahal. In fact, they argue it was constructed as early as 372 A.D., not in 1645.

Investigation of facts holds no problem with the biblical love story. The more one learns of its breadth, length, depth and height, the greater it becomes.

As E. E. Hewitt wrote nearly a century ago,

> What a wonderful salvation!
> For its length and breadth and height
> Far excel the grandest knowledge
> Of the seraphim in light;
> I can never, never fathom
> Half its holy mystery,
> But I know it is for sinners,
> And it just suits me.

It is like the father who took his small son to the top of a high hill, from which the pair could see in every direction. As he pointed to the north, the east, the south, and the west, the enthusiastic parent exclaimed, "Son, God's love is as big as all that!"

Then the little lad, with more wisdom than many a university professor, exclaimed, "Yes, Dad! And just think, we are right in the middle of it!"

In talking about the breadth, length, depth and height of God's love, Paul pleads with the Heavenly Father to help the saints know the unknowable and measure the immeasurable. In fact, the words in the Authorized Version, "that ye may be able," are literally, "that ye may be *fully* able." This should be the goal of "all saints," not just a few.

Some years ago I read in a secular newspaper a love story as beautiful as one could ever hope to read outside of the Bible. It was the account of a young woman who "had run away from a dunghill tribal sty of brutishness and coarseness when she was thirteen. For four years she had lived a nightmare on the streets—used, abused, never excused. . .in and out of the police stations, institutions and hospitals. . .unwanted, unloved, unloving."

Finally, at the age of 17, she was dragged from the scum of the Monongahela River—her second suicide attempt—and a kindly policeman begged an elderly couple to take the human derelict into their home. Although the couple had little and the wife was sickly, they received her and loved her and treated her as if she were their very own daughter.

When I read the account, the former derelict was a lovely 26-year-old woman, married and the mother of a precious little girl, and she had returned to Pittsburgh to be with the man on his deathbed. The wife had died a few months before. After his funeral, the young woman made this statement about them both:

> They had no reason to love me, but they did. They were never ashamed of me. Sending me to a special school and college was a tremendous sacrifice. From them, I learned the beauty of hope.

Yet in what a greater, grander, more glorious manner the Heavenly Father—who had no reason to love us—in a sense bankrupted Heaven to provide a redemption and a life worth living here and hereafter. No wonder Paul wanted the saints to "be fully able to comprehend" the breadth, length, depth and height of this wonderful love.

Bishop Moule, in the *Expositor's Bible,* tells of a dying French saint who embraced her daughter for a final time and said, "My child, I have loved you because of what you are; my Heavenly Father, to whom I go, has loved me *malgre moi,*" that is, "in spite of myself."

Since this is true, how can we fully comprehend it? It is like the lady in Miami Beach, Mildred Fello, who accidentally discarded her $4,000 diamond ring in a plastic bag with garbage. When she realized what had happened, the trash collectors had already gathered up the bag.

Miss Fello chased the truck for two blocks, but by the time she caught up the machinery in the truck had smashed everything together. Going with the crew to the dump and sifting the refuse, she finally came upon the blue bag and, happily, discovered the diamond ring undamaged.

Later, talking to newsmen, she said, "Even in all that mess that ring looked just as beautiful." And in a way I cannot describe, to say nothing of comprehend, the Lord of Glory looked down at me, dwelling in the foul mess of this world's garbage, and I looked "just beautiful" to Him. How great is the breadth, length, depth and height of this love.

How can these four dimensions of love be explained? To take a feeble stab at it, how about John 3:16? "For God so loved the world"—there is its breadth. "That he gave his only begotten Son"—there is its depth. "That whosoever believeth in him should not perish"—there is the length. "But have everlasting life"—there is the height.

Mary Shekleton caught a glimpse of this four dimensional love, writing:

> It passeth knowledge, that dear love of Thine,
> My Jesus, Saviour; yet this soul of mine
> Would of Thy love, in all its breadth and length,
> Its height and depth, its everlasting strength,
>   Know more and more.
>
> It passeth telling, that dear love of Thine,
> My Jesus, Saviour; yet these lips of mine
> Would fain proclaim to sinners far and near
> A love which can remove all guilty fear,
>   And love beget.
>
> But though I cannot sing, or tell, or know
> The fulness of Thy love, while here below,
> My empty vessel I may freely bring:
> O Thou, who art of love the living spring,
>   My vessel fill.
>
> O, fill me, Jesus, Saviour, with Thy love!
> Lead, lead me to the living fount above;
> Thither may I, in simple faith, draw nigh,
> And never to another fountain fly,
>   But unto Thee.

F. Our Enlargement

This is described: "And to know the love of Christ, which passeth knowledge." You see, Paul did not pray merely that the eyes be opened, but the heart as well. This love, since it passes knowledge, cannot be broken down in a chemist's test tube; it cannot be seen through an astronomer's telescope; it cannot be painted on an artist's canvas; nor can it be told by an orator's free-flowing tongue. But, on the other hand, it can be experienced by any humble soul who so desires!

Most metropolitan newspapers have an "answer" section where readers seek information about people or things. Some time ago, in the *Washington Star-News,* some one had written to inquire, "How do you say 'I love you' in Apache?"

The newspaper replied, in part, "It is a very hard question, but here goes. There is no way of translating 'I love you' literally into English from the Apache for several reasons: (1) Apache, we're told, is a language with very few abstractions (such as love, which is not a concrete thing or idea) and, therefore, an Apache would be more likely to say 'You would make a fine hunting partner,' rather than use a romantic phrase."

We have the same problem translating the language of Heaven—when the Father says to the sinner, "I love you"—into the language of earth. It is not so much a matter of *knowledge* as it is *experience.*

It is something like the missionary lady who found a pitiful leper, one who had lost all her fingers and toes to that dread disease, sobbing on the grass, cruel children near by taunting her in her misery. The missionary put her arms around her and the leper, overcome with emotional sobbing, exclaimed, "A human hand has touched me! A human hand has touched me! For seven years no one has touched me!"

In what a greater, grander manner the Heavenly Father touches sinners in love through redemption. As another has expressed it,

> Stronger His love than death or Hell,
> Its riches are unsearchable:

> The first-born sons of light
> Desire in vain its depth to see,
> They cannot tell the mystery,
> The length, and breadth, and height!

Paul prayed that the Ephesians might experience this love which cannot be entered into through mere knowledge.

Did you know that natives formerly offered human sacrifices on the island of Formosa? When a Chinese governor named Goho came into power, he convinced the people to sacrifice an ox or a pig instead of a human. The people agreed and all went well for a few years until, one harvest season, crops were unusually poor. Convinced their gods were angry and human sacrifices would again be necessary, Governor Goho pleaded contrariwise in vain.

Eventually, seeing the people were determined to revert to their paganistic ritual, he instructed them to go the next day to a certain place in the forest where they would find a victim ready. He explained that the man would be wearing the red robe of sacrifice, a red cloth over his head, tied to a tree.

The following day the natives went to the appointed place and found the victim, just as the governor had described him. In a wild frenzy they rushed upon him and the executioner, with one swift stroke of his sword, struck off the victim's head. When the red cloth was removed, the horrified natives discovered they had sacrificed Governor Goho himself. That ended the inhuman practice and from that day to this, no human sacrifice has ever been offered on that island.

In a much greater manner, the Governor of Heaven, Jesus Christ, offered Himself a sacrifice to free us from our sins. Do you know that love which passeth knowledge?

> Love, so vast that nought can bound;
> Love, too deep for thought to sound;
> Love, which made the Lord of all
> Drink the wormwood and the gall.
>
> Love, which led Him to the cross,
> Bearing there unutter'd loss;
> Love, which brought Him to the gloom
> Of the cold and darksome tomb.
>
> Love, which made Him hence arise
> Far above the starry skies,

There, with tender, loving care,
All His people's griefs to share.

Love, which will not let Him rest
Till His chosen all are blest;
Till they all for whom He died
Live rejoicing by His side.

G. Our Enrichment

Paul said, ". . .that ye might be filled with all the fulness of God." *What a climax!*

"That ye might be filled." In other words, self completely obliterated, sin dethroned, and Christ in complete charge.

"With all the fulness of God." Here is another amazing thought which goes far beyond human comprehension. Solomon, when he built and dedicated that great temple, declared, "But will God indeed dwell on the earth? behold, the heaven and heaven of heavens cannot contain thee; how much less this house that I have builded" (I Kings 8:27).

If God was too great to be contained in fullness in that great temple, how can He, in His fullness, be contained in a believer's body?

Someone has suggested that you take a child's sand pail to the seashore, set it on the sand and wait for the tide to roll in, filling the pail. Then one might pick up that pail and truly exclaim, "It is filled with all the fullness of the ocean."

When Paul wrote to the saints at Colosse, he described this truth:

"For in him dwelleth all the fulness of the Godhead bodily. And ye are complete in him, which is the head of all principality and power."—Col. 2:9,10.

III. PAUL'S POSITIVE PRAISE

He closed this prayer with a doxology, exulting:

"Now unto him that is able to do exceeding abundantly above all that we ask or think, according to the power that worketh in us, Unto him be glory in the church by Christ Jesus throughout all ages, world without end. Amen."—Vss. 20,21.

A. The Assurance

"Him that *is able* to do"! How often we desire to *do* something, *help* someone, *comfort* another in an hour of grief, but we cannot, we are unable. God is never thus stumped. He is never even pressed. No matter the need, *He is able!*

B. The Amount

Paul describes it as "exceeding abundantly above all that we ask or think." Note how staggering these statements are when separated into individual thoughts:

Him that *is able.*
Him that is able *to do.*
Him that is able to do *all we ask.*
Him that is able to do all we *think.*
Him that is able to do *above all* that we *ask.*
Him that is able to do *above all* that we *think.*
Him that is able to do *abundantly* above all that we *ask.*
Him that is able to do *abundantly* above all that we *think.*

Him that is able to do exceedingly abundantly above all that we *ask.*

Him that is able to do *exceedingly* abundantly above all that we *think.*

Truly this is beyond human comprehension. Yet scriptural examples abound of this power in amounts of such nature.

There was the time God opened the Red Sea for Israel and caused them to cross on *dry ground.* He did the same later at the Jordan.

Then there was the fire which fell from Heaven for Elijah and consumed the water-soaked sacrifice, the stones, the dust, and the water in the trench.

Then there was the incident when Christ took five barley biscuits and two small fish, blessing and breaking them to feed five thousand men—with His disciples gathering twelve baskets of the fragments that remained.

Beyond question, our God is able to do "exceeding abundantly above all that we ask or think."

C. The According

Paul described this as "according to the power that worketh in us." The thought of the word "according" is that of "being in agreement with," or, "the state of being in harmony." The idea is that God does His "exceeding abundantly" as we are in harmony with Him! Surely we should understand that our life cannot be filled with the discords of sin and still experience great answers to prayer or great feats in service.

Note also that it is the "power that worketh in us." He does the work! Our accomplishments do not come through the efforts of the flesh. Oh, that we might learn, with the poet,

> Once it was my working,
> His it hence shall be;
> Once I tried to use Him,
> Now He uses me.

D. The Aim

This purpose, this intention is described in the final verse: "Unto him be glory in the church by Christ Jesus throughout all ages, world without end." In other words, it is directed toward glory for God in the church by Christ: *"unto all the generations of the age of the ages."* This is a thought of one generation endlessly succeeding another in bringing praise and glory to God. And it will continue throughout all the eternities of the future.

"Amen!" *So be it!*

Conclusion

Lord, open our hearts!

Most of today's Christians, if they recognize the name Russell Conwell at all, associate him with his famous address, "Acres of Diamonds." Near the sunset of this man's ministry, a magazine reporter asked if he could name the outstanding experience of his long and fruitful life.

Surprisingly, he referred to an incident which happened when he was fighting in the army, before his conversion. An orderly named Johnny Ring had been assigned to him and the devotion the lad showed toward his officer was amazing, to say the least. One night, surprised by an enemy attack, Conwell's forces were driven across a bridge. To slow down the pursuit of the enemy, he ordered fire set to the bridge and then discovered he had left, in his haste, his sword in the tent. The orderly, although not instructed to do so, broke away and ran across the burning bridge to retrieve the sword, then raced through the flames the second time, receiving serious third-degree burns. It cost him his life.

Conwell said that as he sat beside the lad's cot and watched him twisting and tossing in agony before he died, the question kept burning in his mind, "Why did Johnny Ring give his life to save my sword?" The only answer he could come up with was that the lad loved him supremely, unworthy though he was. And Conwell said, in describing it to the reporter, "Believe me, I *was* unworthy."

Dr. Conwell went on, "It was just a step from there to the question that had made me a skeptic, 'Why did Christ die for sinners?' I had never been able to understand or to accept the atonement, but suddenly I saw it clearly. Christ, like Johnny Ring, suffered for the same reason, because He loved us." That moment all of his doubts were washed away in the love of God and then and there he received Jesus Christ as Lord and Saviour, promising God he would work for two lives—Johnny Ring and Russell Conwell.

How about you? Have you responded to the love of God and the sacrifice of Christ?

In the East is a New Yorker whose first name is John, married to a woman named Janette. John had a dog named Max Donovan. When the wife filed a separation suit from John, the correspondent, so to speak, was Max! She explained that although Max was "a very lovable Schnauzer dog," she objected to her husband treating her like a dog and Max like a human.

Apparently the wife's complaint was justified. Evidence showed her husband put the dog on the payroll of his Wall Street brokerage firm, and even took out a social security card in Max's name. When the judge asked if the dog paid income tax, the wife replied that she did not know, "But I know that he collected wages."

When one of the witnesses, an employee of the brokerage firm, was asked in her testimony about Max Donovan, she declared: "He is a dog. He had a Social Security number. He drew a salary. And he was on several mailing lists, including a book club's."

Because of this cruel and inhuman treatment during eleven years of marriage, Janette was seeking $250 a week in alimony from her husband. She was tired of being treated like a dog while her husband treated a dog with the affection which should have been given to a wife.

When I read the above story, I could not help but think of how the average individual treats Jesus Christ. The Son of God came from the glories of Heaven and died in agony at Calvary in order to provide a redemption for sinners. Again and again, in sundry ways and divers manners, He appeals to the heart of man for entrance and submission. Yet Max Donovan, the dog, got better treatment from his master than the Lord Jesus Christ receives from the average sinner!

No wonder Hebrews 10:28-31 says:

"He that despised Moses' law died without mercy under two or three witnesses: Of how much sorer punishment, suppose ye, shall he be thought worthy, who hath trodden under foot the Son of God, and hath counted the blood of the covenant, wherewith he was sanctified, an unholy thing, and hath done despite unto the Spirit of grace? For we know him that hath said, Vengeance belongeth unto me. I will recompense, saith the Lord. And again, The Lord shall judge his people. It is a fearful thing to fall into the hands of the living God."

How have you responded to the love of Christ, which passeth knowledge?

***Walking Worthy of
Our Calling
and Commission***

I therefore, the prisoner of the Lord, beseech you that ye walk worthy of the vocation wherewith ye are called,
With all lowliness and meekness, with longsuffering, forbearing one another in love;
Endeavouring to keep the unity of the Spirit in the bond of peace.
There is one body, and one Spirit, even as ye are called in one hope of your calling;
One Lord, one faith, one baptism,
One God and Father of all, who is above all, and through all, and in you all.
But unto every one of us is given grace according to the measure of the gift of Christ.
Wherefore he saith, When he ascended up on high, he led captivity captive, and gave gifts unto men.
(Now that he ascended, what is it but that he also descended first into the lower parts of the earth?
He that descended is the same also that ascended up far above all heavens, that he might fill all things.)
And he gave some, apostles; and some, prophets; and some, evangelists; and some, pastors and teachers;
For the perfecting of the saints, for the work of the ministry, for the edifying of the body of Christ.
Till we all come in the unity of the faith, and of the knowledge of the Son of God, unto a perfect man, unto the measure of the stature of the fulness of Christ:
That we henceforth be no more children, tossed to and fro,

and carried about with every wind of doctrine, by the sleight of men, and cunning craftiness, whereby they lie in wait to deceive;

But speaking the truth in love, may grow up into him in all things, which is the head, even Christ:

From whom the whole body fitly joined together and compacted by that which every joint supplieth, according to the effectual working in the measure of every part, maketh increase of the body unto the edifying of itself in love.—Ephesians 4:1-16.

One of the most amazing stories of practical Christianity ever told relates to a Christian father who, during the fierce fighting of the Korean War, witnessed a wicked, cruel communist soldier torture and then slay his beloved 19-year-old son. When the murderer was captured by the United Nations forces, he was tried before a military tribunal, found guilty, and sentenced to death before a firing squad.

In a fashion truly amazing and equally gracious, the bereaved father pled with the authorities to place the condemned man in his custody, rather than putting him to death, saying, "Let me have him and I will train him."

In action that went way beyond turning the other cheek or traveling the second mile, the Christian gentleman took the communist soldier into his own home, loved him, lived Christ before him, and explained the beautiful plan of redemption to him through both word and deed. He won him to Christ and established him in the faith! Today that ex-communist is a minister of the Gospel of Jesus Christ, pastoring a church in Korea.

That Christian father was not only *sound in the faith,* he was *controlled by the Spirit.* It is the latter which is before us in this text. In the first three chapters of Ephesians, Paul sets forth Christian *doctrine;* in the last three chapters he exhorts relative to Christian *doing.* Just as flowers sprout from pregnant plants, so Paul launches into a duty that springs from doctrine.

When Paul wrote to Timothy, he said: "All Scripture is given by inspiration of God, and is profitable for doctrine, for reproof, for correction, for instruction in righteousness: That the man of God may be perfect, throughly furnished unto all good works" (II Tim. 3:16,17). Paul handled the matter of doctrine in the first chapters of Ephesians, now he settles down to the reproof, the correction, and the instruction in righteousness.

The last are as important as the first. We must know our duty as well as our doctrine, be able to demonstrate truth as well as defend it, have the fire to go with the facts. In other words, it is imperative that our walk match our standard.

The apostle commences with a heartbroken plea, beseeching his converts at Ephesus to "walk worthy." Paul knew souls were lost and dying. He believed in a literal, horrible, eternal Hell. He knew the human heart and how many would reject Christ if Christians were inconsistent in their living. You may be sure the "hypocrites in the church" alibi was as predominant and popular in Paul's day as in ours. He wanted that excuse annihilated at Ephesus—*and wherever else his message would penetrate unto the end of time.*

His opening "therefore" indicates his plea was based upon what he had written in the passage preceding our text, especially the great love and power of Jesus Christ placed at the Christian's disposal (3:16-21). It was a recognition and a reminder of the truth in Philippians 4:13, "I can do all things through Christ which strengtheneth me."

The appeal was a personal one from the very heart of the aged apostle. He says, "I. . .the prisoner of the Lord." What credentials! And what proof of Paul's love and concern for the Ephesians: *writing while in chains!*

Even in his plea he was conscious of the fact—and he wanted his readers to be mindful, too—that his imprisonment was for righteousness' sake. Paul, unlike his companions in the Roman prison, was not guilty of any moral crime; he was as innocent of judicial wrongdoing as a newborn babe. He was there because of his stand for the Son of God! So while Rome might consider him Caesar's prisoner, he considered himself, in truth and in fact, "the prisoner of Jesus Christ."

Really, it mattered little to Paul *where* he was. He served God just as acceptably as a bondman as he did a freeman. If he had liberty to come and go as he pleased, then he went forth to do the will of God. If he were shut up behind prison bars in some filthy dungeon, then he would sing God's praises and do the will of God in the dungeon. As Madam Guyon wrote many centuries later,

> A little bird I am,
> Shut from the fields of air;
> And in my cage I sit and sing
> To Him who placed me there;
> Well, pleased a prisoner to be
> Because, my God, it pleases Thee.

Paul preferred, as would any of us, to mount up with eagle's wings; but if they put him in a cage, he *could* and *did* sing like a canary to the glory of his Saviour and Lord, Jesus Christ. Might we be imitators of him in this today (I Cor. 11:1)!

I. WALKING WORTHY OF OUR CALLING! Vss. 1-6

Paul said, *"I therefore, the prisoner of the Lord, beseech you that ye walk worthy of the vocation wherewith ye are called"* (vs. 1). The Christian's walk is to be based upon his exalted position as a child of God.

Our English word "courteous" is based upon the French "cortis"—court. So the word courteous actually means "in a manner befitting the court," or, "in a courtlike manner." Just so is the Christian's walk to be a courteous one. In other words, it should be in a manner befitting his holy, heavenly calling in the family of divine royalty. Just as it was considered a crime to take the ring of Augustus into a promiscuous place in the days of Tiberius, so the friends and followers of Christ in the twentieth century should earnestly seek to preserve and protect the noble reputation of the Son of God. It is for "his name's sake" that we are to walk "in the paths of righteousness" (Ps. 23:3).

The German Bible renders the opening clause of Hebrews 10:38, *"Der Gerechte aber wird des glaubens leben."* This translates into English, "The right will live his belief." This is what Paul is pleading for; he wants every Christian, justified by faith, to live that belief before an ungodly world, shining as "the light of the world. . .that they may see your good works, and glorify your Father which is in heaven" (Matt. 5:14,16).

If any group of people in the world ought to be unselfish, considerate, outgoing, and concerned about others, it is the company known as Christians.

In a tiny cemetery outside of Leamington, England, is a grave with the following inscription carved on its tombstone:

> Here lies a miser who lived for himself,
> And cared for nothing but gathering pelf,
> Now, where he is, or how he fares,
> Nobody knows and nobody cares.

No Christian should be forced, like Jehoram of old, to "depart without being desired" (II Chron. 21:20). A worthy walk will eliminate this embarrassing possibility.

A. The Position of the Walk in View of Our Calling

Contrary to what some might suppose, this position is not up, but down. Verse 2 says, *"With all lowliness and meekness, with longsuffering, forbearing one another in love."*

Someone tells the story of a circus being moved from one community to another. Through an unfortunate error, a freak, sideshow rooster was put into a van with an elephant. As the vehicle bounced down a rough road, the elephant had difficulty keeping his balance, being forced to keep shifting his feet. After hopping, ducking, dodging and otherwise seeking to stay out of the elephant's way, the masculine chicken finally drew himself as erect as he could, looked the giant behemoth straight in the eye, and said, "Listen here, big boy. Let's get one thing straight. We are not going to have any stepping on one another!"

It is the practice of the world to get ahead by a dog-eat-dog, stepping-on-each-other philosophy for success, but this is not to be the Christian's route.

1. With All Lowliness!

Perhaps, for people in our day, this word might better be rendered "modest," since it carries the thought of a Christian having a modest opinion of himself. Another has rightly observed, "People fall in love with themselves almost immediately after birth. This is invariably the beginning of a lifelong romance. There is no record of infidelity, separation, or divorce between humans and their egos."

A past leader in the China Inland Mission, Dr. Henry W. Frost, told a story of his illustrious uncle, Rev. James Inglis, a gracious gentleman who pastored a large Detroit church. He had been highly educated, a graduate of Edinburgh University and Divinity School, was an unusually eloquent and gifted speaker, and had been marvelously blessed of God in the pastorate. In fact, such throngs jammed his church every Sunday that people sat in the aisles and on the stairs, space being at a premium.

One day in his study, preparing a message for the following Lord's Day, his thoughts were startled by an inward voice seeming to say, "James Inglis, whom are you preaching?"

Amazed and startled, he replied, "I am preaching good theology."

The inner voice insisted, "I did not ask *what* you were preaching, but *whom.*"

Again Inglis answered, "I am preaching the Gospel."

Still again the voice challenged, "I did not ask *what,* I asked *whom.*"

The missionary statesman said his uncle sat silently with head bowed for considerable time, then he raised up and exlaimed, "O God, I am preaching James Inglis!"

We fear a kindred self-examination would result in identical conclusions by many Christian leaders today. Actually, however, not a one of us has anything to be boastful about. Whatever we *have,* whatever we *are* we owe to the matchless, infinite grace of God. Someone has expressed it, "To quell the pride, even of the greatest, we should reflect how much we owe to others and how little to ourselves." It would be humbling reflection, indeed.

When Paul wrote to the Philippians, he pleaded, "Let nothing be done through strife or vainglory; but in lowliness of mind let each esteem other better than themselves" (Phil. 2:3). Contrary to other religions, all of which elevate self, the Christian faith leaves its adherents without a single shred of self-praise.

Apart from the Lord Jesus Christ, the Apostle Paul is probably considered by Christians to be one of the greatest individuals of all time. Yet he said of himself, "I am the least of the apostles, that am not meet to be called an apostle. . ." (I Cor. 15:9). Earlier in Ephesians he passionately declared, "Unto me, who am less than the least of all saints, is this grace given. . ." (3:8).

Dr. S. I. McMillen, in his book, *None of These Diseases,* quotes the prayer of an anonymous supplicant:

> Lord, keep me from becoming talkative and possessed with the idea that I must express myself on every subject. Release me from the craving to straighten out everyone's affairs. Teach me the glorious lesson that occasionally I may be wrong. Make me helpful but not bossy. With my vast store of wisdom and experience it does seem a pity not to use it all—, but Thou knowest, Lord, that I want a few friends at the end. *Amen.*

Do not misunderstand. There is a sense in which the child of God should think highly of himself. Paul in Romans 12:3 declared: "For I say, through the grace given unto me, to every man that is among you, not to think of himself more highly than he ought to think; but to think soberly, according as God hath dealt to every man the measure of faith." The child of God is to think of himself as being too good to live like the world, his calling is too high to walk in paths of sensuality, his heritage is too noble to pursue evil tendencies.

The lowliness of which Paul speaks carries the idea of a willingness to be treated even more insignificantly than one actually is, without any complaint or thought of redress. Unlike the Oriental who must concern himself so much with "losing face," the Christian can be put down without offense.

When D. E. Hoste, who eventually succeeded J. Hudson Taylor as head of the China Inland Mission, first went to that land to serve, he and another brother were sent to establish a remote station in one of the inner provinces. Since their superiors had not indicated which one should be in charge, the other missionary announced to Hoste, "I've prayed about it and I feel the Lord wants me to take the leadership and make whatever decisions need to be made at this station."

Hoste, a very gracious and kindly man, simply replied, "That will be very satisfactory with me."

No one who tells this story today can even give *the name* of the other man. He faded into obscurity. But God exalted Hoste to one of the most influential positions in the field of missions in his day.

Yes, "God resisteth the proud, but giveth grace unto the humble" (James 4:6). His inflexible law is, "For whosoever exalteth himself shall be abased; and he that humbleth himself shall be exalted" (Luke 14:11). So, "Humble yourselves therefore under the mighty hand of God, that he may exalt you in due time" (I Pet. 5:6).

2. With All Meekness

When one is "clothed with humility" he does not react as did the two ladies who sought the office of president in a local church women's organization. After campaigning bitterly for the position to which only one could be elected, those two sisters refused to speak to each other for nearly a year. Kindred tragedies—and they are legion in our churches—could be averted with huge doses of the prescription our Great Physician offers in this passage.

Perhaps Christians could benefit from the advice of the former heavyweight boxing champion, "Jersey Joe" Wolcott. Referring to his former fighting days, he said, "I thought that the fellow who could knock the most people down was the fellow who would reach the top the fastest." Not so, he discovered; today the fighter-turned-lawman says it is "the fellow who can pick up the guy who is a fallen human being and help him find his way" who is the one truly succeeding in life.

As the old spiritual says,

> The quickest way up is down

> The quickest way up is down,
> You may climb up high, and try and try,
> But the quickest way up is down.

3. With Longsuffering

This is talking about patient endurance and literally means "to endure with unruffled temper." If you want the correct understanding of the word, emphasize *"suffering"* and then add *"long."* We are to endure wrongs inflicted by others, no matter the occasion prompting them. As Beecher wrote: "Every man should keep a fair-sized cemetery in which to bury the faults of his friends." Paul pleads for such a cemetery in the life of every believer.

We find fascinating the story of "Squanto," the Indian who befriended the Pilgrims surviving that first Massachusetts winter following arrival at Plymouth Rock. Squanto had been captured years before by a plundering British sea captain, sold into slavery in Spain, then managing to escape to England. There he had been treated kindly and eventually arrived back in his homeland. In the merciful providence of God, he was the Indian who found the small colony of white men, acted as their go-between with the powerful Indian chief, Massasoit, then taught them the rules of survival in this strange land. There is no telling what might have happened to the Pilgrims apart from his kindness.

From the human standpoint, one might say Squanto had every reason to hate the white man because of the mistreatment and suffering at his hands years before. Yet this one whom some would describe as a "savage" was willing to forgive and forget, offering Christians today an illustration of longsuffering.

Do you find it difficult? Learn Jeremiah's secret as expressed in Jeremiah 15. Talking about his troubles, he said in verse 15: "O Lord, thou knowest: remember me, and visit me, and revenge me of my persecutors; take me not away in thy longsuffering: know that for thy sake I have suffered rebuke." What did he do to overcome the enmity, to dispel the hatred, to endure the opposition and persecution? The next verse says, "Thy words were found, and I did eat them; and thy word was unto me the joy and rejoicing of mine heart: for I am called by thy name, O Lord God of hosts."

Here is the secret of triumph for any believer: *it is a digging into the depths of the wonders of God's Word.*

The missionary statesman of yesteryear, A. B. Simpson, told of a lady who took a journey of 50 miles by train through an interesting and beautiful region. Although it was her first railway trip and she had eagerly anticipated the pleasure, it took her so long to get into her seat, adjust her baggage and make herself comfortable that the name of her station was announced before she knew it. As she was hustled off the coach, she exclaimed, "Oh, my! If I had only known we would have arrived so soon, I wouldn't have wasted so much time fussing."

We fear many a saint will have the same reaction when he gets to Glory. If only he had realized how temporary was his earthly journey, he would have eliminated much of the fussing along the way. Let us for Christ's sake endure with unruffled tempers whatever wrongs are inflicted upon us.

4. *Loving Forbearance*

This is literally "to put up with in love." Have you ever admired the beauty of the lily? Did you know that there are numerous members of the lily family which are never used in corsages, in table centerpieces, or telegraphed by absent members to loved ones far away? We refer to garlic, onions, leaks—and even the more noble asparagus! Each of these, horticulturists tell us, is a member of the lily family.

New converts soon discover what older Christians have long known: some members in God's family are less attractive than others, at least when it comes to spiritual graces. It requires a hearty dose of lowliness, meekness, longsuffering and loving forbearance to get along with them. Incidentally, longsuffering might consist of mere passive indifference, but loving forbearance includes an active side to the Christian's endurance. It is putting into practice the old motto, "Be to my faults a little blind, and to my virtues, very kind." Or as another expressed it, "It's nice to be important, but more important to be nice."

It is helpful in practicing loving forbearance to remember that, this side of the grave, we do not have all the facts. The umpire directly behind the plate can call balls and strikes much more accurately than the bleacherite in the left field stands, no matter the latter's confidence to the contrary. Much of our criticism of others would evaporate immediately if we had a close-up view of both the person and the problem.

In short, Paul is saying, "Don't be overly sensitive." Proverbs 10:12 reveals the divine key for putting up with all that is disagreeable and offensive in others when it says, "Hatred stirreth up strife: but love covereth all sins."

Keep in mind that the insults, indignities, opposition and sundry forms of disagreeableness which come into the life of a Christian are there only because God, in His infinite wisdom, has permitted them. J. Hudson Taylor offered sound advice when he wrote:

> How the tendency to resentment and a wrong feeling would be removed, could we take an injury from the hand of a loving Father, instead of looking chiefly at the agent through whom it comes to us! It matters not who is the postman—it is with the writing in the letter that we are concerned; it matters not who is the messenger—it is with God that His children have to do. If we accept all God's Providential dealings as from Himself, we may be sure that they will issue in ultimate blessing; because God is GOD, and therefore "all things work together for good to them that love him."

Yet it is still the *love aspect* which is the primary key. Do you remember the mother whose son had been pardoned from a sentence of death by President Abraham Lincoln? After leaving the great President's presence, she was heard to excitedly say, "I knew it was a copper-headed lie!"

Thaddeus Stevens, who had accompanied the lady during the White House audience, inquired, "To what do you refer?"

She replied with rising vehemence, "They said he was an ugly-looking man. I think he is the handsomest man I have ever met in my life!"

Probably no one who has ever seen a portrait of the Great

Emancipator would agree with that mother's evaluation. Why did he appear so handsome to her? It was because she beheld him through the affectionate eyes of a burning love, grateful for what he had done in behalf of her son. When the old-time religion makes us love fellow believers as we ought to love them, the virtue of loving forbearance will flow from our lives without forcing.

B. The Purpose of Our Walk's Position

This is described in verses 3 through 6: *"Endeavoring to keep the unity of the Spirit in the bond of peace. There is one body, and one Spirit, even as ye are called in one hope of your calling; One Lord, one faith, one baptism, One God and Father of all, who is above all, and through all, and in you all."*

Some time ago we read in a Los Angeles paper of a dog darting across the Santa Ana freeway during the peak traffic of a holiday weekend. It resulted in 40 vehicles smashing together over a stretch of three miles, causing more than $10,000 in damage. Over one-third of the automobiles had to be towed from the scene. Eleven persons required treatment for minor injuries and it took an hour to get the freeway cleared.

The dog was killed.

Yet this is minor compared to the catastrophes which have resulted when God's people have failed to follow the formula of lowliness, meekness, longsuffering and loving forbearance. Legion are the churches which have been split, pastorates which have been terminated, friendships of a lifetime which have been voided—all because of failure here.

Why must Christians endeavor to manifest these virtues? In order that we might "keep the unity of the Spirit in the bond of peace." In fact, if the last two words of the previous verse are added to verse three, the thought comes through even stronger: "In love endeavoring to keep the unity of the Spirit in the bond of peace."

Paul speaks of "endeavoring." In other words, Christians are to make it their aim to keep unity and peace. Success normally falls within the grasp of people who take seriously such goals.

Note also that it is to be the "unity of the Spirit." He is the only source of genuine unity. Forms, creeds and ceremonies cannot make or keep unity. They can provide a togetherness which, on the surface, looks like unity, but it takes the fullness of the Holy Spirit to provide authentic oneness.

When He is in control there will be no need for worldly "how to win friends and influence people" philosophies. This unity does not come through diplomacy. We recall the Southern preacher's definition of this, when he explained to his congregation: "Brethren, my own homespun idea of the matter is that diplomacy is the art of saying the nastiest things one can think of to say to folks, in the nicest way possible."

Note, however, that our responsibility for unity is limited to the scope of the Holy Spirit. There is no "let's all get together for the good of the community" in this command. The ecumenists have seized on this statement by Paul as an opportunity to insist that everyone get together in one big happy family, perhaps in the form of a superchurch. This most certainly was not Paul's intention. Any unity not embraced within the confines of the Holy Spirit's *doctrine* and *practice* is not the unity sought. This is no encouragement to a "good Lord, good Devil" philosophy.

When we were in meetings in Prosperity, West Virginia, a Sunday school teacher told of presenting a lesson to her primary girls on the text, "Love your enemies!" After a rousing lecture session, to make the application more personal for her girls, she had the children write on a piece of paper, "I love _____," instructing them to fill in the blank with the name of some "enemy." Imagine the teacher's chagrin when one little girl, after working laboriously for a few moments, looked up to inquire, "How do you spell 'Devil'?"

This, assuredly, is not what Paul meant! In fact, he carefully listed exactly what he had in mind by describing it as "the unity of the Spirit." This unity (singular) is wrapped up in seven distinct parts: *Inward, outward and Godward.* Seven is the number of completion and this is complete, unblemished, perfect unity.

1. Inward Unity

First he speaks of "one body." This is in reference to the mystical, spiritual body composed only of regenerated people. It is as he wrote to the Corinthians, "For as the body is one, and hath many members, and all the members of that one body, being many, are one body: so also is Christ" (I Corinthians 12:12).

Then he speaks of "one Spirit" and the reference is to the blessed Holy Spirit whereby believers are baptized into that one body. As Paul said in the next verse of the Corinthian passage: "For by one Spirit are we all baptized into one body, whether we be Jews or Gentiles, whether we be bond or free; and have been all made to drink into one Spirit" (vs. 13).

The third aspect of the inward unity is described as "one hope of your calling." This, no doubt, refers to the hope burning within every child of God, looking forward to the time when he will see his Saviour face to face, be transformed into His image, freed from all sin and frailty, when corruption shall put on incorruption and mortal shall have put on immortality. In the words of Romans 8:19, "For the earnest expectation of the creature waiteth for the manifestation of the sons of God."

2. Outward Unity

While the inward elements of the unity of the Spirit relate to that which cannot be seen by man, the outward phases deal with the open aspects of public profession.

This is seen in the "one Lord"—referring to worship, authority, rulership. The child of God has only one head, only one to tell him what to do, where to go, how to live. This is the thought of Luke 6:46, where our Lord questioned, "And why call ye me, Lord, Lord, and do not the things which I say?" Jesus Christ alone is our Lord; the source of our authority is not a pope, nor a church, nor human reason or self-will. It is not anything else or anyone else but the Son of God.

Then he speaks of "one faith." This is not our personal faith which we exercise in daily living, nor is it even saving faith. Quite the contrary, since this is an outward aspect of the unity of the Spirit, it logically refers to the one standard of truth Christians are to proclaim. We have one Gospel; it is *the* faith. The idea here is the same as in Jude 3, where we are told, "Beloved, when I gave all diligence to write unto you of the common salvation, it was needful for me to write unto you, and exhort you that ye should earnestly contend for the faith which was once delivered unto the saints." It is not "faith"; it is "the faith."

This is what Frederick W. Faber was thinking about when he taught us to sing:

> Faith of our fathers! living still
> In spite of dungeon, fire and sword:
> O how our hearts beat high with joy
> Whene'er we hear that glorious word!
> Faith of our fathers! holy faith!
> We will be true to thee till death!

The third aspect of the outward phase in the Spirit's unity relates to "one baptism." Scores of books have been written speculating about the kind of baptism Paul meant here, but the interpretation seems to us very simple. For three specific and definite reasons we are forced to conclude that his reference is to water baptism. First of all, when any baptism other than water is intended, it is clearly labeled. Second, the Holy Spirit has already been considered, right where He ought to be mentioned, in the *inward* phase of the unity. So it is not His baptism under discussion. Third, since this baptism relates to an outward, public expression manifesting allegiance to Christ, it would necessarily have to be water baptism. Surely no one would classify the baptism of (or *in*) the Holy Spirit as an outward, public manifestation.

This should settle once and for all any debate about water baptism. How wrong and how wicked for ministers of Christ to offer converts a choice about water baptism, saying, "If you want to be immersed, I will immerse you. Or if you would prefer to be sprinkled, I will just as happily do that for you. As long as your conscience is clear and you are satisfied in your heart, that is all I ask." But this does not square with the teaching of the Word of

God. The Bible teaching is that there is only one baptism. *There is no choice to make!*

Perhaps a word of caution would be fitting. Since water baptism is an outward expression of allegiance to Christ, signifying that the one being baptized is trusting in the death, burial and resurrection of Christ to take him to Heaven, how terrible for one to have *the outward mark* of allegiance to Christ, yet never be saved and burn in Hell forever! Make sure you have been biblically born again, not simply baptized in water as part of a religious ceremony.

3. Godward Unity

After a trilogy in *inward* and a trilogy of *outward* aspects of the Holy Spirit's unity, the apostle looks Heavenward and sums it up: "One God and Father of all, who is above all, and through all, and in you all" (vs. 6). Again there is a trilogy, this one reminding us of the Trinity. That He is "above all" and "through all" is a matter of fact, but what a glorious truth is summed up in the words "in you all." As Paul said elsewhere, ". . .ye are the temple of the living God; as God hath said, I will dwell in them, and walk in them; and I will be their God, and they shall be my people" (II Cor. 6:16).

Incidentally, note that Paul is not teaching the "universal Fatherhood of God and the brotherhood of man" in this passage, in spite of the liberals' efforts to so interpret it. He designates God as Father *only* to the body of Christ as he has described it in this epistle. Yet how wonderful and thrilling to realize that if you are in that body you can look up to the Almighty God of the Universe and say, "Father, *my* Father!"

Dear Christian friend, walk worthy of such a calling!

II. WALKING WORTHY OF OUR COMMISSION! Vss. 7-16

This section is based upon the gifts the body of Christ has received from the Risen Redeemer.

A. The Commissioned

Here is no secret, select, exclusive fraternity. Verse 7 says, *"But unto every one of us is given grace according to the measure of the gift of Christ."* None is excluded, no matter how feeble, how insignificant, or how unknown he or she may be. Just as the physical body has organs never seen by the human eye, yet play an essential part in the well-being of the individual, so the body of Christ has some members which are prominent and some which are not—*but all are vital and important in the plan and will of God.*

The amazing thing is that even rebellious Christians, stubbornly flaunting the will of God, are commissioned by the ascended Christ and have been given gifts by Him. While such is not clear in the Ephesian passage, the Psalm from which Paul quotes teaches this truth in no uncertain terms. There we read, "Thou hast ascended on high, thou hast led captivity captive: thou hast received gifts for men; yea, for the rebellious also, that the Lord God might dwell among them" (68:18). Yes, even "the rebellious also"!

Paul enlarges on this somewhat in Romans 12:4-8, saying:

"For as we have many members in one body, and all members have not the same office; So we, being many, are one body in Christ, and every one members one of another. Having then gifts differing according to the grace that is given to us, whether prophecy, let us prophesy according to the proportion of faith; Or ministry, let us wait on our ministering: or he that teacheth, on teaching; Or he that exhorteth, on exhortation: he that giveth, let him do it with simplicity; he that ruleth, with diligence; he that sheweth mercy, with cheerfulness."

Do not be discouraged if you have not been given a major gift—such as evangelist, pastor, or teacher. In fact, there are really no *major* or *minor* gifts when considered in the overall plan and program of God. As Paul wrote elsewhere, "Nay, much more those members of the body, which seem to be more feeble, are necessary" (I Cor. 12:22).

In Canada some time ago a tragic crash between a commuter

train and a bus killed nine people and injured others. When the investigation was completed, the report traced the problem to a missing screw from a master switch. It resulted in some wires hanging loose and they made a connection with the steel tracks which, in turn, opened the bus doors and caused the rear brakes to be activated, stopping the bus on the tracks. *The catastrophe was brought about by one missing screw!*

We can only speculate as to the spiritual tragedies resulting from Christians not being in their places, using their gifts which were given by the ascended Son of God. The full story will only be revealed at the Judgment Seat of Christ.

B. The Commissioner

While those who have been commissioned may be feeble, lowly and insignificant, such is not true of the One who commissioned them. We are told:

"Wherefore he saith, When he ascended up on high, he led captivity captive, and gave gifts unto men. (Now that he ascended, what is it but that he also descended first into the lower parts of the earth? He that descended is the same also that ascended up far above all heavens, that he might fill all things.)"

What power, what authority is indicated here!

Who is the Commissioner? It is the One who ascended up on High—Jesus Christ. It is the One who led captive him who held Him captive—Jesus Christ.

The explanation of this is seen in Hebrews 2:14,15, where we are told: "Forasmuch then as the children are partakers of flesh and blood, he also himself likewise took part of the same; that through death he might destroy him that had the power of death, that is, the devil; And deliver them who through fear of death were all their lifetime subject to bondage."

It is interesting that the same expression is found in the song of Deborah and Barak, in Judges 5:12,13, where we read: "Awake, awake, Deborah: awake, awake, utter a song: arise, Barak, and lead thy captivity captive, thou son of Abinoam. Then he made him that remaineth have dominion over the nobles among the people: the Lord made me have dominion over the mighty." Thank God, our mighty enemy, Satan, is a conquered, defeated foe—just as were Sisera, Jabin and the Canaanites after their rout by Israel.

Paul emphasizes that our Commissioner, Jesus Christ, is the One who descended before He ascended. This is not speaking of the location or condition of Christ's soul following death, but of our Lord's humiliation in the incarnation and in the atonement. As H. A. Ironside expressed it: "We are reminded that He who has gone up higher than any other man ever went, once for our redemption went down lower than any other man has gone."

C. The Commissioned

"And he gave some, apostles; and some, prophets; and some, evangelists; and some, pastors and teachers."—vs. 11.

The first two mentioned are apostles and prophets. We were told of them in Ephesians 2:20, "And are built upon the foundation of the apostles and prophets, Jesus Christ himself being the chief cornerstone." The apostolic and prophetic gifts were for the foundation of the building. Since the foundation has long been completed, there is no need for these offices at this end of the present dispensation. Only the cultists, seeking to enhance their error with the prestige of high-sounding titles, claim to have apostles and prophets today.

Next in order comes "evangelists." These are evangels, bearers of glad tidings, and their ministry is in particular to the unsaved, although not limited to them in any sense of the word, as we shall shortly see.

Then Paul speaks of "pastors," or shepherds. These are men whom He had endued with power to guide His own, ones who have a heart for the sheep of Christ. This is the ministry with which Christ challenged Peter in John 21, "Feed my lambs" (vs. 15), and "Feed my sheep" (vss. 16,17).

Next come "teachers," ones with whom He has endowed special ability to instruct His own in Bible truth. They are those gifted in unfolding the precious Word of God in a clear, plain, orderly manner so hearers may both *understand* and *apply* the will of God in their lives.

D. The Commission in Action

This action is threefold:

1. Fixing Up the Saints

Verse 12 says, *"For the perfecting of the saints, for the work of the ministry, for the edifying of the body of Christ."* The punctuation of the King James Version makes it seem that Christ has commissioned apostles, prophets, evangelists, pastors and teachers for a threefold work: to perfect saints, to do the work of the ministry, and to edify the body of Christ. However, the true sense of the passage is best revealed by removing the punctuation, making it read: "For the perfecting of the saints for the work of the ministry for the edifying of the body of Christ." It is not a threefold work, but a single ministry.

Those commissioned by the ascended Christ are to perfect (*lit.*, "mend," "repair") saints—not to get them to Heaven, *but to get them to work!* It is a work that is to continue until the body of Christ is completed and gathered Home. Verse 13 expresses it,

"Till we all come in the unity of the faith, and of the knowledge of the Son of God, unto a perfect man, unto the measure of the stature of the fulness of Christ."

When that has taken place, there will be no need of any ministry by evangelists, pastors, teachers, or anyone else. Incidentally, the expression "unto a perfect man" refers to a "full-grown man," and speaks of maturity and completeness.

2. The Stabilizing of Wavering Children

Verse 14 describes the work of the commissioned: *"That we henceforth be no more children, tossed to and fro, and carried about with every wind of doctrine, by the sleight of men, and cunning craftiness, whereby they lie in wait to deceive."*

Did you know that authorities broke up a school in Las Vegas, Nevada, which was actually in business simply to teach others to cheat in gambling casinos? Police said the school was operating in a swank Las Vegas home where gambling tables had been set up in casino style for practice. Dozens of decks of marked cards and 3,000 pairs of loaded dice were confiscated in the raid.

And did you know that the word "sleight" (Gr., *kubeia*) here in Ephesians—the only time it is used in the entire New Testament—is defined in *Young's Analytical Concordance* as "playing at dice, cheat, artifice"?

Paul is talking about religious cheaters who confuse weak Christians by trickery in handling the Scripture. Just as some gamblers cheat with loaded dice, so some religious leaders cheat and deceive in their handling of the Word of God. Yes, Satan has his religious cheating schools, too!

God has commissioned evangelists, pastors and teachers in our day to help those who have been deceived by modern sects and isms. Have you ever noticed that cults will not work nearly as hard to gain converts among the ungodly as they will in trying to proselyte newly converted Christians? They will compass land and sea the moment they hear of someone getting saved, seeking to trick him, through deceitful handling of the Word of God, into leaving the sound church and uniting with their cult.

God wants His children to grow up! You are aware, of course, of the shortness in a child's attention span. He will play with one toy for one moment, then drop it and go after something else. Especially is this true when another child is present. He will quickly lose interest in what he has and become absolutely fascinated by whatever is in the hands of the other child.

So it is with the spiritually immature. They are "tossed to and fro," carried about with every new religious idea anyone announces, no matter how farfetched or ridiculous.

Babies are cute, sweet and precious but no parent wants his child to remain a baby. He wants him to develop, to grow, to gain knowledge, to become strong. How pathetic are children people refer to, for want of a better description, as retarded. Yet how many spiritually retarded saints we have in our churches across the land and around the world. They just never develop, they never grow up, they never gain any real spiritual depth or perception.

There used to be a girl in Philadelphia who was described as "the oldest baby in the world." She was born into the home of Mr. and Mrs. Patrick Henry on May 15, 1876. Everything was fine until she reached the age of seven or eight months, then all development was suddenly arrested. She never walked, she never developed teeth, she never learned to talk. Even though she lived to a ripe old age, she never got past the "baby food" stage, nor did she ever pass the frailties and helplessness of an infant. It was a pathetic thing.

Yet such is no more tragic than a Christian who never grows up, who never matures. No wonder the Bible pleads, "Hold fast the form of sound words, which thou hast heard of me, in faith and love which is in Christ Jesus" (II Tim. 1:13). And how fitting the appeal of Peter, "But sanctify the Lord God in your hearts: and be ready always to give an answer to every man that asketh you a reason of the hope that is in you with meekness and fear" (I Pet. 3:15).

In other words, evangelists, pastors and teachers are to carefully and thoroughly instruct Christians in the Word of God. Truth is not merely to be tenaciously *held,* it is to be thoroughly *taught.*

3. Joining, Binding the Body in Unity

Not only are the commissioned to mend the saints and stabilize the wavering, but the final verses of our text explain:

"Speaking the truth in love, may grow up into him in all things, which is the head, even Christ: From whom the whole body fitly joined together and compacted by that which every joint supplieth, according to the effectual working in the measure of every part, making increase of the body unto the edifying of itself in love."

Note the individual responsibility here: "*every joint* supplieth." Every joint, every part, every separate organ of the body is to work for the upbuilding of the whole. Paul speaks of the body being fitly joined together and compacted; that is, bound in a perfect unity.

4. An Important Qualification

Paul highlights a vital essential which is to govern the commission in action. If the results outlined in this passage are to become reality, not only must truth be manifested, it must be manifested *in love!* Note the opening words of verse 15 again: "But speaking the truth in love. . . ."

Probably the most justified criticism hurled at Fundamentalists relates to the lack of charity sometimes demonstrated in our defense of the faith. According to what Paul told the Ephesians, it is possible to defend the truth in love. Just as one cannot have real love apart from real truth, so you cannot have real truth apart from real love. While modernists are wrong in trying to promote love with truth, so Fundamentalists are wrong when and if they promote truth without love.

Paul elsewhere wrote:

"If I speak in the tongues of men and of angels, but have not love, I am only a resounding gong or a clanging cymbal. If I have the gift of prophecy, and can fathom all mysteries and all knowledge, and if I have a faith that can move mountains, but have not love, I am nothing. If I give all I possess to the poor and surrender my body to the flames, but have not love, I gain nothing"—I Cor. 13:1-3, TNIV.

Conclusion

The only summary possible is to join Paul in beseeching, in pleading, in begging you to *walk worthy.* You owe it to yourself, to your fellow believers, to the church, to the lost in your community, but most of all to Him who paid such a tremendous price to purchase your soul at Calvary.

As someone expressed it,

> Lord, may I walk all worthy of the One whom I adore;
> Yea, worthy of my calling, to the things which lie before;
> In lowliness and meekness, I would manifest Thy love;

Forgiving and forbearing, till I reach Thy throne above;
And may I ever faithful keep the unity divine,
The bond of peace the Spirit gives, the oneness that is Thine.

Walking Worthy of Our Creation and Cleansing

This I say therefore, and testify in the Lord, that ye henceforth walk not as other Gentiles walk, in the vanity of their mind,

Having the understanding darkened, being alienated from the life of God through the ignorance that is in them, because of the blindness of their heart:

Who being past feeling have given themselves over unto lasciviousness, to work all uncleanness with greediness.

But ye have not so learned Christ;

If so be that ye have heard him, and have been taught by him, as the truth is in Jesus:

That ye put off concerning the former conversation the old man, which is corrupt according to the deceitful lusts;

And be renewed in the spirit of your mind;

And that ye put on the new man, which after God is created in righteousness and true holiness.

Wherefore putting away lying, speak every man truth with his neighbour: for we are members one of another.

Be ye angry and sin not: let not the sun go down upon your wrath:

Neither give place to the devil.

Let him that stole steal no more; but rather let him labour, working with his hands the thing which is good, that he may have to give to him that needeth.

Let no corrupt communication proceed out of your mouth, but that which is good to the use of edifying, that it may minister grace unto the hearers.

And grieve not the holy Spirit of God, whereby ye are sealed unto the day of redemption.

Let all bitterness, and wrath, and anger, and clamour, and evil speaking, be put away from you, with all malice:

And be ye kind one to another, tenderhearted, forgiving one another, even as God for Christ's sake hath forgiven you.— Ephesians 4:17-32.

A few years ago one of Boston's leading chest surgeons, Dr. Richard Overholt, told delegates at a cancer seminar in Phoenix, Arizona, "Doctors who smoke should be ashamed of themselves." Calling smoking "more of a health menace than radioactive fallout," the surgery professor from Tufts College charged his medical brethren, "We have an obligation to humanity to give up smoking" because the tobacco habit could shorten the user's life "by as much as nine years" and can "accelerate lung cancer."

Appealing to the physicians to follow his own example in abandoning the filthy habit, he offered the following twofold benefits: (1) The influence it would set for the non-medical man; (2) The better health the doctors themselves would enjoy!

In our text, the Apostle Paul continues his appeal for the Ephesian saints to follow his example in a worthy walk. His theme might be summed up in the same pair of benefits Dr. Overholt offered: the influence on others and the personal blessing in the life of the individual who so walks.

He opens this section with the words, "This I say therefore," basing his remarks upon all that has gone before. A worthy walk should be the logical outgrowth of our spiritual blessings in the heavenlies; the work of the Trinity of our redemption; the hope of our calling; the riches of the glory of His inheritance in the saints; the exceeding greatness of His power to usward who believe; our salvation past, present and future; the true church, God's hidden mystery; the love of God which passeth knowledge; and the "exceeding, abundantly, above all" power that worketh in us. Especially is this to be true in the light of our calling and our commission in Christ.

Note carefully also his expression, "and testify in the Lord." This is simply another declaration, another claim of divine inspiration. Paul speaks as one who is in fellowship with the Lord, one who knows the mind of God. His is no mere casual witness on some incidental subject; this is a solemn calling upon God as a witness regarding matters of utmost importance. It is not a passage to consider lightly, but to meditate upon solemnly, seriously and soberly.

I. WALKING WORTHY OF OUR CREATION!
Vss. 17-31

This section of the appeal is based upon the fact that we became new creatures in Christ upon conversion. As II Corinthians 5:17 says, "Therefore if any man be in Christ, he is a new creature: old things are passed away; behold, all things are become new." Yet, as Paul makes plain in this Ephesian passage, the Christian with a *new* nature is still very much plagued with the *old* nature, a problem he will have throughout the duration of his earthly sojourn. Paul's concern is that the new nature, not the old one, have the upper hand and be dominant in the believer's life.

The Bible Expositor and Illuminator told of a Christian named John who was rather eccentric. He had a small farm where he raised turkeys and one day a passing motorist hit one of his birds, killing it, but then graciously stopped to apologize. Instead of accepting the apology, however, John was so enraged he threw a stone through the car's windshield and gave the driver a bitter, vitriolic tongue-lashing. The offended motorist reported the incident to the police, signed a complaint, and had him arrested.

When the trial came up, John said to the judge, "Your Honor, it was not the new John who threw that stone. It was the old John!" Then he explained about the two natures a Christian has, blaming his rash act on the "old man."

The judge thoughtfully replied, "I see! You are a kind of dual personality and the old man threw the stone."

Thinking he had won his point, the farmer explained, "That's it, your Honor!"

"I am sorry," the judge responded, "but I'm afraid both of you will have to go to jail."

Since Paul did not want anything like this for the Ephesians, he instructed them as to what to put *off*, what to put *on*, and what to put *away*.

A. What to Put Off: Walk of the Unsaved

He said:

"This I say therefore, and testify in the Lord, that ye henceforth walk not as other Gentiles walk, in the vanity of their mind. Having the understanding darkened, being alienated from the life of God through the ignorance that is in them, because of the blindness of their heart: Who being past feeling have given themselves over unto lasciviousness, to work all uncleanness with greediness."—Vss. 17-19.

Note these items in Paul's description of the walk of the unconverted:

(1) It is a walk of a deceived, delusioned mind. He calls it "the vanity of their mind."

(2) It is a walk with a darkened understanding. How reminiscent this is of I Corinthians 2:14, where we read, "But the natural man receiveth not the things of the Spirit of God: for they are foolishness unto him: neither can he know them, because they are spiritually discerned."

(3) It is a walk alienated from the life of God. The Bible knows nothing of unregenerate man having any spark of divinity in him, as suggested in the theology of the liberals.

(4) It is a walk filled with ignorance and blindness of heart. Second Corinthians 4:3,4 expresses it: "But if our gospel be hid, it is hid to them that are lost: In whom the god of this world hath blinded the minds of them which believe not, lest the light of the glorious gospel of Christ, who is the image of God, should shine unto them."

(5) It is a walk of those who are "past feeling"; that is, they no

longer have any pangs of conscience concerning their evil doing. They are beyond pain. However, just as numbness in the body is a danger sign, so numbness of the soul is a warning from God of imminent danger and eternal destruction.

(6) It is a walk wherein the travelers have given themselves over to lasciviousness, being sold out completely to sin and Satan.

(7) It is a walk of greediness, working all uncleanness.

Having emphasized the fruits of unregeneracy, the apostle hastens to exclaim: "But ye have not so learned Christ" (vs. 20). Quite the contrary, "The fruit of the Spirit is love, joy, peace, longsuffering, gentleness, goodness, faith, Meekness, temperance: against such there is no law" (Gal. 5:22,23).

How have you learned Christ? Paul reasoned that the Ephesians would agree with him, "If so be that ye have heard him, and have been taught by him, as the truth is in Jesus" (vs. 21). In other words, if we are truly, personally acquainted with the Lord Jesus Christ, we ought to be like Him in our lives. Peter expressed it, "For even hereunto were ye called: because Christ also suffered for us, leaving us an example, that ye should follow his steps" (I Pet. 2:21).

We are to put off the former manner of living of the old man, the kind of individuals we were before we got saved. *Why?* Because it is corrupt according to deceitful desires, it yearns after the fool's gold of sin's glitter. Paul explains it, "That ye put off concerning the former conversation the old man, which is corrupt according to the deceitful lusts" (vs. 22).

There is a humorous story along this line in Volume II of Spurgeon's autobiography. It seems he had gone to preach for his friend, John Offord, arriving late for his appointment, something quite unusual for him. He offered two excuses, one being that the road had been blocked at one point, the other that he had stopped to vote on the way.

His friend exclaimed in surprise, "To vote! I thought you were a citizen of the New Jerusalem."

Spurgeon's response was simply, "So I am, but my 'old man' is a citizen of this world."

"Ah," suggested Offord, "you should mortify your 'old man.' "

Spurgeon beamed broadly and replied, "That is exactly what I did! My 'old man' is a Tory, and I made him vote for the Liberals!"

B. What to Put On: The New Man

Paul wrote: *"And be renewed in the spirit of your mind; And that ye put on the new man, which after God is created in righteousness and true holiness"* (vss. 23,24).

The new man is a new creation, as we saw in II Corinthians 5:17: "Therefore if any man be in Christ, he is a new creature: old things are passed away; behold, all things are become new." This new man is to be "put on" in a very realistic way in the believer's life; it is much more than some theological dictum regarding a saint's standing before God.

Just as the eastern luggage manufacturer advertised, "A man is judged by his baggage," so it is with the child of God. Society is much more interested in how you *live* than in what you *claim*. The world is wanting and waiting for proof.

When we were a thousand miles up the mighty Amazon River in Manaos, Brazil, a few years ago, some of our missionary friends took us into the jungle to visit a leper colony. We conducted services in the little chapel and, my, how pitiful the *outside* of some of those dear Christians appeared. Some had stubs for hands and feet, others had nose or ears eaten away by that dread, deadly disease.

Yet the *inside* was so completely different and the beauty of the interior shone through upon their disfigured outward features while they lustily, happily sang the songs of Zion and drank in the Word of God. They had an inward peace and beauty that a woman as attractive as an Elizabeth Taylor or a man as handsome as a Rock Hudson could know nothing about apart from Christ. Beauty, wealth, position, power, fame and all else are helpless to give what comes to the child of God through a new birth experience.

This new creation is one created "after God," Paul tells us. In other words, it is according to His standards and therefore perfect. First John 3:9 explains, "Whosoever is born of God doth not commit sin; for his seed remaineth in him; and he cannot sin, because he is born of God."

Paul tells us that this new man, because it is created according to God's standards, is "in righteousness." This relates to the *external* and refers to right dealings with man. But it is also in "true holiness," speaking of the *internal*. This pictures a heart fully separated unto God.

We think it is significant that Paul specified "true" holiness. If there is a true holiness, there must be a false holiness. In other words, not everyone talking about holiness, or professing holiness, has the kind of holiness of which the Bible speaks.

Paul was talking about putting on this new man when he said to the saints at Rome:

"And that, knowing the time, that now it is high time to awake out of sleep: for now is our salvation nearer than when we believed. The night is far spent, the day is at hand: let us therefore cast off the works of darkness, and let us put on the armour of light. Let us walk honestly, as in the day; not in rioting and drunkenness, not in chambering and wantonness, not in strife and envying. But put ye on the Lord Jesus Christ, and make not provision for the flesh, to fulfill the lusts thereof."—Rom. 13:11-14.

C. What to Put Away: Sins of the Flesh! Vss. 25-29,31

1. Falsehood!

Verse 25 says, *"Wherefore putting away lying, speak every man truth with his neighbour: for we are members one of another."* In Colossians 3:9,10, he expressed it: "Lie not one to another, seeing that ye have put off the old man with his deeds; And have put on the new man, which is renewed in knowledge after the image of him that created him."

What a terrible sin is lying! Oliver Wendell Holmes said, "Sin has many tools, but a lie is the handle which fits them all."

What is a lie? It is anything less than the truth! Our generation could well be described as a lying generation. Parents lie to their children about Santa Claus, reindeer flying through the sky, Easter bunnies laying eggs, storks bringing babies, and a thousand-and-one other matters. Manufacturers lie to the public about the performance of their products to such an extent intelligent people find radio and television commercials more hilariously entertaining than the programs themselves. Businessmen lie to prospective customers about the value, nature and performance of their merchandise.

Altogether too many, even evangelical church members, feel like the little lad who was asked by his Sunday school teacher for a definition of a lie. He answered, "A lie is an abomination in the sight of God, but a very present help in time of trouble."

The youth was certainly right in the first half of his definition! God hates lying with a vengeance, listing it as one of the "Ten Commandments" and demanding, "Thou shalt not bear false witness against thy neighbour" (Exod. 20:16; Deut. 5:20). The Bible speaks of "lying vanities" (Ps. 31:6), "lying tongues" (Ps. 109:2), "lying lips" (Prov. 12:22), "lying children" (Isa. 30:9), "lying words" (Jer. 7:4,8), "lying wonders" (II Thess. 2:9), and "lies in hypocrisy" (I Tim. 4:2). It speaks of a "false oath" (Zech. 8:17), "false swearers" (Mal. 3:5), "false prophets" (Matt. 7:15), "False Christs" (Matt. 24:24), "false witnesses" (I Cor. 15:15), "false apostles" (II Cor. 11:13), "false brethren" (Gal. 2:4), "false accusers" (II Tim. 2:3), and "false teachers" (II Pet. 2:1).

It should go without saying that the world has a right to expect to be able to trust a follower of Jesus of Nazareth to the limit, believing anything and everything emanating from his mouth. All of us ought to be like the small boy being suddenly pulled up short, charging, "Your father has been telling you how to testify, hasn't he?"

Without hesitation the lad replied in the affirmative.

"Ah," glowed the gleeful barrister, "please tell us exactly what instructions your father gave you."

"Well," was the modest, quiet response, "he told me the lawyers would try to get me mixed up in my testimony, but if I would just be careful to tell the truth, I could repeat the same thing every time!"

Abraham Lincoln, you will recall, listed as one of the benefits of always telling the truth the fact that it would not be necessary to remember what had been said.

Paul uses a special reason for teaching that a lie is never justifiable, however. He says, "For we are members one of another." In other words, we are in *the same family*; even more, we are members of *the same body*. Whoever heard of a hand attempting to deceive a mouth, an eye trying to beguile a foot, or an ear seeking to victimize a mind? It would be the height of illogic!

We are to put away lying.

2. *Sinful Wrath*

This is expressed in verse 26, *"Be ye angry, and sin not: let not the sun go down upon your wrath."*

How natural and easy it is for one to become angry, especially when wrong has been done to the individual.

On one occasion when J. Hudson Taylor was traveling in China, he arrived at a river and immediately hired a boat to take him across. Before he could depart, however, a wealthy Chinese businessman approached the dock and attempted to hire the same boat. The boatman declined, explaining that a foreigner had already engaged the craft. It was then that the Chinese noted Mr. Taylor and, without saying a word, doubled his fist and hit the missionary a stunning blow between the eyes.

Mr. Taylor staggered back a step or two, recovered himself, then noted his assailant was on the edge of the dock, between himself and the river. He was a man with a naturally quick temper and he raised his hands to push his adversary into the water.

Suddenly he stopped, dropped his hands to his side, and said, "Notice how easily I could have pushed you into the river. However, the Jesus whom I serve would not let me do it. You were wrong in hitting me, since the boat was rightfully mine, but

I forgive you. Since the boat is mine, allow me to share it with you. Come with me across the river."

Such a response in a circumstance like this is possible only through the new man. Yet *ignoring* an insult is always much better than *retaliation* for anyone. Someone has said, "The only graceful way to accept an insult is to ignore it; if you cannot ignore it, top it; if you cannot top it, laugh at it; if you cannot laugh at it, it's probably deserved."

President Abraham Lincoln's Secretary of War, Edwin Stanton, was given to repeated ridicule of his leader. On one occasion he called Lincoln a fool. When the latter learned of the taunt, he merely laughed and noted that if Stanton said it, it must be true, since Stanton was a very wise man.

An unknown poet wrote,

> When I have lost my temper, I have lost my reason, too.
> I am never proud of anything which angrily I do.
> When I have talked in anger and my cheeks were flaming red,
> I have always uttered something which I wish I hadn't said.
> In anger I have never done a kindly deed or wise,
> But many things for which I felt I should apologize.
> In looking back across my life, and all I've lost or made,
> I can't recall a single time when fury ever paid.
> So I struggle to be patient, for I've reached a wiser age;
> I do not want to do a thing or speak a word in rage.
> I have learned by sad experience that when my temper flies
> I never do a worthy thing, a decent deed or wise.

Driving down the highway one day in Michigan I picked up an unknown radio preacher on my dial. Although I never learned who he was, what church he pastored, or anything about him, one statement he made that day has remained. He pointed out that "anger" is only one letter short of "danger." How true this is in life's realities! Perhaps that is why a rattlesnake, when cornered, can become so excited, so in a frenzy it may accidently bite itself with its deadly fangs. Many a human rattlesnake has done the same!

It might help us refrain from flying off the handle if we remembered the wise words of Sir John Lubbock:

> Always be patient. We know if children are fractious it is, in nine cases out of ten, because they are suffering, and men and women are but grown-

up children in this respect as in others. In most cases, if we knew all the circumstances, if we knew what they were feeling, we should be sorry for, and not angry with, people who are cross.

If a baby cries, it is normally because something is disturbing him. Either he is wet, or hungry, or a pin is sticking him, or something else is wrong. And when people say or do things which ignite our emotions, usually it is because of inner problems they are facing. *Try to remember that!*

Note, however, there is a wrath that is right. Paul definitely commands his readers, "Be ye angry. . . ." Sometimes it is wrong *not* to be angry. For example, in Mark 10:14, at the time our Lord's disciples were trying to keep the little children from Him, we read: "But when Jesus saw it, he was much displeased, and said unto them, Suffer the little children to come unto me, and forbid them not: for of such is the kingdom of God."

On another occasion, when the religious leaders were waiting to see whether Jesus would heal the man with the withered hand on the Sabbath, Mark 3:5 says, "And when he had looked round about on them with anger, being grieved for the hardness of their hearts. . . ." Here was holy anger, but even it was mingled with grief for the wicked men with their evil hearts.

For our Lord not to have been angry on such occasions would have been wrong. So, today, for us not to be angry *at* sin *is* sin. This principle has been summed up by another, "I am determined so to be angry as not to sin, therefore to be angry at nothing but sin." This is it exactly!

Notice, also, the admonition, "Let not the sun go down upon your wrath." When you do sin in anger, the wrong should be made right at once. The earthly sun should not sink behind the western horizon until apologies have been made and, hopefully, accepted.

3. Giving Place to Satan

This prohibition is summed up in a terse six-word statement: "Neither give place to the devil." This nemesis of the saint, this adversary who goes about as a roaring lion seeking whom he may devour, must not be listened to or tolerated in even the slightest respect. He is like the proverbial camel who gets his nose in the tent; if he does, it is not long until he is completely inside and has totally taken over. Or, like the salesman who tries to get his foot in the door, knowing that if he can it will not be long until he is in the house displaying his wares. So Satan looks for advantages in the life of the believer, openings in his armor where a crippling blow can be struck.

Perhaps it would be wise to point out that Satan tries to trip up Christians in *little* things. He does not come to a saint and suggest something like murdering a mate, robbing a bank, or overthrowing the government. He seeks to succeed in so-called minor matters, realizing that sins are like snowballs rolling downhill, the more the momentum, the bigger the ball.

We subscribe, in our office, to the "Official Airline Guide." It enables us to plan our own flight itineraries, not being dependent upon a travel agency or an airline. The OAG formerly sent a magazine, *Air Travel,* to subscribers once a month and, glancing through it one day, I noted an item reminiscent of the old ditty, how, for want of a nail, a kingdom was lost.

The writer told of being present when one of the airlines conducted a briefing for all supervisory personnel. One problem discussed was a flight cancellation which had been necessitated by an unavailable spare part. The writer went on:

> And why wasn't the part there? It seems that standard procedure calls for an original and two carbons of such shop orders, and when the time came to make out this particular order, there was only one sheet of carbon paper on hand. A box was on order, but it hadn't arrived. So only one copy was made instead of two, and the chap whose primary responsibility was to get the part never saw the order. Thus, for a lack of a sheet of carbon, a part was not available, a flight was cancelled, and the airline suffered a loss of hundreds of dollars, to say nothing of a loss of good will.
>
> As so often happens in many phases of airline operations, a human being failed. The guilty party never explained just why he couldn't have gone next door or down the street and either bought or borrowed a sheet of carbon paper.

In truth and in fact, a major airline flight was cancelled because of a lack of one single sheet of carbon paper. In like manner, Satan uses little things to cancel many of God's plans and programs in the life of the believer. This is why Paul pleaded with the Christians at Ephesus not to give place to the Devil for a single moment, and it is why the intreaty is equally applicable for us today.

4. Stealing

Part of the old nature is wrapped up in larceny and evidence of it is manifested at an early age, perhaps in toddlers stealing cookies out of cookie jars, appropriating things not one's own. In the case of some, it is a childish vice not thwarted with the arrival of adulthood and thievery becomes a way of life. So our text says: *"Let him that stole steal no more: but rather let him labour, working with his hands the thing which is good, that he may have to give to him that needeth"* (vs. 28).

We like the story of the Negro lad on the block at a Southern slave market years ago. Since he seemed smart, healthy and active, a tenderhearted master, thinking how sad it would be for such a youth to have a cruel owner, stepped up to him and inquired, "If I buy you, will you be honest?"

The Negro boy, with a look that cannot be described on paper, raised himself erect, looked the gentleman in the eye, and passionately declared, "I will be honest whether you buy me or not!"

Ah, that is what we need. Most people are willing to be honest if it is to their advantage; Christians must be honest whether it is expedient or inexpedient.

Yet how this country is plagued with stealing. In fact, many good church members steal from the government when making out income tax returns, fraudulently misrepresenting the facts to gain additional deductions. Others steal petty things under the guise, "Let's take home a souvenir."

The manager of a single hotel in New York City, the Hotel Astor, reported his establishment lost, in just one year's time, 4,112 bath towels, 7,570 face towels, 12,613 napkins and 19,292 silver teaspoons. All of this was done, he lamented, "only in a spirit of remembrance."

Some may call it *souvenirs;* God calls it *stealing.*

It is in areas such as this where true Christianity is determined. Psalm 37:21 says, "The wicked borroweth, and payeth not again; but the righteous showeth mercy, and giveth."

In fact, Paul points out that the ex-stealer is especially obligated to give to the destitute, appealing for him to get an honest job, "working with his hands the thing which is good, that he may have to give to him that needeth." Galatians 6:10 describes it, "As we have therefore opportunity, let us do good unto all men, especially unto them who are of the household of faith."

5. Corrupt Communication

"Let no corrupt communication proceed out of your mouth, but that which is good to the use of edifying, that it may minister grace unto the hearers" (vs. 29). The idea of *corrupt* is decayed, rotten. Such speech should be eliminated entirely from a Christian's vocabulary.

Yet what a problem this is for all! James 3:5,6 warns us:

"Even so the tongue is a little member, and boasteth great things. Behold, how great a matter a little fire kindleth! And the tongue is a fire, a world of iniquity; so is the tongue among our members, that it defileth the whole body, and setteth on fire the course of nature: and it is set on fire of hell."

Previously James said: "For in many things we offend all. If any man offend not in word, the same is a perfect man, and able also to bridle the whole body" (James 3:2).

Here is how Christians are defiled. Jesus told His disciples, "Not that which goeth into the mouth defileth a man; but that which cometh out of the mouth, this defileth a man" (Matt. 15:11). The Ancient Greek philosopher, Diogenes, upon being asked what animal had the most deadly bite, responded, "Of wild beasts, the backbiter; of tame, the flatterer."

Paul makes his appeal for proper speech both in the *negative* and in the *positive*. He refers to the negative first, saying that no corrupt communication is to proceed out of a believer's mouth. He is to completely cleanse it of all foulness and impurity.

Some time ago the Australian House of Representatives voted

a revision of its House behavior code. Members decided to forbid further reference to each other by such names as: *asinine, blood-drinker, cad, cur, gasbag, ignoramus, lap dog, mendacious mongrel, miserable body-snatcher, rat, sewer rat, and slimy reptile!* No doubt they felt such a crippling of the members' vocabulary would give them a much more peaceful atmosphere in which to work.

It might not be a bad idea if some churches incorporated the same resolution into their constitutions and by-laws. James 3:11 asks, "Doth a fountain send forth at the same place sweet water and bitter?" Then neither should a Christian's mouth and tongue!

After all, we have been born again; we are expected to be different. This is why our Lord warned His disciples in Matthew 12:35,36: "A good man out of the good treasure of the heart bringeth forth good things: and an evil man out of the evil treasure bringeth forth evil things. But I say unto you, That every idle word that men shall speak, they shall give account thereof in the day of judgment."

No wonder Augustine is reported to have had engraved upon his dining table the words, "There is no place at this table for anyone who loves scandal." It might be well if the same message were inscribed on the Lord's Table.

Charles Haddon Spurgeon, commenting on Psalm 15:3, quotes John Trapp as saying that "the tale-bearer carrieth the devil in his tongue, and the tale-hearer carries the devil in his ear." Then Spurgeon observed:

> "Show that man out!" we should say of a drunkard, yet it is very questionable if his unmannerly behaviour will do us so much mischief as the tale-bearer's insinuating story. "Call for a policeman!" we say if we see a thief at his business; ought we to feel no indignation when we hear a gossip at her work? Mad dog! Mad dog! is a terrible hue and cry, but there are few curs whose bite is so dangerous as a busybody's tongue. Fire! Fire!! is an alarming note, but the tale-bearer's tongue is set on fire of hell, and those who indulge it had better mend their manners, or they may find that there is fire in hell for unbridled tongues.

The biography of the late T. T. Shields tells how that noble gentleman handled the matter of tale-bearing. In Shield's own words:

> A woman came into my office—she is not with us now. She came in and carefully closed the door and wanted to tell me something about another member of our church. I opened the desk drawer and took out a sheet of paper and handed her a pen and said, "Now, you write that down. It is a very serious matter. Write it down and sign it."
>
> "Oh!" she said, "I don't want you to mention my name. I do not want to be in it at all."
>
> I said, "Write it down and sign it."
>
> "No, no, I couldn't do that."
>
> I said, "Do you see that door? Go out, and don't dare to come here again and find fault with anyone unless you are willing to write down what you say."

Most of us could very profitably say with Job, "Teach me, and I will hold my tongue. . ." (Job 6:24). Or, as Psalm 34:13 expresses it, "Keep thy tongue from evil, and thy lips from speaking guile." Remember,

> A careless word may kindle strife,
> A cruel word may wreck a life;
> A bitter word may hate instill,
> A brutal word may smite and kill;
> A gracious word may smooth the way,
> A joyous word may light the day;
> A timely word may lessen stress,
> A loving word may heal and bless.

Most of us need to learn the lesson the tourist received when he entered a Vermont country store and tried to engage in conversation the local men idling by the big wood stove. After several fruitless efforts he exclaimed, "Well, is it against the law to talk in this town?"

One of the natives replied, "Ain't no law against it, but around here a man don't speak unless he's sure he can improve on the silence."

Abraham Lincoln is quoted, "Better to remain silent and be thought a fool, than to speak and remove all doubt." Alexander Pope expressed it, "Wisdom is divided into two parts: (a) having a great deal to say, and (b) not saying it." Or, as Solomon was inspired to write, "Whoso keepeth his mouth and his tongue keepeth his soul from troubles" (Prov. 21:23).

However, Paul was not merely interested in the negative—*no corrupt communication emanating from the mouth*—he was vitally concerned about the positive as well: *"but that which is good to the use of edifying, that it may minister grace unto the hearers."* The believer's mouth should be filled to overflowing with truth, goodness and grace. As Colossians 4:6 says, "Let your speech be alway with grace, seasoned with salt, that ye may know how ye ought to answer every man."

Honest praise—and we emphasize *honest*—is one form of ministering grace through the mouth. A preacher friend in Florida tells of having an old deacon in his first church who, although lacking an abundance of formal education, enthusiastically loved the Lord and lived it in his daily life. Every time he would leave the little country church, he would say to his pastor, "By jiminy, Bob, you've done it again!" That may not have been the most refined way to express appreciation for a sermon, but it was a word of encouragement that reached the pastor's heart like cold water to a thirsty soul.

A poem, *Just a Word,* translated from old Norwegian by Rachel E. Michell, goes like this:

> A word, a little worthless word,
> Can kill the joyous laughter,
> Destroy a live hope, sparkling bright,
> Make dark the road hereafter.
> A little word, live coal from Hell,
> Burns, blightens love and courage,
> Tears down a heart's sincere desire
> And wrecks life's upward voyage.
>
> A word, just kind and meaning well
> Can cheer the lone and weary;
> Cause grief and sorrow deep to flee
> And gladden face so cheery.
> The little word like angel bloom
> Can heal the hurt and bleeding,
> New courage give, and scatter gloom;
> Lift up the faint and needing.
>
> A word, a little word of grace,
> Can raise to life the dying
> And cause a soul, so dark, so dead
> To be with angels vying.
> God's Spirit, speak within my heart

> So hate and vengeance flee,
> And love and joy and peace impart,
> That Christ the world may see.

6. *Malice and Its Evil Friends*

In verse 31, Paul mentions several fruits which hang on a single tree. He pleads, *"Let all bitterness, and wrath, and anger, and clamour, and evil speaking, be put away from you, with all malice."*

We are to put away "bitterness." This is a sin which harms the individual more who harbors it, usually, than the one toward whom the feelings are manifested. Yet how commonplace and ordinary is this sin in our day.

Dr. Lee Roberson tells of a member of Congress who, although plagued with the double fault of inability to remember either names or faces, nonetheless was greatly loved by his constituents. He had the knack of making each person he met feel he knew him personally and was vitally interested in his every problem.

Asked how he pulled it off when he could neither remember a person's name or even recall having seen him before, the Congressman confessed: "When I meet someone I don't know from Adam, and I see he expects me to know who he is, I take him warmly by the hand, look straight into his eyes, and say, *'And how's the old complaint?'* I have never known it to fail."

Alas and alack, all of us have our "old complaints" and we hug them to our bosom as if they were of great value, instead of putting them off as the apostle begs us.

We are also to put away "wrath." Wrathfulness is the act of submission to temper's temptation. If it is seen in a child, we call it a temper tantrum, but we have more refined terminology for adults who allow their emotions to succumb to passion in the same way. At any rate, it is certainly a direct contradiction to the appeal for tenderheartedness in the next verse.

Dr. Robert G. Lee tells of seeing a picture of a rattlesnake with the words above it: "A rattlesnake can strike and coil in less than one-half second!" Tongues can equal or better the snake's record and, as Dr. Lee pointed out, a rattlesnake sometimes *looks* just like a tongue.

We are also to put away "anger." While wrath may be the sudden outrage, anger is the continuation of such a spirit, mingled with the venom of bitterness. It is a harboring of the resentment, actually adding fuel to the fire of hatred.

We are to put away "clamour." W. E. Vine says this is "an onomatopoeic word, imitating the raven's cry." It is a sudden, loud, uncontrollable racket of the tongue; what we might today call "shooting from the hip."

It reminds us of a Pennsylvania hunter who decided to go into the wilds of Wyoming in quest of antelope and deer. Admittedly overeager in his excitement to bag big game, this Yankee dude fired several shots on a ranch near Wheatland. When he got to where his "big game" had fallen, this is what he discovered had resulted from his seven shots: four dead horses, two wounded horses, plus a shot that [fortunately] missed! The hunter left Wyoming with a much lighter wallet than when he arrived, the consequence of paying a rancher for the six steeds.

It is a pretty good idea to know what you are shooting at before you fire. This is not only true in big game hunting, but in all walks of life—especially with shots that come from the dangerous and deadly mouth-gun. Christians should remember what the mamma whale is supposed to have told the baby behemoth: "It's only when you're spouting that you get harpooned."

We are to put away "evil speaking." Elsewhere Paul explained that evil speaking emanates from pride. He said in I Timothy 6:4, "He is proud, knowing nothing, but doting about questions and strifes of words, whereof cometh envy, strife, railings, evil surmisings." Pride, with its desire to make the speaker look good, tries to bring someone else down in order to elevate self. It never really works that way, since "pride goeth before destruction, and a haughty spirit before a fall" (Prov. 16:18).

Perhaps we could learn here from the Chinese. The three symbols making up their ideograph for *slander* are the ones for *words, mountain* and *mouth.* Literally, it simply means "making a mountain out of a molehill." Most evil speaking is based upon some fact, but the speaker cannot overcome the temptation to embellish. G. Campbell Morgan observed that some people would scratch through a bushel of chaff to find a single grain of wheat, while others scratch through a bushel of wheat looking for one bit of chaff.

You are probably familiar with the practice of the Roman Catholic Church to use a "Devil's advocate" in its system. It is this official's responsibility to call attention to every failure and sin of a candidate under consideration for beatification or canonization. When one such official died, the Rt. Rev. Salvatore Natucci, the Vatican reported he had argued against at least 100 sainthood candidates.

Unfortunately, while Protestants have no *official* designation of Devil's advocate, most churches have them by the score—all amateurs. These "accusers of the brethren" are ever ready to bring up every choice tidbit of gossip ever heard about practically anyone and everyone. And if there are no tidbits available, they are only too happy to manufacture some!

We need to remember the claim of Proverbs 11:9, "An hypocrite with his mouth destroyeth his neighbour." And we would do well to acknowledge that no one can be an evil speaker unless there is a ready evil listener.

In a periodical which occasionally crosses our desk we read of a Dr. McLean and his experience in relating a serious matter about another to a friend. To his embarrassment and chagrin, the friend opened his Bible to Deuteronomy 13:12,14 and solemnly read: "If thou shalt hear say in one of thy cities, which the Lord thy God hath given thee to dwell there, saying. . .Then shalt thou enquire, and make search, and ask diligently; and, behold, if it be truth, and the thing certain, that such abomination is wrought. . . ."

Dr. McLean's friend then turned and quietly asked:

"Have you, dear brother, 'inquired'? Have you 'made search'? Did you 'ask diligently'? Did you try to find out if the story were 'truth'? Did you make sure the thing was 'certain'? Dear brother, is it certain that 'such abomination is wrought'?"

The embarrassed Dr. McLean had to acknowledge ruefully that he had not fulfilled a single one of the biblical conditions.

We pointed out previously how one letter changes anger into danger. In like manner, if you drop the "o" from your voice it will become vice. Don't let your voice deteriorate into vice.

Finally, we are to put away "malice." This is the heart, the root of it all. If it were not for malice, there would be no bitterness, no wrath, no anger, no clamor, no evil speaking. Vine's *Expository Dictionary of New Testament Words* defines the Greek word translated malice, *kakia,* as "badness in quality (the opposite of *arete,* excellence) 'the vicious character generally' (Lightfoot)."

How pitiful it is that so many today, as Titus 3:3 expresses it, are "living in malice." Yet maliciousness is listed along with all unrighteousness, fornication, covetousness, murder, being haters of God, and the other vices enumerated in Romans 1:28-32 as characteristic of those whom God has given over to a reprobate mind. Certainly malice does not belong in the life or heart of a born-again believer.

Notice that we are to put away **all of it.** No allowances are to be made for any form of supposed extenuating circumstance; there is no manner of so-called situation ethics which will excuse these sins. Sometimes we think our predicament is different and that we have justification for malice, but such is never the case.

7. Anything, Everything
"Paining" the Holy Spirit

Including and adding to all he has listed, the apostle broadens out his "disposal program" by summarizing: *"And grieve not the holy Spirit of God, whereby ye are sealed unto the day of redemption"* (vs. 30).

How sensitive is He! How carefully we should seek to yield to His promptings and follow His leading!

The saintly F. B. Meyer told of an elderly lady who came to him at the close of a service and said she had heard him speak with great blessing two decades previously. She had returned home with the glow and glory of God in her soul which lasted until mid-morning the following day. At that time she sensed the prompting of the Holy Spirit to go and seek reconciliation with her sister. She did not go and the glory had dimmed. Sadly she told Dr. Meyer how, in all the succeeding years, it had never been recovered.

Of course, the preacher told her to bind the thread of obedience where it had been broken, even yet going to her sister. Ah, but the loved one had already stepped into eternity and it was too late to seek reconciliation. Here was a woman with twenty wasted years behind her that could never be redeemed.

Some have misunderstood this passage as teaching that the Holy Spirit can be grieved out of the life of a Christian. Such is not the case, as the Saviour made very clear to His disciples when He said in John 14:16, "And I will pray the Father, and he shall give you another Comforter, *that he may abide with you for ever.*"

Paul adds to this security by noting that the believer is "sealed unto the day of redemption" by the Spirit. Obviously, this could not refer to the redemption of the soul since he was writing to those whose souls had already been redeemed. No, he spoke of the redemption described in Romans 8:22,23: "For we know that the whole creation groaneth and travaileth in pain together until now. And not only they, but ourselves also, which have the first fruits of the Spirit, even we ourselves groan within ourselves, waiting for the adoption, to wit, the redemption of our body." The believer is sealed until he receives from his Redeemer a glorified, perfect body.

Earlier in the epistle Paul noted that the seal of the Holy Spirit is a mark of His ownership. He declared,

"In whom ye also trusted, after that ye heard the word of truth, the gospel of your salvation: in whom also after that ye believed, ye were sealed with that holy Spirit of promise, Which is the earnest of our inheritance until the redemption of the purchased possession, unto the praise of his glory" (1:13,14).

We might point out also that the admonition about grieving the Holy Spirit is further proof that He is a Person. It is utterly, totally impossible to grieve an influence!

Yet, how blessed it is to follow His leading, responding to His guidance, and seeing Him work *in* and *through* our lives. One evangelist tells of a layman in Charleston, West Virginia, who was heading home from his place of business. As he crossed the South Charleston bridge he observed a man standing alongside the railing. Immediately he was impressed by the Holy Spirit to stop and offer the gentleman a ride.

Now, the man was not hitchhiking and the Christian ordinarily did not pick up hitchhikers anyway. Nor was he at all a fanatic, yet the impression was so strong he braked the car, stuck his head out the window, and inquired, "Would you like a ride?" The man hesitated for a moment, stuttered a little bit, then said he guessed he would and got into the car.

As they rode along the Holy Spirit again impressed the Christian businessman, "Sing this man a song. Sing him *Softly and Tenderly Jesus Is Calling.*" It just so happened that this particular Christian could not carry a tune to save his life, but he began to quietly sing: "Softly and tenderly Jesus is calling, calling for you and for me. . . ."

The tears started rolling down the cheeks of the other occupant of the automobile, and he said, "My mother used to sing that song as she worked in the kitchen and labored about the house." Then he went on to tell how he had been on the bridge, contemplating jumping off and ending his life, when the businessman stopped and offered him a ride.

Naturally, the Christian brother then took out his New Testament and carefully explained the beautiful plan of redemption to the desperate soul, leading him into the glory and peace of eternal redemption. He took him home that night, fed him, gave him a good night's sleep and a good breakfast the following morning, then sent him on his way rejoicing in Christ.

How *beautiful* to follow the leading of the Holy Spirit; how *pitiful* when we fail to do as He impresses.

Not only are we to walk worthy of our creation in Christ, the apostle also speaks of

II. WALKING WORTHY OF OUR CLEANSING! Vs. 32

This part of a worthy walk is based upon the salvation and redemption we presently have in Christ. Paul says: *"And be ye kind one to another, tenderhearted, forgiving one another, even as God for Christ's sake hath forgiven you."*

The late Bob Ripley described a lady whom he called "the cleanest woman in all history." She was the Countess D'Angiviller, born in 1725 and living to the ripe old age of 83. Ripley said that throughout the last eleven years of her life she spent one entire day every week in the bathtub. On the other days, she bathed for six hours every morning, then spent the remainder of the day in bed.

Yet all of her scrubbing, all of her soaking, all of her soaping only cleansed the outside of the countess. We dispute Ripley's claim that she was the cleanest woman in all history, since any soul cleansed by the blood of Jesus Christ is far cleaner! John testified, "The blood of Jesus Christ his Son cleanseth us from all sin" (I John 1:7).

But how are we to walk worthy of this cleansing?

A. Manifesting Divine Grace: "Be Ye Kind"

The Roman philosopher Seneca, although not a Christian, expressed this sentiment: "I had rather never *receive* a kindness than never *bestow* one."

Paul begged his followers to manifest kindness, and the primitive meaning of the word is usefulness. The kindness of which he speaks evidences itself in action promoted and prompted by love.

When we talk of love we do not refer to the sticky sentimentalism that is known as love by today's world. Dr. Louis T. Talbot wrote wise words when he penned: "What is love? *Love is the consuming, absorbing desire for and delight in another's highest good.*"

Real love is entirely unselfish. It loses sight utterly of self-interest and sets itself to seeking the interest of the person loved." It is not difficult for such love to be kind!

Duncan McNeil wrote:

> God, make me kind!
> So many hearts are breaking,
> And many more are aching,
> To hear the tender word.
>   God, make me kind!
> For I myself am learning
> That my sad heart is yearning
> For some sweet word to heal my hurt.
>   O Lord, do make me kind!
>
> God, make me kind!
> So many hearts are needing
> The balm to stop the bleeding,
> That my kind words can bring.
>   God, make me kind!
> For I myself am learning
> The cure in someone's keeping
> He should impart to my sick heart.
>   O Lord, do make me kind!

B. Manifesting Divine Compassion: "Tenderhearted"

God wants us to have hearts that are tender. Isn't it amazing that we can shed so many tears over a dead dog, yet fail to spend a single sleepless night or one agony-driven day for a lost world? How calloused we have become to never soak down our pillows at night over our generation on its toboggan slide to Hell. Instead of being tenderhearted we are, if anything, hardhearted.

Why? No doubt the answer lies in lack of love. It is certainly impossible for one to be tenderhearted apart from love; in fact, all the problems relating to the things we have been implored to put away would no longer be problems if our hearts were tender. It would then be simple to follow the advice of the unknown poet:

> If you see a tall fellow ahead of the crowd,
> A leader of men, marching fearless and proud
> And you know of a tale whose mere telling aloud
> Would cause his proud head to in anguish be bowed,
>   It's a pretty good plan to forget it.
>
> If you know of a skeleton hidden away

> In a closet, and guarded and kept from the day
> In the dark, whose showing, sudden display,
> Would cause grief and sorrow and lifelong dismay,
> > It's a pretty good plan to forget it.
>
> If you know of a spot in the life of a friend,
> (We all have such spots concealed, world without end),
> Whose touching his heartstrings would play on and rend
> Till the shame of its showing no grieving could mend,
> > It's a pretty good plan to forget it.
>
> If you know anything that will darken the joy
> Of a man or a woman, a girl or a boy,
> That will wipe out a smile or the least way annoy
> A fellow, or cause any gladness to cloy,
> > It's a pretty good plan to forget it.
>
> If you know of a thing, just the least little sin,
> Whose telling would cork up a laugh or a grin
> On a man you don't like, for the Lord's sake keep it in!
> Don't be a knocker, right here stick a pin—
> > It's a pretty good plan to forget it.

C. Manifesting Divine Mercy: "Forgiving One Another"

We are to forgive as God has forgiven us! *How is that?* He has removed our sins as far as the east is from the west (Ps. 103:12). He has blotted them out, as a thick cloud (Isa. 44:22). He has buried them in the depths of the deepest sea (Micah 7:18,19). He has put them behind His back (Isa. 38:17). He has completely forgotten them, promising never to remember them any more (Heb. 10:17).

How unlike God are most of us. We more easily identify with the sweet, gentle Irish lady who spoke of going to confession, and a friend said, "Surely, Brigit, you have no sins to confess."

"Ah, yes. I had to confess using a strong word when I couldn't get the ice cube tray out of the refrigerator. And I also confessed that my anger was so intense I chased my mother-in-law out of the kitchen with a broom."

The friend said, "But that happened last year. Surely you've been to confession since then!"

With a shy smile, Brigit responded, "I have, indeed; but I confess it every time. I do so love to remember it!"

Therein lies a problem faced by all: *we love to remember!*

How has God forgiven us? All summed up, He has made us faultless and blameless in His eyes. Can your mind fathom what would be true if we forgave those who trespassed against us in a like manner, making them faultless and blameless in our eyes?

We would certainly not be like the two ladies who had been brought to the parsonage by the pastor, seeking reconciliation after years of feuding. He pleaded with them to forgive and forget, shaking hands in mutual pledge of peace.

After a silence that lengthened to the point of acute embarrassment, one lady said, "Well, I wish you all that you wish me."

Then the other snapped back, "Now who is saying nasty things?"

And the feud was on again!

Perhaps this entire section of Ephesians could be summarized with the "six points of Methodism," which John Wesley drew up for the early followers of the Wesleyan movement to sign. They covenanted:

(1) That we will not listen to, or willingly inquire after, any ill concerning each other.
(2) That if we do hear any ill of each other, we will not be forward to believe it.
(3) That as soon as possible we will communicate what we hear, by speaking or writing to the person concerned.
(4) That till we have done this, we will not write or speak a syllable of it to any person whatsoever.
(5) That neither will we mention it, after we have done this, to any other person whatsoever.
(6) That we will not make any exception to these rules, unless we think ourselves absolutely obliged in conscience to do so.

Conclusion

There is no better way to wrap up this section than to quote the writer who, in another letter, pleaded: "Finally, brethren, whatsoever things are true, whatsoever things are honest, whatsoever things are just, whatsoever things are pure, whatsoever things are lovely, whatsoever things are of good report: if there be any virtue, and if there be any praise, think on these things" (Phil. 4:8).

Paul surely meant these to be matters meditated not alone with the head, but with the heart as well. We are convinced that anyone who *thinks* on the things set forth in Ephesians 4, earnestly pleading with God for their fulfillment in his life, cannot help but *walk worthy*.

Walking as Imitators of God

> *Be ye therefore followers of God, as dear children;*
> *And walk in love, as Christ also hath loved us, and hath given himself for us an offering and a sacrifice to God for a sweetsmelling savour.*
> *But fornication, and all uncleanness, or covetousness, let it not be once named among you, as becometh saints;*
> *Neither filthiness, nor foolish talking, nor jesting, which are not convenient: but rather giving of thanks.*
> *For this ye know, that no whoremonger, nor unclean person, nor covetous man, who is an idolater, hath any inheritance in the kingdom of Christ and of God.*
> *Let no man deceive you with vain words: for because of these things cometh the wrath of God upon the children of disobedience.*
> *Be not ye therefore partakers with them.* —Ephesians 5:1-7.

Paul reminds believers that they are to be *followers*, something not always easy. We think of the noted cleric of a previous generation who was discovered by a friend, pacing back and forth across the floor of his living room. As he proceeded to wear down the carpet, his companion inquired, "What seems to be troubling you?"

The classic reply, which would fit all of us at one time or another, was, "I'm in a terrible hurry—**and God isn't!**"

"Be ye therefore followers of God." This is at once the Christian's greatest duty and his most blessed privilege. Following God is an "all-out" business; there is no room for pussyfooting or halfheartedness. Certainly this is the only conclusion one can garner from our Lord's interviews with the three men who said

they were willing to "follow" Him.

Luke 9:57-62 records the conversations:

"And it came to pass, that as they went in the way, a certain man said unto him, Lord, I will follow thee whithersoever thou goest. And Jesus said unto him, Foxes have holes, and birds of the air have nests; but the Son of man hath not where to lay his head. And he said unto another, Follow me. But he said, Lord, suffer me first to go and bury my father. Jesus said unto him, Let the dead bury their dead: but go thou and preach the kingdom of God. And another also said, Lord, I will follow thee; but let me first go bid them farewell, which are at home at my house. And Jesus said unto him, No man, having put his hand to the plough, and looking back, is fit for the kingdom of God."

Earlier our Lord had said to all, "If any man will come after me, let him deny himself, and take up his cross daily, and follow me. For whosoever will save his life shall lose it: but whosoever will lose his life for my sake the same shall save it" (Vss. 23,24). Discipleship is mighty serious business.

No greater honor or testimony could be given mortals than the one summed up in that wonderful statement about the undefiled 144,000 in Revelation 14:4, "These are they which follow the Lamb whithersoever he goeth." Is this true of you? Can you sing with E. W. Blandly:

> Where He leads me I will follow,
> Where He leads me I will follow,
> Where He leads me I will follow,
> I'll go with Him, with Him all the way.

There is *a price* to this kind of discipleship. Hebrews 13:12,13 point out: "Wherefore Jesus also, that he might sanctify the people with his own blood, suffered without the gate. Let us go forth therefore unto him without the camp, bearing his reproach." Probably John summed it up best, "Beloved, follow not that which is evil, but that which is good. He that doeth good is of God: but he that doeth evil hath not seen God" (III John 11). The test of whom or what one is following is best determined by what that one is doing.

However, the word Paul uses in our text, translated "followers," has a more definite meaning than what we usually associate with following, and most translators, along with the majority of Bibles containing marginal notes, render it "imitators." It includes more than mere action; it involves motivation, even character.

Just as a physician might go through all the proper procedures in treating his patients, yet have no heart sympathy with their sufferings, so children of God can perfunctorily go through their duties, carefully dotting every "i" and crossing every "t" in service with full accord to the letter, yet have no heart empathy, no genuine burden. We are to copy God as children copy fathers—even more so since the child is only playing; to the Christian it is serious business.

There are several things we should note about this imitation of God. First, it is based upon Calvary. Paul's "therefore" looks back to the previous verse, the final one in chapter 4: "And be ye kind one to another, tenderhearted, forgiving one another, **even as God for Christ's sake hath forgiven you.**" Second, this imitation can be accomplished only by the children of God. Before one can be an *imitator* of God, he must be a *partaker* of His nature. Third, the imitation is to be done because we are not only His children, but His "dear children." This is a service performed, not as slaves or even hirelings, but as His own precious children who have been so bountifully blessed and tenderly treated by Him.

The gist of what Paul is saying in this passage has been summed up by John in I John 2:6, "He that saith he abideth in him ought himself also so to walk, even as he walked."

How is that?

I. IMITATORS OF GOD'S LOVE!

Paul said, *"Be ye therefore followers of God, as dear children; and walk in love, as Christ also hath loved us, and hath given himself for us an offering and a sacrifice to God for a sweetsmelling savour"* (vs. 2).

Walk in love! Dr. Lee Roberson tells of an ugly man who

resided in the Dutch village of Ide. His name was Hans Bergen and he lived a lonely, loveless life because others would have nothing to do with him. When his days mercifully came to a close, it was learned he had left his entire estate, worth about $40,000, to a young girl by the name of Ann Martin.

No one could understand why he had bequeathed the fortune to her until his Will was read and they discovered she had smiled at him on one occasion. He wrote in the Will, "All the rest of you have frowned and looked away when I passed down the street. But Ann, when I met her one day, gave me a friendly smile, *the only one in all of my life.*"

How little love there is in our world! Perhaps this is one of the reasons God so repeatedly appeals for His followers to manifest it.

The German philosopher and poet, Goethe, wrote, *"Man lernt nichts kennen als was man liebt."* Translated, it is, "Man learns to understand only what he loves."

Isn't this true also in the spiritual realm? The more we love God, the more we understand Him. And the more we love one another, the more we understand each other.

How are we to imitate God's love?

A. Whom Are We to Love?

Our love is to be dispensed in several directions.

1. Love to God

Beyond any question, we are to advance in love to our Redeemer. First John 4:19 says, "We love him, because he first loved us." If He had not taken the first step, if He had not initiated love in our behalf, we would never have known how to love Him. Our goal now is the one Christ declared to the lawyer who demanded to know which was the law's greatest commandment: "Thou shalt love the Lord thy God with all thy heart, with all thy soul, and with all thy mind. This is the first and great commandment" (Matt. 22:37,38).

This should pose no problem for the Christian.

It is as Mordecai Ham responded when a young lady inquired of him, "How can I love God? I can't *make* myself love Him."

He noted, "I understand that you cannot make yourself love anyone, but you love your mother, do you not?"

"Oh, yes, that is natural."

"And so will it be natural for you to love God when you are born of God," he told her. "You won't have to make yourself; you cannot do that. But if you are saved, that is, born of God, it is just as natural to love Him as it is to love your natural mother."

It takes only brief meditation on Calvary's truths to inspire love and devotion to Christ. We can sympathize with the African chieftain who, along with others in his village, was being told by a missionary the message of the cross. As the servant of God related the story of the humiliation, the beatings, the crowning with thorns, the agonies of the crucifixion, the chief interrupted to cry, "Stop! He ought not to be there. I ought to be there." He spoke the sentiments of every born-again believer.

Augustine said he was amazed that God could love man so much and man could love God so little. Probably it is because we so seldom stop to think about His love for us. One of the purposes in the Lord's Supper is to compel believers to think about Calvary every so often.

2. *Love to the Brethren*

Christ intended this love to be an identifying badge of discipleship. He said in John 13:34,35, "A new commandment I give unto you, that ye love one another; as I have loved you, that ye also love one another. By this shall all men know that ye are my disciples, if ye have love one to another." He added in John 15:12, "This is my commandment, That ye love one another, as I have loved you."

Officials in Venezuela must understand the value of love. It is our understanding that the post office department there allows love letters to be mailed at one-half the usual rate, the only condition being that the missives be placed in special bright red envelopes. In other words, the sender must be willing to unashamedly identify his letter as an affirmation of love for the recipient.

God wants our declarations of love for each other to be public. First John 4:20,21 remind us, "If a man say, I love God, and hateth his brother, he is a liar: for he that loveth not his brother whom he hath seen, how can he love God whom he hath not seen? And this commandment have we from him, That he who loveth God love his brother also."

When Paul wanted his dearly beloved brother Philemon to receive Onesimus, he based his appeal on love rather than obligation. He said, "Wherefore, though I might be much bold in Christ to enjoin thee that which is convenient, yet for love's sake I rather beseech thee, being such an one as Paul the aged, now also a prisoner of Jesus Christ" (Philemon 8,9).

3. Love to Enemies!

This gets down to the nitty-gritty of the matter. It is not hard, or at least it shouldn't be, for Christians to love God and one another. However, we are as obligated to love our enemies as anyone else! Listen to our Lord's words in His famous mountain sermon:

"Ye have heard that it hath been said, Thou shalt love thy neighbour, and hate thine enemy. But I say unto you, Love your enemies, bless them that curse you, do good to them that hate you, and pray for them which despitefully use you, and persecute you; That ye may be the children of your Father which is in heaven: for he maketh his sun to rise on the evil and on the good, and sendeth rain on the just and on the unjust. For if ye love them which love you, what reward have ye? do not even the publicans the same? And if ye salute your brethren only, what do ye more than others? do not even the publicans so? Be ye therefore perfect, even as your Father which is in heaven is perfect."—Matt. 5:44-48.

Probably Christians fail here more seriously than in any other duty. No wonder the little girl prayed, "Lord, make all the bad people good, and all good people nice."

Actually, love is God's way for "eliminating" enemies. It is like the little boy who discovered, while playing in a hilly area not far from his home, an echo. He did not know who was answering his shouts, but since he felt the unknown one was mocking him by yelling back the same words, the lad eventually cried, "I'll fight you!"

The voice answered, "Fight you!"

The lad responded, "I hate you!"

The voice came back, "Hate you."

Frightened, he ran home and told his mother there was a boy out in the hills who mocked him and threatened him. His wise mother, understanding what had happened, smiled and replied, "Go out and shout 'I love you,' and see what happens."

The boy went out to the hills and cried: "I love you."

Back came the sweet reply, "Love you."

Do you remember what Elisha did when his enemies, the Syrians, fell into his hands? Instead of smiting them, as his own king wanted, he fed them, gave them drink, and then liberated them. Rather than smiting our enemies, how much better to provide for them and evidence love.

We are to walk, to go forward, to advance in this kind of love for God, for each other, and for our enemies.

How are we to do it?

B. What Does Love Do?

There are several things worthy of note.

1. Love Forgives

Isn't that what Paul said in Ephesians 4:32, ". . .forgiving one another, even as God for Christ's sake hath forgiven you"? Colossians 3:13 says, "Forbearing one another, and forgiving one another, if any man have a quarrel against any: even as Christ forgave you, so also do ye."

Do you remember our Lord's message to Peter in Matthew 18:21,22? Peter said, "Lord, how oft shall my brother sin against me, and I forgive him? till seven times?" Obviously he felt this was a tremendous concession—to forgive seven times—but Jesus replied, "I say not unto thee, until seven times: but, Until seventy times seven."

Christ gave kindred advice to His disciples in Luke 17:3,4, "Take heed to yourselves: if thy brother trespass against thee, rebuke him; and if he repent, forgive him. And if he trespass against thee seven times in a day, and seven times in a day turn again to thee, saying, I repent: thou shalt forgive him." Obviously, the love our Lord has in mind doesn't know how to hold a grudge!

2. *Love Warns!*

Should spiritual love be any less than ordinary human love? A parent who loves a child will warn the toddler against playing with a knife, getting close to a hot stove, or any other action which might bring the child harm. Love is not silly sentimentalism which never opposes anything, never offends, never rebukes, or never plainly speaks out against that which is wrong. Christ, who exhibited the world's greatest love, spent much of His time warning, rebuking, exhorting.

3. *Love Gives of Self*

Paul, in our text, reminds us that the love of Christ resulted in His having "given himself for us an offering and sacrifice to God." This is the example of love we are to copy, to imitate. The great love chapter, I Corinthians 13, tells us love "seeketh not her own" (vs. 5). Philippians 2:4 exhorts, "Look not every man on his own things, but every man also on the things of others." Galatians 6:10 comes to mind here also, "As we have therefore opportunity, let us do good unto all men, especially unto them who are of the household of faith."

Paul says this is "for a sweetsmelling savour." That is, "an odor of a sweet smell." It is one that meets God's requirements, one that is acceptable and pleasing unto Him. Philippians 4:18 illustrates this meaning, "But I have all, and abound: I am full, having received of Epaphroditus the things which were sent from you, an odour of a sweet smell, a sacrifice acceptable, wellpleasing to God."

Some time ago we read of a stocky, friendly Negro in Florence, South Carolina, who had done a wonderful job in the crusade against children's diseases. His fight began when his childhood sweetheart died of polio. In twenty-four years he raised the amazing total of $148,659.71 during various fund drives, principally the March of Dimes.

Most of his efforts were made by riding his bike from the railroad station, where he worked as a redcap, to the downtown area, a mile distant. He would select a position on a strategic street corner near a bank, or wherever people gathered, then hold out a large glass jar with the name of the fund inscribed on the outside. The year we read the account, he had collected $7,660.86 for the March of Dimes, not counting the final day's take.

One paragraph stood out sharply in our mind when we read of his heroic exploits. It said, *"He's given up many vacations, off-duty days, holidays and Saturday nights. Rain or cold has made little difference."*

Would to God those of us who have been redeemed by His precious blood might express our love in a kindred fashion! Do you love Jesus Christ enough to give up vacations, off-duty days, holidays and Saturday nights to serve Him and introduce Him to those who know Him not?

4. Love Obeys!

There will be no disagreement when we say that defiance, rebellion, disobedience, disloyalty and other such ugly manifestations are not fruits of love. First John 2:4,5 reveal, "He that sayeth, I know him, and keepeth not his commandments, is a liar, and the truth is not in him. But whoso keepeth his word, in him verily is the love of God perfected: hereby know we that we are in him." John follows this up by insisting, in II John 5,6, "And now I beseech thee, lady, not as though I wrote a new commandment unto thee, but that which we had from the beginning, that we love one another. And this is love, that we walk after his commandments. This is the commandment, That, as ye have heard from the beginning, ye should walk in it."

Does love obey? Note how Jesus proved His love for the Father. With His face set as a flint toward Calvary and the agonies of the cross, He said in John 14:31, "But that the world may know that I love the Father; and as the Father gave me commandment, even so I do. Arise, let us go hence."

Our love is to be love in action, not merely a verbal expression. As I John 3:18 insists, "My little children, let us not love in word, neither in tongue; but in deed and in truth." We are to live our love!

5. Love Always Does Right!

A Christian's love should not be dependent upon outward circumstances or what others are doing. Two Christians were walking down the street one day when one stopped to purchase a paper. The man at the newsstand was sour-faced and mean looking. When the Christian accepted the paper he graciously said, "Thank you, Sir." The other made no response whatsoever.

As they walked on up the street, the friend said to his companion, "Do you say 'thank you' to that surly fellow every afternoon when you buy your paper?"

The Christian gentleman replied, "Why, yes, I can't let someone else decide how I am going to act."

Ah, that is the idea exactly! Paul, in the great love chapter referred to previously, wrote:

"Love is patient, love is kind, and is not jealous; love does not brag and is not arrogant, does not act unbecomingly; it does not seek its own, is not provoked, does not take into account a wrong suffered, does not rejoice in unrighteousness, but rejoices with the truth; bears all things, believes all things, hopes all things, endures all things. Love never fails. . . ."—I Cor. 13:4-8a, New American Standard Bible.

Dr. Theodore H. Epp gives a good illustration of love in action. When he was in a pastorate years ago, his deacons heard a very damaging story about him which had originated in a neighboring church. The men got together, spent a season of earnest prayer about the issue, then set out to get to the root of the problem. They traced it to the neighboring town and church, found the man responsible for starting the gossip, faced him with his falsehood, made him acknowledge its untruthfulness, then insisted he go to everyone he had told the story and confess that it was completely false. Dr. Epp did not even know about the situation until the men had the matter completely settled.

That was love in action!

Paul follows this positive with a negative, pointing out that believers are to be,

II. IMITATORS OF GOD'S HATRED OF SIN!

He says:

"But fornication, and all uncleanness, or covetousness, let it not be once named among you, as becometh saints; Neither filthiness, nor foolish talking nor jesting, which are not convenient: but rather giving of thanks. For this we know, that no whoremonger, nor unclean person, nor covetous man, who is an idolater, hath any inheritance in the kingdom of Christ and of God. Let no man deceive you with vain words: for because of these things cometh the wrath of God upon the children of disobedience."—Vss. 3-6.

A. The Depths of the Degradation Into Which Man Can Sink!

Paul lists six things—the number of man—in this section. Ephesus abounded in the vilest of sins and impurities, some even used in worship, and he wanted followers of the Son of God to understand that their life must be different "in Christ."

1. Fornication

This is a term we understand to be synonymous with adultery. One of the Ten Commandments, the seventh, forbade the scarlet sin. Exodus 20:14 says bluntly, with no reservations or exceptions, "Thou shalt not commit adultery." Christ reaffirmed this prohibition when He instructed the rich young ruler, "Thou shalt do no murder, Thou shalt not commit adultery, Thou shalt not steal, Thou shalt not bear false witness" (Matt. 19:18).

2. *All Uncleanness*

This is any form of impurity. Such an exhortation was not needed in an Ephesus of long ago any more than it is in an America today. The pornographic magazines, the X-rated motion picture theaters, the so-called adult bookstores are daily dispensing picturing uncleanness too filthy to describe on these pages.

Children of God are not to be partakers! Although the Bible does not say "cleanliness is next to godliness," as so many seem to think, the principle is certainly there. While we are not sure that cleanliness is always godliness, godliness is certainly always cleanliness!

Biographers of the Robert Moffats tell us that when Mary began reaching so many of the African women for Christ the husbands came to Robert and asked him to stop his wife's labors. The Africans explained they could no longer afford what was happening. It seemed their wives were now requiring too much soap and calico! In other words, the women were now bathing and dressing properly and the husbands were objecting that it was costing them too much.

There is something wrong with a conversion that does not make the individual want to *clean* up and *dress* up!

3. *Covetousness*

Any covetousness is wrong; in fact, it is forbidden in the Ten Commandments. However, in this particular case keep the context in mind. Paul is speaking of covetousness in line with the sins of the flesh. It is the type of covetousness described in Matthew 5:28, where Christ said, "I say unto you, That whosoever looketh on a woman to lust after her hath committed adultery with her already in his heart."

4. Filthiness

Again, keep the context in mind. This is indecency; it is filthy conduct, including filthy speech. When the heart is wrong, the mouth will be wrong. Jesus said, "It is from the heart's overflow that the mouth speaks; a good man utters good words from his store of goodness, the wicked man, from his store of wickedness, can utter nothing but what is evil" (Matt. 12:35, Knox Translation).

5. Foolish Talking

This is no mere idle conversation. Trench sums it up as "that 'talk of fools' which is foolishness and sin together." Profanity is certainly one form of fool's talk. Someone showed us a card, the size of a normal business card, on which the words had been printed: "PROFANITY is the Public Announcement of STUPIDITY!" This evaluates it succinctly.

Yet how popular today is vulgarity of speech. Tom Malone, Jr., tells of an incident which happened when he worked at Sears and Roebuck. He and some other men, truck drivers, were sitting at a loading dock when a lady stormed up, highly indignant about some package. She turned the air blue with her yelling, cursing and vulgarity. Finally one of the men interrupted and said, "Please, lady. There are some truck drivers present!"

Martin Luther wrote some wise words about profanity:

> It is no mark of a gentleman to swear. The most worthless and vile, the refuse of mankind, the drunkard and the prostitute swear as well as the best dressed and educated gentleman. No particular endowments are requisite to give a finish to the art of cursing. The basest and meanest of mankind swear with as much tact and skill as the most refined; and he that wishes to degrade himself to the very lowest level of pollution and shame should learn to be a common swearer.
>
> Any man has talents enough to learn to curse God, and imprecate perdition on himself and his fellow men. Profane swearing never did any man any good. No man is the richer or wiser or happier for it. It helps no one's education or manners. It commends no one to any society.
>
> It is disgusting to the refined, abominable to the good, insulting to those with whom we associate, degrading to the mind, unprofitable, needless and injurious to society; and wantonly to profane His name, to call His vengeance down, to curse Him, and to invoke His vengeance is perhaps of all offenses the most awful in the sight of God.

6. Jesting

This is no criticism of a sense of humor. Proverbs 17:22 assures us, "A merry heart doeth good like a medicine: but a broken spirit drieth up the bones." So there is nothing evil or sinful about good, sanctified humor.

Vine tells us this word "jesting" is literally "ribaldry." So it is *suggestive* humor, the *double entendre* form of jesting to which the apostle is objecting. He is opposing what the world calls "dirty stories" and other forms of vulgarity in speech.

Of these six forms of degradation, Paul says, "Let it not be once named among you." It is like the street sign in Needham, a southwestern suburb of Boston, which advises motorists, "Don't Even THINK of Parking Here!" These are sins of a nature Christians should **never** be guilty of, *not even one time.*

Why? Paul says, "as becometh saints." We are sons and daughters of the King of kings. The dignity of our position is far above stooping to such debasement.

Sam Jones tells of an eastern king whose twelve-year-old son was turned over to a tutor for an education and training befitting his position. The lad was wild and unruly, a managing problem of major proportions for the tutor.

At first he could not even begin to control him, but then he got the idea of pinning a small bow of ribbon on the lapel of the boy's coat. He explained, "That is a sign of your royal character, an emblem signifying you are a king's son." After that, whenever the boy started to misbehave, the tutor merely had to point to the bow and the rebellion was halted immediately, and an apology forthcoming.

7. Instead, "Giving of Thanks"

A tongue profuse with praise will not have room for profanity or filth. How much we have to thank God for! When we are consumed with a sense of all that God has done for us and all we owe to Him, the problems described in this passage will not even be a temptation.

Have you learned the secret of praise? First Thessalonians 5:18

says, "In every thing give thanks: for this is the will of God in Christ Jesus concerning you."

B. The Damnation Such Degradation Deserves!

Paul has been talking about vile sins and now he says: *"For this ye know, that no whoremonger, nor unclean person, nor covetous man, who is an idolater, hath any inheritance in the kingdom of Christ and of God. Let no man deceive you with vain words: for because of these things, cometh the wrath of God upon the children of disobedience"* (Vss. 5,6).

"For this ye know." Here is a certainty based upon the infallible Word of a holy God. Some things may be misunderstood, but the apostle wants this crystal clear. Heaven is barred to the unchaste, the sensual, the lustful. He says such "hath any inheritance"; that is, none whatsoever. What a blow this is to the universalist's teaching that every man will eventually receive inheritance in God's kingdom.

In fact, Paul goes on to say, "Let no man deceive you." He earnestly intreats his readers, "Don't let anyone fool you on this point, however plausible his or her argument might appear." Sin simply doesn't pay. God's Word is final. Hebrews 13:4 notes, "But whoremongers and adulterers God will judge," and so He will.

Observe that these upon whom the wrath of God will fall are "children of disobedience," not children of God. The judgment of God will come upon them; it *cannot* fall upon a child of God. As Romans 8:1 promises, "There is therefore now no condemnation to them which are in Christ Jesus." No damnation to the believer; nothing but condemnation for the sensualist.

III. IMITATORS OF GOD'S HOLINESS!

Verse 7 of our text says, *"Be not ye therefore partakers with them."*

No one is perfect, all claims to the contrary notwithstanding. We read once of a preacher who asked anyone in his congregation who thought he was perfect to raise his hand. None responded. Then he asked if anyone had ever heard of someone being perfect and, to his surprise, one brother lifted his hand high. The startled clergyman gasped, "You have heard about someone who was perfect?" And the brother replied, "Yes, my wife's first husband!"

We know better. Elsewhere God said anyone claiming to be without sin was deceiving himself, lying, accusing God of lying, and the truth was not in him (I John 1:8,10). But that doesn't mean we are not to work at being as nearly perfect as possible and Paul has just listed serious sins he tells believers they must not be partakers of in any form, shape or manner.

This is sound advice, imperative for preserving a Christian's character and his testimony. Miguel de Cervantes well said, "Tell me thy company and I'll tell thee what thou art." Joseph C. Salak added, "People are also judged by the company they keep away from." Paul is pleading that believers keep away from all such company and all such deeds.

An unknown poet penned:

> When some alluring glimpse of golden pleasure
> Is held before my captivated sight,
> There comes some questions that my soul must answer
> Beside the common question: Is it right?
> Fresh from its scenes and gay associations
> Can I to prayer and sweet communion go?
> Will it affect the bond of close relation
> Between my heart and Him who loves me so?
> Whatever renders me less influential
> With men for whom my Lord and Savior died,
> Whatever mars to others my profession,
> These for His sake must all be put aside.

The Bible is clear about the holiness Christians should manifest. Peter was talking about imitating God's absolute purity when he said, in I Peter 1:15,16: "But as he which hath called you is holy, so be ye holy in all manner of conversation; Because it is written, Be ye holy; for I am holy." And Paul wrote to the young preacher Timothy, "But refuse profane and old wives' fables, and exercise thyself rather unto godliness. . . godliness is profitable unto all things, having promise of the life that now is, and of that which is to come" (I Tim. 4:7,8). He added, "But godliness with contentment is great gain" (I Tim. 6:6).

This holiness for which our text pleads is in the form of separation. We understand that in the English House of Commons when members are ready to vote on a matter, instead of calling for the question as we might do, they cry, *"Divide, divide!"* In other words, members are to get on one side of the fence or the other. Paul is crying, *"Divide, divide!"* to all believers, insisting they identify themselves on the side of Christ and holiness, not on the side of Satan and perversion.

He is appealing for purity in the church. We cannot help being in the world, and Christ said He did not save us to take us out of the world, but that does not mean the world is to be in us. An unknown poet wrote:

> All the water in the world,
> However hard it tried;
> Could never sink a ship
> Unless it got inside.
>
> All the evil in the world,
> The wickedness and sin,
> Can never sink the soul's craft
> Unless it gets inside.

Paul tells us to have nothing to do with men or sins of the character described in our text. He expressed it in II Corinthians 6:14-7:1:

"Be ye not unequally yoked together with unbelievers: for what fellowship hath righteousness with unrighteousness? and what communion hath light with darkness? And what concord hath Christ with Belial? or what part hath he that believeth with an infidel? And what agreement hath the temple of God with idols? for ye are the temple of the living God; as God hath said, I will dwell in them, and walk in them; and I will be their God, and they shall be my people. Wherefore come out from among them, and be ye separate, saith the Lord, and touch not the unclean thing; and I will receive you, And will be a Father unto you, and ye shall be my sons and daughters, saith the Lord Almighty. Having therefore these promises, dearly beloved, let

us cleanse ourselves from all filthiness of the flesh and spirit, perfecting holiness in the fear of God."

Isn't it strange how professing Christians will madly plunge along with the world, following the dictates of the latest fashions, completely ignoring the commands of God for separation and the divine consequences for failing to heed? Well known are the antics of sheep, how they will follow one another even to destruction. But did you know that buffalo do the same? As a matter of fact, in the days of the old West, sometimes a herd of buffalo, roaming together in great numbers, would become frightened and a stampede would start. Hundreds of buffalo would dash madly across the prairie and, sometimes, the path of their mad dash would take them to a precipice. Those dumb brute beasts would just pour over, one after another, plunging to instant death on the rocks below. Don't be a mad buffalo! Separate yourself from the heard headed for destruction.

The story of the conversion and separation of Jenny Lind, known to history as the Swedish Nightingale, is sweet indeed. She came from Sweden to New York for a series of concerts. On one occasion she visited a boat in the harbor being used as a chapel. Olaf Hedstrom was the minister in charge and she eagerly listened to him preach. He talked frankly about sin, salvation, judgment, Heaven, Hell and redemption only through the Lord Jesus Christ. After the service she talked privately to the man of God and he led her to Christ. That happened at the height of her fame and influence in the musical world, in 1851, and she set out immediately to follow her Redeemer.

After just a short time she announced that she was leaving the theatrical world and the operatic stage. As might be expected, she received all kinds of abuse and criticism from the world, not understanding her decision. However, she kept her promise and never again appeared in opera, using her gifted voice only for spiritual songs and occasional concerts for philanthropic purposes.

Some time after abandoning the theatrical world, a visitor dropped in and found her reading her Bible. The friend inquired,

"Jenny, tell me truthfully. Why did you leave the stage?"

Pointing off to a beautiful sunset in the west, Miss Lind replied simply, "Because it blinded my eyes to that." Then, her eyes dropping down to the Word of God in her lap, she added, "And because it blinded my eyes to this."

Ah, that is the trouble with the world! It blinds the eyes of an individual to spiritual light as revealed in the wonderful creation of God and in the blessed Word of God. This is just one more reason God insists upon separation from the world and worldlings, demanding that His children not be partakers with them in their sins.

There is a poem entitled, "You Tell on Yourself," which we gleaned from a church bulletin. No author was credited although it sounds like something Edgar Guest might have written. It declared:

> You tell on yourself by the friends you seek,
> By the very manner in which you speak,
> By the way you employ your time,
> By the use you make of dollar and dime.
>
> You tell what you are by the things you wear,
> By the spirit in which you burdens bear,
> By the kind of things at which you laugh,
> By the records you play on the phonograph.
>
> You tell what you are by the way you walk,
> By the things of which you delight to talk,
> By the manner in which you bear defeat,
> By so simple a thing as how you eat.
>
> By the books you choose from the well-filled shelf:
> In these ways and more, you tell on yourself;
> So there's really no particle of sense
> In an effort to keep up false pretense.

Conclusion

We are to be imitators of God. Some imitations are good and others are bad, of course. This is true with all kinds of imitations, whether they be of music, of actors, of paintings, or whatever.

Our youngest son, Ron, is currently a student at the Herron School of Art in Indianapolis. As part of the training, students in certain classes go to the Indianapolis Museum of Art and "imitate" the works of the masters. At the time of this writing he is copying a work, "Sleeping Cupid," by the Italian master, Polidoro da Caravaggio. The purpose is to examine the painter's techniques, style and other matters, copying them as perfectly as possible.

So the Christian is to study the techniques of his Master, noting His style and reproducing His character in his own life as nearly as possible.

All professing Christians claim to be imitating God. How are you progressing with your imitation? Oh, that we might all settle down to business in this matter, be in dead earnest, and become as close to the Original as possible.

In paintings, some imitators do the job so well they pass for the original. Wouldn't it be wonderful if you were mistaken in such a manner?

Walking in Light and Wisdom

For ye were sometimes darkness, but now are ye light in the Lord: walk as children of light:
(For the fruit of the Spirit is in all goodness and righteousness and truth;)
Proving what is acceptable unto the Lord.
And have no fellowship with the unfruitful works of darkness, but rather reprove them.
For it is a shame even to speak of those things which are done of them in secret.
But all things that are reproved are made manifest by the light: for whatsoever doth make manifest is light.
Wherefore he saith, Awake thou that sleepest, and arise from the dead, and Christ shall give you light.
See then that ye walk circumspectly, not as fools, but as wise,
Redeeming the time, because the days are evil.
Wherefore be ye not unwise, but understanding what the will of the Lord is.—Ephesians 5:8-17.

There is a manufacturer in Birmingham, England, making deluxe beds which carry a $7,000 price tag! These beauties by D. V. Bliss have bedspreads of mink, adjustable and electrically heated mattresses, built-in television sets, phonographs and radios, among other items. Thirteen had been manufactured when we read the story and purchasers included sheiks of Quatar and Bahrein, along with an unnamed American.

While we cannot fathom paying such an outlandish, unreasonable price for an object to rest the body, we suppose that if one were weary enough, he would pay any kind of a price for what Shakespeare called "sleep that knits up the ravell'd sleave of care." Many today, stricken by a tormenting conscience, know nothing of a good night's rest. One lady recently called us twice from Wisconsin in a period of less than two days, pleading with us to pray for her because she could not sleep.

There is a repose and a peace that comes through a conscience right with God, knowing one is in His will, doing His pleasure and serving Him in a manner acceptable. Paul pleads with those who have experienced rest and peace in Christ to now go forward and advance in their walk with Him.

Have you noticed how often Paul speaks of the believer's walk in Ephesians? In 2:10, he appeals to believers to walk in good works. In 4:1, it is a walk worthy of our vocation. The theme of 4:17 is a walk not like the sinner's walk. The walk of 5:2 is a walk in love, imitating God. In 5:8 it is a walk in light, and in 5:15 it is a walk in wisdom. These are only the *direct* references to walk; indirectly the idea runs throughout the entire epistle. For example, it relates to family instructions, to warfare directions, and many other matters.

How important must be our walk as Christians! It *does* matter how we live. An unnamed poet wrote:

> I am my neighbor's Bible,
>   He reads me when we meet;
> Today he reads me in my home—
>   Tomorrow in the street.
>
> He may be relative, or friend,
>   Or slight acquaintance be;
> He may not even know my name,
>   Yet he is reading me.
>
> And, pray, who is this neighbor
>   Who reads me day by day,
> To learn if I am living right,
>   And walking as I pray?
>
> Oh, he is with me always,
>   To criticize or blame;
> So worldly-wise in his own eyes—
>   And 'Sinner' is his name.
>
> Dear Christian friends and brothers,
>   If we could only know
> How faithfully the world records
>   Just what we say and do;

> Oh, we would write our record plain,
> And come in time to see
> Our worldly neighbor won to Christ,
> While reading you and me.

This is one reason why our walk is so vital.

I. WALKING IN LIGHT!
Vss. 8-14

A. "FACT" of Our Walk in Light

Verse 8 says, *"For ye were sometimes darkness, but now are ye light in the Lord: walk as children of light."*

1. A Look of Retrospect

This is what we were: **darkness!** Matthew 4:16 describes our Lord's sojourn in Capernaum as being a fulfillment of Isaiah's prophecy: "The people which sat in darkness saw a great light; and to them which sat in the region and darkness of death light is sprung up." The believer, before conversion, was one seated in darkness and the shadow of death. Darkness is, of course, absence of light. When descriptive of the spiritual realm, it indicates absence of holiness, absence of purity, absence of righteousness.

Our Lord described these two classes, those seated in darkness and those seated in light, when He said: "The light of the body is the eye: therefore when thine eye is single, thy whole body also is full of light; but when thine eye is evil, thy body also is full of darkness" (Luke 11:34).

The American Protestant Episcopal bishop of Minnesota, Henry Benjamin Whipple, had a blessed ministry among North American Indians. On one occasion he told of an Indian who traveled some 600 miles to visit him. When he reached his door, he dropped on his knees at the clergyman's feet, crying, "I kneel to tell you of my gratitude that you pity the Red Man!"

The visitor went on to describe the agony of his mind and soul for many years, knowing he and his people were perishing. Since his father had told him there was a Great Spirit, he would often go into the woods and cry out to that Great Spirit for help. He lamented, "I only got the sound of my voice."

Then he added frantically, "You do not know what I mean. You never stood in the dark and reached out your hand and took hold of nothing." Yet that is the condition of every individual outside of Christ and it describes the universal experience of us all before salvation.

2. A Look of Realization!

This is what we are: **light!** Just as darkness is absence of light, so light is absence of darkness. In the spiritual realm, just as darkness is sin, iniquity and the disfavor of God, so light signifies purity, holiness and righteousness. And this is the believer's actual position *right now* in Jesus Christ. We **are** light!

Since we are light, it ought to be manifest in and through our lives. D. L. Moody once said:

> I remember hearing, some years ago, of a blind man who sat by the wayside with a lantern near him. When he was asked what he had a lantern for, as he could not see the light, he said it was that people should not sumble over him. The eyes of the world are upon us. I think it was George Fox who said, "Every Quaker ought to light up the country for ten miles around him."

How true this is!

However, note the qualifying phrase about Christians being light: **"in the Lord."** It is not our own light; we are only reflectors. When it comes to a consideration of the true light, we think of John 1:4, "In him was life; and the life was the light of men." Or as Jesus said in John 8:12, "I am the light of the world: he that followeth me shall not walk in darkness, but shall have the light of life."

George Dana Boardman had an interesting observation about Christians as light, writing:

> Distinguish between doing right in order to help others, as when one lights a beacon in order to guide the sailor; and doing right in order to be praised by others, as when one stands in the full blaze of a chandelier in order to display his own jewelry. It is one thing to shine for the sake of illuminating others, and so helping them; it is another thing to shine for the sake of illuminating ourselves, and so be seen to advantage.

The Spirit-filled Christian will use his light to benefit others.

3. A Look of Responsibility

The look of retrospect ("ye were sometimes darkness"), and the look of realization ("now are ye light in the Lord"), is followed by the look of responsibility ("walk as children of light"). This relates to what we should do as Christians: **walk as children of light!** Someone has rendered it, "lead the life of children of light."

What is that? Well, light is made to shine. In the Sermon on the Mount our Lord taught: "Ye are the light of the world. A city that is set on a hill cannot be hid. Neither do men light a candle, and put it under a bushel, but on a candlestick; and it giveth light unto all that are in the house. Let your light so shine before men, that they may see your good works, and glorify your Father which is in heaven" (Matt. 5:14-16).

In one of D. L. Moody's messages he described the two lights at the mouth of the Cleveland harbor. Located one on each side of the bay, they were called the "lower" and "upper" lights. To enter the harbor safely at night, it was necessary for a vessel to sight both lights and sail in between them.

He related how upon one dark, stormy night a steamer had been trying to enter the harbor. Considerable time elapsed and the lower light had not been seen, causing the pilot and captain to become alarmed that they had passed it. When they finally saw a light their fears were confirmed; it was light from the bluff, the "upper" light. Looking back they could see the dim outline of the lower lighthouse against the sky. Alas, the light had gone out.

Moody said an attempt to turn the helm of the ship in the wild storm proved fruitless and the vessel crashed against the rocks, sinking to the bottom of the bay with great loss of life.

He made the application that Christ Himself is the "upper" light for the world and we are the "lower" lights. It is vital to His redemptive program that the lower lights keep burning. The great musician, P. P. Bliss, heard Moody tell the story and went to his room to write that immortal gospel song:

> Brightly beams our Father's mercy
> From His lighthouse evermore,
> But to us He gives the keeping
> Of the lights along the shore.
>
> Dark the night of sin has settled,
> Loud the angry billows roar;
> Eager eyes are watching, longing,
> For the lights along the shore.
>
> Trim your feeble lamp, my brother;
> Some poor sailor tempest tossed,
> Trying now to make the harbor,
> In the darkness may be lost.
>
> Let the lower lights be burning!
> Send a gleam across the wave!
> Some poor fainting, struggling seaman
> You may rescue, you may save.

How great is our responsibility! We think of the dying lighthouse keeper who suddenly raised himself upon one elbow and asked those grouped about the bed, "Is the lamp burning in the tower? You know we must not let it go out tonight. Someone will be watching for it." Assured that the lamp was burning, the faithful keeper dropped back on the bed, saying gratefully, "Then I can rest."

How can we rest today unless our lamps are burning brightly and the light of Christ is shining through us to a world lost in the bitter darkness of sin and despair?

B. "FRUIT" of Our Walk in Light

Verse 9 says: *"For the fruit of the Spirit is in all goodness and righteousness and truth."* Many translations other than the King James, along with various Bibles containing marginal notes, point out that this should be rendered "the fruit of the Light." Actually, there is little difference; it is merely another way of expressing the same truth.

However, this is the test of the reality of the light in the believer's life. Where there is light and life, there will be fruit.

Again referring to our Lord's Sermon on the Mount, He said there:

"Beware of false prophets, which come to you in sheep's clothing, but inwardly they are ravening wolves. Ye shall know them by their fruits. Do men gather grapes of thorns, or figs of thistles? Even so every good tree bringeth forth good fruit; but a corrupt tree bringeth forth evil fruit. A good tree cannot bring forth evil fruit, neither can a corrupt tree bring forth good fruit. Every tree that bringeth not forth good fruit is hewn down, and cast into the fire. Wherefore by their fruits ye shall know them."—Matt. 5:15-20.

Or, as Solomon expressed it in Proverbs 20:11, "Even a child is known by his doings, whether his work be pure, and whether it be right."

Note the trilogy of light's fruit as Paul gives it.

1. Goodness

We will have a benevolent, kindly consideration for other people if the light shines in our life. Someone has pointed out that this is how heavenly grammar differs from worldly grammar. Instead of the first person being "I," it is "he" or "she." In the Christian's grammar, "I" is the third person.

This is the thought in I John 3:16, "Hereby perceive we the love of God, because he laid down his life for us: and we ought to lay down our lives for the brethren."

2. Righteousness

What is the idea of righteousness in this context? It is simply doing whatever is right! It can be something a group is doing, as in Proverbs 14:34 ("Righteousness exalteth a nation"), or it can be the action of individuals. First John 1:4-7 says,

"And these things write we unto you, that your joy may be full. This then is the message which we have heard of him, and declare unto you, that God is light, and in him is no darkness at all. If we say that we have fellowship with him, and walk in

darkness, we lie, and do not the truth: But if we walk in the light, as he is in the light, we have fellowship one with another, and the blood of Jesus Christ his Son cleanseth us from all sin."

3. Truth

Thinking of Psalm 51:6, this has to do with inward sincerity: "Behold, thou desirest truth in the inward parts: and in the hidden part thou shalt make me to know wisdom." It speaks of truthfulness in our dealings with God and in our dealings with our fellow man.

C. "FELLOWSHIP" of Our Walk in Light

Someone tells of eating in a restaurant where the customers obviously preferred darkness to light. He was led by the hostess into a dimly-lit room, fumbled for a chair, and then held the menu inches from his nose, trying to read it. When his order was served, he started eating by faith and not by sight.

Interestingly enough, however, after he had been in the room for some time his eyesight improved considerably. He could make out the people around him and even objects on the other side of the room. Natural eyes get used to the dark.

Unfortunately, the same is true spiritually. When we have fellowship with the works of darkness, we become more and more like them. The farther we get from the light, the easier it becomes to operate without it. There is a sense in which we *use* it or *lose* it.

1. The Positive Aspect: PROVING!

Paul says in verse 10: *"Proving what is acceptable unto the Lord."* This does not mean to prove in the sense of proving a point, although our walk in light should certainly do this. The word means to test, to examine, to discern. It is not so much proof for others as it is to ourselves.

Do you as a believer do this in your life? Do you test everything to discover whether or not it is acceptable "unto the Lord"? No scientist ought to test his theories with any more care in a laboratory than a Christian tests his actions to determine if they are in accordance with the Word of God.

2. The Negative Aspect: REPROVING!

This reproof will take several forms. Verse 11 says, *"And have no fellowship with the unfruitful works of darkness, but rather reprove them."* This is **separation** and the classic passage in II Corinthians 6:14-18 immediately comes to mind. The child of God cannot mingle with the unfruitful works of darkness without becoming contaminated to some degree.

This "no fellowship" even includes those who profess to be "brethren," but who do not walk in the light. First Corinthians 5:11 insists, "But now I have written unto you not to keep company, if any man that is called a brother be a fornicator, or covetous, or an idolator, or a railer, or a drunkard, or an extortioner; with such an one no not to eat." What a warning this is against fellowship with modernists and modernism, since idolatry—worshiping any god other than the one true God—is one of the grievous sins mentioned demanding separation.

There is an old Civil War story told by C. A. Hobbs. He and his men had marched all night and fought most of the day in a fierce battle. They were desperately trying to hold a hill without any prospect of reinforcements.

While they fought the enemy directly below, suddenly a large body of cavalry appeared to the right. Seeing the Confederate gray uniforms, the increased body of enemy soldiers presented them with overwhelming and despairing odds. Hobbs said it was hard to describe the great depression that came over his troups.

Just as they were ready to make a "do or die" battle, the commanding officer shouted: "Hold your fire! I see blue uniforms beneath the thick covering of dust. These are our friends, not our enemies!"

Many Christians, because they have been failing in the matter of separation, are wearing uniforms not discernible as friendly to Christ. The gray dust of the world has covered the royal blue of their heavenly citizenship. Paul is saying, "Shake off the dust from your uniform!" We are to have absolutely no fellowship with the unfruitful works of darkness.

However, the believer not only reproves by separation, he also reproves by **silence.** Verse 12 says, *"For it is a shame even to speak of those things which are done of them in secret."*

How we can reprove by silence is explained in the next verse: by **shining!** As verse 13 says, *"But all things that are reproved are made manifest by light: for whatsoever doth make manifest is light."*

Light has the capacity to show up everything for what it really is. When one lives the life of light, it will show up everything that is evil. Bob Jones told of visiting his neighbor at twilight and the man's wife invited him in, yet did not turn on the light. He wondered why until her little boy walked into the room and started to perform that simple chore. She interrupted him, saying, "Son, don't turn on the light. Your mother's hair isn't combed." She feared the revealing light since it would manifest her failure.

To put this in scriptural language, John 3:19-21 says:

"And this is the condemnation, that light is come into the world, and men loved darkness rather than light, because their deeds were evil. For every one that doeth evil hateth the light, neither cometh to the light, lest his deeds should be reproved. But he that doeth truth cometh to the light, that his deeds may be made manifest, that they are wrought in God."

D. "FEATURE" of Our Walk in Light

This is set forth in verse 14 and it is the main message of our walk: *"Wherefore he saith, Awake thou that sleepest, and rise from the dead, and Christ shall give thee light."*

1. The People Addressed: "Thou That Sleepest"

Does not this remind you of the ten virgins? While five were described as wise and five as foolish, all ten slumbered and slept while waiting for the bridegroom to make his appearance. The "prepared" were as sound asleep as the "unprepared." So many today are sleeping "among the dead." Why? Because of coldness of heart and indifference of soul.

Dr. McVicar of Montreal tells of being at a boarding house in Northern China when a lamp he was given burned brightly for only a short time, then dimmed. Complaining to the landlord, the latter disappeared with the lantern and then came back with it shining brightly once more. However, the same problem with dimness took place again after a matter of minutes.

Inquiring as to the problem, he learned that the oil was frozen. The landlord had taken it to the fire and thawed it a little and the melted oil burned well, but the frozen oil would not burn at all. There is a powerful lesson applicable for every Christian, in this parable.

Too many Christians are like the old Southern mammy who explained, "When I walks, I walks hard. When I sits, I sits loose. And when I sees work coming, I takes a nap."

It is like the fellow who had just recovered from a serious illness. Explaining to a friend about how he was sleeping, the convalescent said: "I sleep pretty good nights, and not so bad in the mornings; but in the afternoons I just twist and turn." Too many Christians are sleeping around the clock when it comes to spiritual activity.

2. The Plea Announced:
"Awake! Arise!"

No one can be of service to others while he is asleep. If Christians are to perform a work for Christ, and do good in His service, they must wake up.

Dr. Alfred Byrne, writing in the *London Clinic Medical Journal,* shared his secret of staying awake and alive while driving on long automobile trips at night. Simply summed up, it is: *take off your shoes!* Dr. Byrne explained, "Driving in bare or stocking feet awakens the nerves of the sole and brings the body into new alertness."

Not only so, *it tickles!*

We could only wish that some researcher or good doctor would come up with a solution for keeping Christians awake. A "new alertness" for them could come only through awakening "the nerves of the soul." The disciples in Gethsemane's garden slept when they should have been praying. Christians all down through the ages have been guilty of the same.

Paul not only wanted the Ephesians to *wake* up, but to *rise* up. This implied activity. It involved *doing something* for God. This is the kind of "light shining" that Matthew 5:16 describes, which requires others seeing "your good works." Shining is not merely a passive thing, it includes action.

3. The Promise Assured: "Christ Shall Give Thee Light"

Here is a guarantee that Christ will shine upon those believers who *wake up* and *rise up*. It is, perhaps, another way of saying, "Thanks be to God, which giveth us the victory through our Lord Jesus Christ. . .forasmuch as ye know that your labour is not in vain in the Lord" (I Cor. 15:57,58).

Every religion has its appeals for its followers to do good. *Brahmanism* says: "This is the sum of duty; do naught unto others which would cause pain if done unto you." *Buddism* says: "Hurt not others in ways that you yourself would find hurtful." *Confucianism* expresses it: "There is one maxim of loving kindness; do not unto others what you would not have them do unto you." The appeal of *Islam* is: "No one of you is a believer until he desires for his brother that which he desires for himself." *Taoism* teaches: "Regard your neighbor's gain as your own gain, and your neighbor's loss as your own loss." *Zoroastrianism* says: "That nature alone is good which refrains from doing unto another whatsoever is not good for itself." But while all religions have high ideals, Christianity alone offers the inner *light* and inner *power* to make those goals reality.

II. WALKING IN WISDOM!
Vss. 15-17

A. This Walk Enjoined

First of all, Paul pleads negatively. He says in verse 15, ". . . *not as fools"*; adding in verse 17, *"be ye not unwise."*

Then he approaches it positively, saying in verse 15, *"as wise,"* and in verse 17, *"understanding."* This kind of being made wise involves, of course, learning the wisdom of God.

The God of the Old Testament said, "Get wisdom, get understanding: forget it not; neither decline from the words of my mouth. Forsake her not, and she shall preserve thee: love her, and she shall keep thee. Wisdom is the principal thing; therefore get wisdom: and with all thy getting get understanding" (Prov. 4:5-7). The God of the New Testament put it like this: "Behold, I send you forth as sheep in the midst of wolves: be ye wise as serpents, and harmless as doves" (Matt. 10:16).

B. This Walk Explained

It is a walk that is *circumspect*. It is to be careful. The child of God is to look all around and be cautious of pitfalls, quagmires, traps and other things that would hinder his advance in spiritual matters.

You may be sure the Devil has a lot of snares for the child of God. *Watch out for them!* Like a mountain climber who carefully tests each step before placing his weight, so the child of God should carefully watch where his feet lead him, making certain he is on solid, scriptural ground.

He is also to walk *conservatively;* that is, "redeeming the time." This is literally, "buying up opportunities." Just as an earnest, effective shopper watches for a good buy, then snaps it up, so the child of God should be watching for opportunities to witness for Jesus Christ.

Here is an earnest plea for using time to its best value. We pay no price for time, but once it is used it will never return; it is gone forever. How we should seek to use it wisely for the glory of God!

Most Christians are only playing at the job. Writing several years ago, James A. Stuart said of the communists in Italy: "In all my travels throughout postwar Europe, I have never seen their equal for earnestness, aggressiveness, and a sacrificial passion for the spreading of the message of the Kremlin. They have little halls everywhere, something similar to mission halls. Loud speakers blare out the message at almost every street corner."

No wonder communism has overrun Europe and is now rapidly taking control of Africa. What dedication communists have to a falsehood! Would to God the followers of Jesus Christ were as dedicated to truth.

Horatius Bonar pleaded:

> The time is short!
> If thou wouldst work for God, it must be now;
> If thou wouldst win the garland for thy brow;
>   Redeem the time!
>
> Shake off earth's sloth!
> Go forth with staff in hand while yet 'tis day;
> Set out with girded loins upon the way;
>   Up! Linger not!
>
> Withstand the foe;
> Die daily, that forever thou mayest live;
> Be faithful unto death! the Lord will give
>   The crown of life.

Paul exhorts not only for a walk circumspectly and conservatively, but *understandingly* as well. He says: "... *understanding what the will of the Lord is*" (vs. 17).

The Christian who understands what the will of God is knows that he will eventually triumph. He experiences no such pessimism as Ibn Ezra expressed in the 12th century, when he wrote:

> My labor's vain,
>   No wealth I gain.
> My fate since birth
>   Is gloom on earth.
>
> If I sold shrouds
>   No one would die.
> If I sold lamps,
>   Then in the sky

> The sun for spite
> Would shine at night.

How could one profess to be truly wise and yet not know the will of God? Yet how can one know the *will* of God unless he knows the *Word* of God? This is why the believer needs to dig into the Holy Scriptures with a passionate earnestness. He needs to *read* it. He needs to *memorize* it. He needs to *meditate* upon it. It is only thus that he will become a wise Christian, one whose light will shine effectively for Jesus Christ.

Conclusion

There is a work to be done, there is a life to be lived, there is a road to be walked for Christ. Someone has expressed it, "The greatest need in our churches today is trained teachers who will put their whole mind into their preparation, their whole soul into their presentation, and their whole life into their illustration." That is what Paul is talking about in this passage.

Where you start is of little importance. There is a story of General Sheridan, in the midst of the Civil War, being approached by a tentative recruit and asking where he should "step in." The fiery general is reputed to have thunderously responded, "Step in? Step in anywhere. There's fighting all along the line!"

It is not *starting* that is important here; it is *continuing*.

Walk in *light!*

Walk in *wisdom!*

"Be Filled With the Spirit"

And be not drunk with wine, wherein is excess; but be filled with the Spirit;
Speaking to yourselves in psalms and hymns and spiritual songs, singing and making melody in your heart to the Lord;
Giving thanks always for all things unto God and the Father in the name of our Lord Jesus Christ;
Submitting yourselves one to another in the fear of God.— Ephesians 5:18-21.

A bishop, on a preaching mission in another city, was walking along a busy thoroughfare one morning when he noted an urchin with his nose pressed against the glass window of a fruit store. Everything about the lad's countenance pictured an inner longing for the goodies inside the market. The kindly clergyman went up to the boy and said, "Let's go in. You pick out anything you want and I will pay for it all!"

The amazed boy bounced into the shop and loaded up with apples, oranges, bananas and other delicious fruits. He jammed every pocket to the brim, then took off his sweater and used it for a sack, rolling it up to hold the fruit.

As he paid the owner of the market for the produce, the last sight the bishop had of the boy, he was hurrying up the street with fruit bulging out from everywhere. And Bishop Berry said he turned his eyes Heavenward and prayed, "Dear Lord, let the satisfying fruit of Thy Spirit stick out all over me in order that the needs of hungry men, women and children might be met." Surely that is what the Apostle Paul had in mind in this passage relative to the Holy Spirit's fullness.

A. Why Needed?

"Be filled with the Spirit!" Here is one of Christendom's most needed and yet most neglected Bible commands. God's people today, for the most part, are trying to do God's work without God's power. They are like the lady L. E. Maxwell described who drove her automobile into a gas station on "Candid Camera." She asked the attendant to check her oil and water, but when he lifted the hood he looked dumbfounded for a moment, then turned and said, "Madam, you ain't got no motor." The car was a late model, had a shiny finish, and was adorned with expensive chrome. It *looked* like an outstanding car, but it *lacked* the main ingredient whereby power could be generated to make it run—the motor was missing!

Isn't that like many of today's evangelical churches? We have beautiful buildings, talented musicians, highly educated ministers, along with all kinds of other physical and material benefits. However, there seems to be no source of power and these churches are simply not doing a real job for God.

Nearly two decades ago, in my book, *Evangelism: The Church on Fire,* I quoted Dr. Jared Gerig as saying:

> It is not new that America is losing her grip and fast slipping from her spiritual moorings. In spite of increased membership in the churches, only approximately 8 per cent of the population is in the Sunday morning worship at any one time, and only 2 percent at night. The majority of churches make no excuses for not having midweek prayer services any longer.

In the same volume I repeated Roland Q. Leavell's lament about church members:

20 per cent never pray
25 per cent never read their Bible.
30 per cent never attend church.
40 per cent never give to any cause.
50 per cent never go to Sunday school.
60 per cent never attend Sunday evening service.
70 per cent never give to missions.
80 per cent never go to prayer meeting.
90 per cent never have family worship.
95 per cent never win a soul to Christ.

The cause for this pitiful condition—and it is getting worse every year—lies in the neglect and disobedience to God's command about being filled with His Spirit.

Dr. Lee Roberson tells of riding into Birmingham one day with the friend who officiated at his wedding, Dr. C. B. Miller. The latter had one of those huge, fancy LaSalle automobiles, so popular in that day. Yet the motor was sluggish and the car seemed to have no power at all. Dr. Miller couldn't imagine what was wrong and he complained constantly all the way into Birmingham.

Suddenly, just as they were about in the center of the city, Dr. Miller turned to his illustrious passenger and exclaimed, "What do you think of that! I still have the car in second gear!"

Most churches today are in second gear. By and large they have ignored the blessed Holy Spirit and, as a result, they are miserably suffering the consequences in barrenness, fruitlessness and powerlessness.

Spurgeon was discussing this problem one day and he said:

> Have you ever read *The Ancient Mariner*? I daresay you thought it one of the strangest imaginations ever put together, especially that part where the old mariner represents the corpses of dead men rising up to man the ship. Dead men pulling the ropes, dead men at the oars, dead men steering, dead men spreading the sails! I thought, *What a strange idea!* And yet I have lived to see that. I have gone into churches where there was a dead man in the pulpit, a dead man reading the notices, a dead man rendering the solos, a dead man taking the collection, and the pews were filled with the dead.

We need to join in the prayer of Isaac Watts:

> Come, Holy Spirit, Heavenly Dove, with all Thy quickening powers,
> Kindle a flame of sacred love in these cold hearts of ours.
>
> Look! How we grovel here below, fond of these earthly toys;
> Our souls can neither fly nor go to reach eternal joys.
>
> In vain we tune our formal songs; in vain we strive to rise;
> Hosannas languish on our tongues, and our devotion dies.
>
> Dear Lord, and shall we ever live at this poor dying rate,
> Our love so faint, so cold to Thee, and Thine to us so great?
>
> Come, Holy Spirit, Heavenly Dove, with all Thy quickening powers;
> Come shed abroad a Saviour's love, and that shall kindle ours.

B. Why Neglected?

One reason the Holy Spirit has been neglected in our day is summed up in the single word—*ignorance.* As someone has said, "The Holy Spirit is not overworked, He is overlooked." Many have ignored Him because they do not understand the teaching about Him and His power. When Paul asked the disciples at Ephesus if they had received the Holy Spirit, they replied, "We have not so much as heard whether there be any Holy Ghost" (Acts 19:2). We fear that most Christians in our day, if questioned about whether they were filled with the Spirit, would reply, "We have not so much as heard whether there be any fullness of the Holy Spirit."

Another cause of His neglect is *fear.* The subject has been so misused, so abused, so perverted by fanatics, many are afraid to mention it, study it, or seek it. In some circles, just to mention the *fullness,* or *anointing,* or *unction,* or even *baptism* of the Spirit is to conjure up thoughts of babbling in some unknown tongue, or rolling on the floor, or some other such wild and fanatical experience.

This ought not to be so! Light is what is needed and the only thing that will dispel the darkness of ignorance and error on the subject of the Holy Spirit and His fullness is to discover what the Bible actually says about it.

Still another reason for the neglect of this subject can be summed up with the familiar phrase, *"love of sin."* While few would express it as being *their* problem, many Christians had rather have some particular sin than God's power. We readily agree that one cannot have both, but we do not acquiesce for a moment that *any sin* is worth the loss of His power.

One religious writer tells of going fishing in a rowboat on a small lake with a man who served as first mate on a huge ocean liner. The preacher rowed out to a good fishing hole and they spent considerable time fishing. When the hour rolled around to head for land, the sailor suggested that he would like to row to shore, a rather novel experience for him in spite of his profession.

They changed seats and the sailor picked up the oars, confidently commencing to dip them into the water. He was not very proficient at it and after a while, since he could see land was no closer than when he first started, he suggested the minister take over once more.

They changed seats again and the first thing the preacher did was to *pull in the anchor,* then he rowed back to shore in a matter of minutes. Here was a professional sailor, a master of ocean liners, yet a complete failure in a small rowboat—*because he had forgotten to take in the anchor.* How many Christians have sins, like anchors, preventing them from making any significant progress in spiritual service for their Master!

Indifference is another reason for the neglect of our subject. Multitudinous are the number who seem to feel they can't be bothered, or they are not interested, or they are too busy with other things. A popular philosophy in our ranks today seems to be, "I am saved. Christ died for me. His cross, His blood, His life will keep me out of Hell. That is all I care about."

It is imperative that we change our attitude! As the late Dr. William Bell Riley said:

> We join absolutely with those enthusiastic students who believe that the church of the twentieth century needs to study the Book of Acts, revive its message, re-adopt its methods, and, above all, re-enthrone its dominating Spirit—the Holy Ghost Himself. If this Book teaches anything, it teaches the presidency of the Holy Spirit in the church of God, and until such time as the church is complete and "caught away," that presidency can only be ignored at the cost of the church itself, and to the unspeakable detriment of the cause of Christianity.

There are three timely thoughts in this passage we wish to emphasize.

I. A TERRIBLE EXCESS TO BE FORSAKEN!

Paul commands in verse 18: *"But be not drunk with wine, wherein is excess; but be filled with the Spirit."*

A. The "CURSE" of Spirits!

There is nothing in the wine cup but woe. How many are the

statements of Scripture emphasizing the anguish of strong drink and commanding the children of God to abstain completely. Proverbs 20:1 says, "Wine is a mocker, strong drink is raging: and whosoever is deceived thereby is not wise."

Proverbs 23:29-32 carries the message in even more vigorous language:

"Who hath woe? who hath sorrow? who hath contentions? who hath babbling? who hath wounds without cause? who hath redness of eyes? They that tarry long at the wine; they that go to seek mixed wine. Look not thou upon the wine when it is red, when it giveth his colour in the cup, when it moveth itself aright. At the last it biteth like a serpent, and stingeth like an adder."

Isaiah joined his voice in crying out against this curse. He declared:

"Woe unto them that rise up early in the morning, that they may follow strong drink; that continue until night, till wine inflame them!. . .Woe unto them that are mighty to drink wine, and men of strength to mingle strong drink: which justifieth the wicked for reward, and taketh away the righteousness of the righteous from him!"—Isa. 5:11,22,23.

Habakkuk 2:15 says: "Woe unto him that giveth his neighbour drink, that puttest thy bottle to him, and makest him drunken also, that thou mayest look on their nakedness!"

It's all like someone's definition of frog gin:

> "Drink a little,
> Hop a little,
> And then croak."

There is nothing of blessing or benefit in the booze bottle; quite the contrary, it is a blight and a burden. How can one miss its curse? The answer is so simple it is surprising so many are ignorant of it: *have nothing to do with it!* As Solomon said, "Look not upon it" (Prov. 23:31).

Nathanael P. Willis wrote:

> Look not upon the wine when it

> Is red within the cup;
> Stay not for pleasure when she fills
>   Her tempting beaker up;
> Though clear its depths, and rich its glow,
> A spell of sadness lurks below.
>
> They say 'tis pleasant on the lip,
>   And merry on the brain;
> They say it stirs the sluggish blood,
>   And dulls the tooth of pain.
> Aye, but within its gloomy deeps
> A stinging serpent unseen sleeps.
>
> Its rosy lights will turn to fire,
>   Its coolness change to thirst;
> And by its mirth within the brim
>   A sleepless worm is nursed.
> There's not a bubble at the brim
> That does not carry food to him.
>
> Then dash the burning cup aside
>   And spill its purple wine;
> Take not its madness to thy lips—
>   Let not its curse be thine.
> 'Tis red and rich, but grief and woe
> Are hid those rosy depths below.

In other words, have as much sense as the hog Mr. Thompson, superintendent of Georgia's anti-saloon league in pre-prohibition days, told about. It seems he had a friend who owned a large saw mill in South Georgia. Every payday he would bring a keg of beer and demijohn of corn whiskey, letting the men help themselves. One day some of the hands, trying to be funny, put a quantity of the liquor in the trough of an old sow that lived around the sawmill. To their delight, she swigged it up in nothing flat, then amused the crowd with her antics as she staggered around the premises. Eventually she made it to a mud puddle, burrowed herself in, and slept it off.

When the next payday rolled around, the men, thinking they would have more fun, dumped booze into her feeder again. The sow waddled up, sniffed, then put her long snout underneath the trough and overturned it. She then stuck her head high in the air and marched off, curly little tail bouncing behind.

Thompson claimed that the owner of the mill, standing nearby, picked up an axe and burst both the beer keg and the whiskey demijohn. When the hired hands remonstrated with him over his action, he replied, "I don't mean to let a common, razorback, piney woods sow have more sense than I have. I'll never take another drink as long as I live." And Thompson says he never did.

Total abstinence is the only way to avoid the curse of the wine cup.

B. The "COMPARISON" of the Spirit!

What did Paul mean when he told the Ephesians not to be drunk with wine? Was he teaching moderation, intimating it would be all right for them to booze it up a little, just as long as they didn't go to excess? **Of course not!** The Holy Spirit of God, who inspired Paul to write these words, couldn't be that irrational—even if a few red-nosed winebibbers are!

It is only when one has drunk *to excess* that he is controlled by a spirit foreign to himself, the spirit of alcohol. He *does* things, he *says* things, and he *goes* places he otherwise wouldn't. He is not himself!

Roger and Margaret Thompson were boozing it up at a California tavern in the wee hours of the morning. They had a disagreement. Mrs. Thompson left in her car and Mr. Thompson followed in his. Driving into a muddy field next to the saloon, they started ramming each other's automobiles until both cars—a Dodge and a Chevrolet—were totaled. They certainly would not have done that had they been in their right minds.

In Daytona Beach, Florida, the city dog warden and superintendent of the Humane Society spent a day of beer drinking, then murdered his wife by jabbing into her stomach two shots of an anesthetic which he kept to kill small kittens and dogs. He told State's Attorney W. W. Judge that his wife was the "best woman in the world" and he had no idea why he murdered her. Said the killer, Walter R. Hoffman, "I can't understand any of this. I have been begging the Lord to give me an answer as to why I did it." The answer lies in the fact that he was controlled by a spirit foreign to himself, the demon spirit of alcohol.

Up in Wisconsin, Wilfred and Gladys Jackson had a family drinking party in their own home, then Wilfred decided he wanted to go out to a bar. She wanted to go to the tavern also, but he didn't want to take the children. A drunken argument followed. When he went out and got into the car, she told him she was going to place their baby, Jacqueline, in the driveway behind the car to prevent his leaving. She did—and he backed over the baby, killing her instantly. Why? They were both filled with a spirit foreign to themselves.

Down in Florida, twenty-year-old Emmett Cline had been "drinking heavily" with friends while attending drag races at the Hollywood Speedway. On a dare, he drove his automobile out on the dragstrip and started speeding the wrong way up the strip toward two racing youngsters who had just left the starting line. He got his car up to about ninety miles per hour, then applied his brakes. Apparently they locked and his car slid sideways into the wall near the crowded starting line. When he slammed into the concrete wall he not only injured himself but, far more tragically, killed a 13-year-old youth from Ft. Lauderdale. Cline was controlled by a spirit foreign to himself.

Did you know that more than half the murders committed every year in the city of Dallas are the result of arguments started in bars? We suppose this is typical of other major cities as well. It is part of the "contentions" and "wounds without cause" which come about when individuals are controlled by this spirit foreign to themselves, the evil spirit of alcohol. No doubt all the people described above were pretty decent people when they were sober. But under the curse of alcohol, controlled by this demon, they committed demonical acts.

Paul is simply pleading for Christians to be controlled by the Holy Spirit rather than an evil spirit, such as the spirit of wine. They, too, will *do* things, *say* things, and *go* places they would not apart from being under the control of God's Spirit. Unlike the winebibbers, however, their words and actions will be dominated by "a sound mind" (II Tim. 1:7). You will recall that the disciples at Pentecost, filled with the Holy Spirit, were accused of being "full of new wine" (Acts 2:12-21).

II. A TREMENDOUS EXHORTATION TO BE FOLLOWED!

How sublime are these five words: *"be filled with the Spirit."* Here is the true secret in service for any child of God. We, being human, look to talents, finances, human abilities and other matters, yet none of these is the key.

A professor of elocution went to hear Bishop Simpson preach in London's Memorial Hall years ago. The clergyman preached quietly, calmly and nondramatically, but with such power that at the conclusion of the address the entire audience rose to its feet as one—then, after a moment or two, dropped back into the seats.

A friend of the professor's, who knew he had gone to the meeting just to criticize, approached him later and inquired, "What did you think of the bishop's elocution?"

"Elocution!" he exclaimed. "That man doesn't need elocution! He has the Holy Spirit!"

That was the truth. We do not need preachers today like those described in Jude 19, who were "sensual, not having the Spirit." The word "sensual" there is the same one translated "natural" in I Corinthians 2:14. It simply refers to teaching and preaching with only natural, human abilities. That is not the kind of service Paul wanted for the Ephesians. He wanted their ministry, like his, to be "in demonstration of the Spirit and of power" (I Cor. 2:4).

A. What Does It Mean to Be Filled?

It means what it says! Why all the confusion, all the error, all the ignorance, all the controversy about it? E. M. Bounds quoted a renowned Scotsman as describing unction:

> There is sometimes that in preaching which cannot be ascribed either to matter or expression and which cannot be described or discerned as to whence it cometh; yet with a sweet violence it pierceth into the heart and affections, and comes immediately from the Lord. But if there be any way to obtain such a thing, it is by the heavenly disposition of the speaker.

We are not primarily interested in the *terminology* with which the experience is ascribed by men, although we prefer biblical language. Here is a plain command to be "filled with the Spirit," yet men spend hours trying to explain what being "filled" is, or, in some cases, explaining it away.

Sometimes Christians, when the matter of the Holy Spirit's fullness is brought up, will say, "You don't need more of the Holy Spirit; He needs more of you!" We will not quibble about the fact that the Holy Spirit *does* need more of the Christian. He wants a deeper commitment, a more complete surrender to Him. Yet that is begging the issue. When an automobile needs gas do you say, "The car doesn't need any more gas; the gas needs more of the car"? Of course not. If language means anything, to "fill" is to put more in!

Another argues, "The word 'filled' means 'controlled.' When Paul commanded the Ephesians to be filled with the Spirit, he was merely saying that the Holy Spirit should control them." While we would not for a moment deny that one who is *filled* with the Spirit will, beyond disputation, be *controlled* by the Spirit, that is not the idea of the command. The Greek word Paul used is *pleroo*. James Strong says it is from *pleres* (replete, covered over), and means *"to make replete, i.e. (lit.) to cram* (a net), *level* up (a hollow), or (fig.) to *furnish* (or *imbue, diffuse, influence*), *satisfy, execute* (an office), finish (a period or task), verify (or *coincide* with a prediction), etc." W. E. Vine agrees, saying it denotes "to make full, to fill to the full."

Sometimes Christians try to explain away the force of this command in Ephesians 5:18 by saying, "You can't have more of a 'person' and the Holy Spirit is a Person." We would not deny for a moment the personality of the Holy Spirit, but, again, that is begging the issue. These matters cannot be comprehended clearly with human terminology. If the Holy Spirit is a Person, and He is, *how can more than one Christian have Him?*

Here is a congregation of thirty saved people, all with the blessed Holy Spirit dwelling within. In come ten unconverted sinners; they hear the Gospel and get saved. According to the human understanding of *person,* how could these ten receive the Holy Spirit when the other thirty already have Him? Don't you see, those who try to explain away the fullness of the Holy Spirit in this manner are confusing the Person with a physical form. A human personality is confined within a body; the Holy Spirit has no such limitation. A personality not restricted to one body is not limited in giving "more" to another. The fact that the Holy Spirit can be received in "more" or in "less" is shown from the words of John the Baptist about Christ, "For he whom God hath sent speaketh the words of God: for God giveth not the Spirit **by measure** unto him" (John 3:34). The inference is that the Holy Spirit is given "by measure" to others.

The expression "be filled" is in the present tense and, in the Greek, this speaks of continuous action. Paul was saying, "Be continuously filled to the overflowing with the Holy Spirit of God." He meant for this to be an every day realization, not some occasional emotional experience at the climax of a church service.

Dr. Bob Wells quotes the British Bible teacher, Rev. W. W. Martin, in a message on the Holy Spirit at an English Keswick in 1938: "The filling of the Holy Spirit is a crisis which becomes a process." This crisis is simply a time of surrender, a full yieldedness to God, a climactic laying everything on the altar of submission to Jesus Christ. This does not necessarily mean an emotional experience, although any kind of dedication to God would contain some emotion, surely.

The greatest and most effective servants of God down through the ages have claimed to have had this crisis filling of the Holy Spirit. We think of Jonathan Edwards, John Wesley, A. T. Pierson, J. Wilbur Chapman, R. A. Torrey, Dwight L. Moody and Charles Finney. The latter called it "highly criminal" for a servant of God *not* to be filled with the Holy Spirit. We recall hearing the late Charles E. Fuller tell of the crisis experience of his filling, which so overwhelmed him he eventually had to "ask the Lord to shut the glory off."

Ah, no wonder the little girl, after listening to her mother read some Bible stories, cried out, "Oh, Mommie, God must have been exciting then!" The truth of the matter is, He wants to be just as exciting in our day, but there are so few empty vessels waiting and willing for Him to fill.

B. Why Do We Need to Be Filled?

The answer is obvious: *for power in service!* The last thing our Lord told His disciples before returning to Glory was, "But ye shall receive power, after that the Holy Ghost is come upon you: **AND YE SHALL BE WITNESSES UNTO ME** both in Jerusalem, and in all Judaea, and in Samaria, and unto the uttermost part of the earth" (Acts 1:8).

The subject of the fullness of the Holy Spirit is never mentioned in either the Old or New Testament apart from testimony or service. Quite frankly, there can be no *useful* service or *effective* testimony apart from His fullness. Wallie Criswell tells of visiting, with his wife, Spurgeon's former church in London and listening to the preacher read his sermon word-for-word. It was a boring experience and two elderly men immediately behind the Criswells commenced a conversation. One asked the other if he had ever heard Spurgeon preach.

"Yes, many times. He was my pastor."

The first man persisted, "What was it like? How did he preach?"

The elderly saint responded, "It is hard for me to describe, but if I could say it without reflecting on my present pastor, I'd put it like this: when I come to church now it seems that I just hear a lecture on the Bible; but when Spurgeon preached, **there was power in it.**" That is the difference between sermons in the fullness of the Holy Spirit and sermons apart from it.

If any read these lines who think they are above being filled with the Spirit, recall how our example, the Lord Jesus Christ, was filled. Listen to some of the statements of Luke 4. In verse 1 we read, "And Jesus being full of the Holy Ghost. . .was led by the Spirit. . . ." Verse 14 tells us, "And Jesus returned in the power of the Spirit. . . ." It says in verse 18 that He applied Isaiah's prophecy to Himself, "The Spirit of the Lord is upon me, because he hath anointed me. . . ."

No wonder "all bare him witness, and wondered at the

gracious words which proceeded out of his mouth" (vs. 22), and "they were astonished at his doctrine: for his word was with power" (vs. 32). It seems the people of our Lord's day were not accustomed to hearing the Word of God preached with power. Sadly, neither are the majority in our day.

"Be filled with the Spirit." This is a command and a blessing for every believer, not merely pastors and evangelists. Each Christian, in his own particular sphere of service, needs the fullness of the Holy Spirit. Dr. Robert G. Lee points out that a foundryman adds seven-tenths of one per cent chromium to low carbon steel and it increases the tensile strength of that metal from fifty-five thousand pounds to the square inch to one hundred thousand pounds—nearly double. So our service, when the fullness of the Holy Spirit has been added, is that much more powerful and effective.

Yet some think that because Finney, Wesley, Moody and others had an experience with the Holy Spirit and became mighty evangelists, preaching to great multitudes, all who are filled will become the same, regardless of their calling. The passage in I Corinthians 12:4-11, dealing with the gifts of the Holy Spirit, shows how foolish and baseless is such a conclusion. God does not want us all to be evangelists, but He does desire all to be filled with His Spirit. He does not want us all to be pastors, but He wants every Christian to experience the fullness of the Holy Spirit in his or her particular sphere of service.

What is your principal calling? Is it to be a mother? Then you need the fullness of the Holy Spirit to be a better mother. Is it to be a businessman? Then you need the fullness of the Holy Spirit to be the kind of honest, effective, useful businessman your community needs. The fullness of the Holy Spirit is necessary for teaching Sunday school classes, directing youth activities, singing in the choir, even ushering at the services of the church.

C. Can We Be Filled? You and I Today?

We recall listening to Dr. Robert J. Wells, with great pleasure and profit, bring a message on this subject at the 1945 Sword of the Lord Conference on Evangelism at Winona Lake, Indiana. He set forth six logical conclusions regarding the matter: (1) *It is a command of God's.* It is not Paul's command, nor the command of any other mortal. (2) *God expects obedience to His commands.* He never gives meaningless instructions. (3) *God would never demand obedience to a command impossible to obey.* Since God has commanded us to be filled, it is a possibility for us. (4) *We should obey God's command,* earnestly seeking to fulfill it. (5) *We should know whether or not we are filled,* just as we know whether or not we are saved. (6) *We should thank Him for filling us,* even as we thank Him for saving us.

So it is not a question of *can we,* but **will we?** God is ready when we are ready.

J. Wilbur Chapman, the noted Presbyterian evangelist, gave his testimony in these words:

> I had been struggling for five years. I had had visions of His power and glimpses of what I might be if I were "filled with the Holy Spirit"; but all this time, like the disciples at Ephesus, there was a great lacking. At last I reached the place where I felt that I was willing to make a surrender. I reached it by the path marked out by one who said, "If you are not ready to surrender everything to God, are you ready to say, 'I am willing to be made willing about everything'? That seemed easy, and alone before God I simply said, "I am now willing."
>
> Then He made the way easy. He brought before me my ambition, then my personal ease, then my home, then other things came to me, and I simply said, "I will give them up." At last all my will was surrendered about everything. Then, without any emotion, I said, "My Father, I now claim from Thee the infilling of the Holy Spirit." From that moment to this He has been a living reality.

III. A THREEFOLD EXPRESSION TO BE FOUND!

What are the results of being filled with the Spirit of God? How will His fullness be manifested in the life of the believer?

A. An Expression of Praise

Paul said, in verse 19: *"Speaking to yourselves in psalms and hymns and spiritual songs, singing and making melody in your heart to the Lord."*

Ingrates are not Spirit-filled. During the Cuban missile crisis a pastor of a church on the Atlantic Coast called for an evening of special prayer. The church auditorium, to his pleasant surprise, was packed and jammed. Later, when the crisis had abated, he felt constrained to request another special service, this one of praise to God for answered prayer. He was even more amazed when only a handful of people responded.

What was the explanation? Carnal Christians, not filled with the Spirit of God, had no note of praise. Only those who were under the dominion of the Holy Spirit wanted to express praise to God for what He had done.

You see, Spirit-filled Christians are happy, joyful, praising Christians. The early church was described in Acts 2:46,47: "And they, continuing daily with one accord in the temple, and breaking bread from house to house, did eat their meat with gladness and singleness of heart, Praising God, and having favour with all the people. . . ." When Paul described the fruit of the Spirit, he started: "But the fruit of the Spirit is love, joy. . ." (Gal. 5:22).

During an evangelistic crusade one time, the host minister picked up the guest speaker to take him to an appointment. He politely, and probably only formally, inquired, "How are you today?"

The evangelist responded, "Oh, I am just loaded down!"

Thinking he referred to problems, the preacher asked, "Do you want to tell me about it?"

Then the happy evangelist triumphantly enthused, "He daily loadeth me with benefits" (Ps. 68:19)! The realization of these benefits, then praising God for them, is part of the fruit of His fullness.

Do you remember the battle which the people of Judah won with a song? The account is in II Chronicles 20 and tells how King Jehoshaphat appointed singers unto the Lord who "should praise the beauty of holiness." They went ahead of the army, shouting, "Praise the Lord; for his mercy endureth for ever." It was "when they began to sing and praise," we are told, the Lord undertook for them and they won the battle.

Paul tells us that this praise is to be in the form of "singing and making melody in your heart." Those without musical ability are not exempted from this fruit. In fact, some who couldn't carry the proverbial tune in a bucket can rejoice the most in heart, making the melody that is sweetest to divine ears.

And that is what it is all about. Paul tells us it is "to the Lord."

Should it be hard to praise Him? Not for one who has experienced redemption. W. B. Riley tells of an American army entering a small French village during World War I, after driving out the Germans. The remaining inhabitants rushed out to greet them singing, dancing, sobbing, and acting in general like people who were beside themselves. When one of the American officers commented, "I am glad to help these people, but I don't see why they should act so crazy about it," and aged lady spoke up, saying, "Ah, M'sieur, that is because you don't know what you saved us from."

Since we know—at least in part—what our Lord has saved us from in this life and the life to come, how excited and thrilled we ought to be, and how profuse should be the praise from our lips and the melody in our hearts!

No wonder John Newton wrote:

> Joy is a fruit that will not grow
> In nature's barren soil;
> All we can boast till Christ we know,
> Is vanity and toil.
> But where the Lord has planted grace,
> And made His glories known;
> There fruits of heavenly joy and peace
> Are found, and there alone.

B. An Expression of Thanksgiving

Paul continues with the manifestations of the Spirit's filling, saying, *"Giving thanks always for all things unto God and the Father in the name of our Lord Jesus Christ"* (vs. 20). He answers five questions here about a single phase of our responsibility to God.

What? *"Giving thanks."*
When? *"Always."*
For what? *"For all things."*
To whom? *"Unto God and the Father."*
How? *"In the name of our Lord Jesus Christ."*

How little of thankfulness we see today in the professing church. The story of the ten lepers is far too often true in the twentieth century. After our Lord had healed the ten, only one, a Samaritan, returned to give thanks (Luke 17:12-19). You might say there were nine carnal Christians and only one who was Spirit-filled.

C. An Expression of Humility

The third manifestation of the Holy Spirit's fullness in a believer's life, which Paul mentions, is humility. In verse 21 he said, *"Submitting yourselves one to another in the fear of God."* Thanksgiving and humility are associated together since pride is incompatible to a thankful heart. Henry Ward Beecher once said, "Pride slays thanksgiving, but an humble mind is the soil out of which thanks naturally grows. A proud man is seldom a grateful man, for he never thinks he gets as much as he deserves."

A Spirit-filled Christian will realize that anything and everything he is able to accomplish is the direct result of the Holy Spirit's working, not any ability of his own. First Peter 5:5 tells us, "Likewise, ye younger, submit yourselves unto the elder. Yea, all of you be subject one to another, and be clothed with humility: for God resisteth the proud, and giveth grace to the humble."

A Spirit-filled Christian does not seek the preeminence. In the language of Philippians 2:3, "Let nothing be done through strife or vain glory; but in lowliness of mind let each esteem other better than themselves."

Are you a Spirit-filled Christian? Do you have the evidences in your life? Are you filled with praise? Are you abounding with thanksgiving? Are you clothed with humility?

Conclusion

If one were to ask what we considered the most important prerequisite to His fullness, we would reply in the words of Acts 5:32, "And we are witnesses of these things; and so is also the Holy Ghost, **whom God hath given to them that obey him.**" Disobedient Christians need not expect to be filled with the Holy Spirit.

During some of the darkest days of the Civil War, General Grant and his army, along with a fleet of gunboats under Commodore Foote, besieged Fort Donaldson. There was strong resistance but, after four days of fierce fighting, the rebels hoisted a white flag and asked for terms.

General Grant responded, "There are no terms other than unconditional surrender."

So, today, Christians seeking to be filled with the Holy Spirit of God cannot expect success in flying flags of truce. Only unconditional surrender to the Word and will of God will result in His fullness.

> Come, O Breath! Be this the hour!
> Come, O Breath of God, with power,
> Ere the depths of Hell devour
> Those who sleep in sin!
>
> Come, O Breath! Thy might we crave!
> Hear our cry! Make haste to save!
> Speak and call them from their grave!
> Bid new life begin.

God's Ideal Marriage

Wives, submit yourselves unto your own husbands, as unto the Lord.

For the husband is the head of the wife, even as Christ is the head of the church: and he is the saviour of the body.

Therefore as the church is subject unto Christ, so let the wives be to their own husbands in every thing.

Husbands, love your wives, even as Christ also loved the church, and gave himself for it;

That he might sanctify and cleanse it with the washing of water by the word,

That he might present it to himself a glorious church, not having spot, or wrinkle, or any such thing; but that it should be holy and without blemish.

So ought men to love their wives as their own bodies. He that loveth his wife loveth himself.

For no man ever yet hated his own flesh; but nourisheth and cherisheth it, even as the Lord the church:

For we are members of his body, of his flesh, and of his bones.

For this cause shall a man leave his father and mother, and shall be joined unto his wife, and they two shall be one flesh.

This is a great mystery: but I speak concerning Christ and the church.

Nevertheless let every one of you in particular so love his wife even as himself; and the wife see that she reverence her husband.—Ephesians 5:22-33.

Dr. Charles Thompson told of an old preacher who used to introduce his marriage ceremony with the words: "John, matrimony is a blessing to a few, a curse to many, and an uncertainty to us all. John, will you venture?"

It is natural to want to venture. God said, "Whosoever findeth a wife findeth a good thing, and obtaineth favour of the Lord" (Prov. 18:22). He said again, "Marriage is honourable in all. . ." (Heb. 13:4).

In the United States during 1975, 4,200,000 people ventured forth in 2,100,000 marriages. However, for the first time in the history of this great nation, divorces numbered in excess of one million and 2,052,000 men and women went their separate ways via the divorce courts, previous promises of "till death do us part" notwithstanding. This means approximately one divorce—which psychologist Dr. Sonya Kiel-Friedman defines as "the only game in which everybody can turn out to be a loser"—for every two marriages. It contrasts with about one divorce for every four marriages in 1950 (using round figures: 1,667,200 marriages; 385,000 divorces), one for every seven marriages in 1925 (1,188,300 marriages; 175,000 divorces), and one divorce for every thirteen marriages at the turn of the century (909,000 marriages; 55,750 divorces). One does not need to be a prophet nor a son of a prophet to see that things are getting progressively worse with each passing year.

We can sympathize with the Los Angeles magistrate who asked to be transferred from a divorce court, saying he was fed up with this type of case. Judge R. J. Dunne explained to the *Los Angeles Examiner:* "I am against divorce. I am against parents so unmindful of their duties and obligations to their children that they place their own selfish interests before their children's happiness. I am against persons who enter marriage lightly and expect to escape just as easily."

We have not yet reached the stage of the Balanta tribe in Africa, where a bride was compelled to remain married only until her wedding gown was worn out—and if she wanted a divorce before that time, all she needed do was rip up the bridal garment!

It has been fashionable to look askance down our snobbish noses at France's "grave injuries" divorce grounds, allowing dissolution for such immature matters as a husband identifying the murderer on the title page of his wife's mystery books, or a wife being forced to keep time with a flyswatter while her husband played his bagpipes. Yet are we much—if any—different?

In Hollywood, a woman divorced her husband because he left her alone when company came, going off to his room to play with his electric trains. In Iowa, a preacher divorced his wife of thirty-one years because she embarrassed him, walking out of church just as he began his sermons. In Indiana, one couple requested dissolution of their marriage because one wanted the bedroom window partly open and the other wanted it completely closed. Another wanted a divorce because they had an argument over whose father to visit on Father's Day, ending up with each visiting his own. In Philadelphia, a woman filed for divorce because, when her mouth was wired shut due to a fractured jaw, her husband nagged her and she couldn't talk back. A nineteen-year-old flaunter of the sanctity of the home in the author's area wanted the judge to sever her marriage bond because her husband insisted she read the Bible, wear skirts instead of blue jeans, and attend church. In this case, Circuit Judge John J. Niblack refused the petition, ruling the husband was "well within his rights on all three points."

Yes, how trivial are the grounds on which most divorces are granted. Incompatibility, irreconcilable differences and other indefinable terms cover the most flimsy excuse like a wet blanket. In fact, Aldous Huxley, not a Christian in any sense of the word, suggests in his *Brave New World:*

> In a few years, no doubt, marriage licenses will be sold like dog licenses, good for a period of twelve months, with no law against changing dogs or keeping more than one animal at a time. As political and economic freedom diminishes, sexual freedom tends compensatingly to increase.

Even the so-called marriage experts find themselves marching into divorce courts with increasing frequency. The head of a scientific marriage center in Denver, who makes money telling others how to have happy homes, was embarrassed when her husband of twenty-two years filed suit for divorce, charging she had inflicted "great mental suffering through extreme and repeated cruelty." She immediately filed a cross-complaint charging him with the same. The red-faced folks at the marriage counseling agency passed it off by saying the two were mismated and never should have married in the first place.

The noted newspaper advice columnist, Ann Landers, is another case in point. Before us as we dictate these lines is a long feature article taken from a metropolitan newspaper. It is titled "Down-to-Earth Advice on Marriages Made in Heaven" and was written by Ann Landers. In her regular column she frequently referred to happiness in marriage and boasted how happy was her own marriage. However, with great embarrassment, she was forced to publicly announce that her thirty-six-year marriage to Jules W. Lederer was "over" and a divorce had been filed.

Yet God never intended anyone to *want* or *need* a divorce. He expects all of us to have happy homes and successful marriages— a sample of what Glory will be like. As another has said, "When a home is ruled by Christ, angels might be asked to stay all night and they would not find themselves out of their element." Paul, in this passage, is telling how it can be attained.

The Bible has the answer to everything practical. God never asks anything of anyone but what He explains how it can be accomplished. When He commands men to be saved, He explains exactly how forgiveness of sins may be received. When He requests service, He tells us how to effectively perform it. And when He wants His children to experience happily married lives, He carefully explains how this can be achieved. No Christian ought ever be in the dark concerning the will of God.

So that none may misunderstand his instructions about a happy home, Paul uses the simplest form of teaching in this passage: the object lesson. Christ and the church are illustrated as the perfect pattern.

It should be understood that the passage takes for granted both husband and wife are born-again Christians. This advice is not for communists, who glory in divorce. The *People's Daily* in China quotes a communist jurist, gloating over the rise in China's divorce rate, as saying: "Marriage is too often wrongly regarded as a result of love rather than a union founded on a common political understanding in mutual endeavor in building up socialism. Love for love's sake is entirely a bourgeois concept." We would not expect Christ-rejecting, atheistic communists to be helped by this study.

The truth of the matter is that the people of God are the best marriage risks. Over a quarter of a century ago the American Institute of Family Relations took a survey and discovered that the most successful marriages were enjoyed by those couples *actively engaged* in a local church. The second most successful group involved those who have continued attending Sunday school and church into their adult years, not dropping out with the passing of youth. Reports such as these are certainly not surprising since the people of God understand that marriage is not something to try out to see if it works—**it is for keeps!** As someone has said, "Marriage is like a violin. After the beautiful music is over, the strings are still attached." The Christian understands this when he takes his vows, no matter whether "for better or for worse."

God planned marriage to be a sample of what Heaven will be like. What Robert Browning described of a kiss could be used to explain a Christian marriage:

All the breath and the bloom of the year in the bag of one bee;
All the wonder and wealth of the mine in the heart of one gem;
In the core of one pearl all the shade and the shine of the sea;
Breath and bloom, shade and shine—wonder, wealth, and—how far above them—
Truth that's brighter than gem,
Trust that's purer than pearl,—
Brightest truth, purest trust in the universe—all were for me
In the kiss of one girl!

I. GOD'S IDEAL WIFE!
Vss. 22-24

Jeremy Taylor said, "A good wife is Heaven's last, best gift to man, her voice his sweetest music, her smiles his brightest day, her lips his faithful counselors; and her prayers the ablest advocate of Heaven's blessing on his head."

To these mates Paul demanded:

"Wives, submit yourselves unto your own husbands, as unto

278 / SAVED BY GRACE . . . FOR SERVICE!

the Lord. For the husband is the head of the wife, even as Christ is the head of the church: and he is the saviour of the body. Therefore as the church is subject unto Christ, so let the wives be to their own husbands in every thing."

Someone has quaintly offered this thought:

> A good wife should be like three things which three things she should not be like. 1. She should be like a snail, to keep within her house, but she shall not be like the snail to carry all she has upon her back. 2. She should be like an echo, to speak when spoken to, but she should not be like an echo, always to have the last word. 3. She should be like the town clock, always to keep time and regularity, but she should not be like a town clock, speaking so loud all the town may hear her.

A. The Command

Wives are to submit to their husbands in exactly the same manner as they would if their husbands were God! Satan and his forces of Hell have led wives to seek and demand equality with husbands. *It is of the pit!* This wrong leads to trouble, grief, heartache, and untold suffering. *Never once* has it resulted in a happy home!

What if a Christian wife is married to an unconverted husband? The Bible says she can win him to Christ if she means business in this area of submission! It is a strange, startling truth that believing wives can either save or damn unbelieving husbands through their response in this very area. First Peter 3:1,2 says plainly: "Likewise, ye wives, be in subjection to your own husbands; that, if any obey not the word, they also may without the word be won by the conversation of the wives; While they behold your chaste conversation coupled with fear."

The clear conclusion is that nagging, bossy, rebellious wives send their husbands to Hell. Some women remind us of the vagabond in England who, tired and hungry, found himself at a roadside inn which was identified by its sign as "George & the Dragon." He banged on the front door and when the innkeeper's wife stuck her head out an upstairs window, the traveler inquired, "Could you spare a poor man something to eat?"

She looked at his shabby appearance, shouted **"No!"** and slammed the window.

The vagabond banged on the door the second time. Again the window went up, the head came out, and the woman screamed, "What now?"

"Do you suppose," he inquired hopefully, "that I might have a word with George?"

Unfortunately, some Christian women talk so nice in church but so abusive at home. Someone has suggested that it is utterly impossible to understand how much or how suddenly a human voice can change until he hears a woman stop scolding her husband to answer the telephone.

True, many women nag because they are trying to improve their husbands—they had rather be called expeditors than naggers. However, it has been humorously pointed out that the only time a woman ever really succeeds in changing a male is when he is in diapers. *It rarely is accomplished after a marriage ceremony!* One fellow even got a divorce in Las Vegas because his second wife had been insisting he attend seances, then claimed he must obey her orders since she was getting instructions from his first wife!

This is not the way to win an unconverted husband, however. As Peter explained through the Holy Spirit, unconverted husbands **can** be won by subjection and obedience.

D. L. Moody tells of a woman who came to him with a request to pray for her husband. Moody agreed, but said, "First, tell me about him." The woman responded with a narration explaining how she was a church member, was present every time the doors were open, but her husband wouldn't come near the church.

Moody quietly studied the lady for a moment, then requested permission to ask some very personal questions. When she consented, he inquired, "Do you ever become irritable and say hard or harsh things to your husband?"

"Yes, I'm afraid I'm guilty of that."

"Do you ever become angry and say harsh things to your servants, to your children, or to your neighbors?"

Dejectedly, she hung her head and acknowledged, "Yes, Sir;

I'm afraid I'm guilty of that, too."

Moody said, "Then perhaps I had better pray for you, first." Tearfully she agreed and together they went to their knees as first Moody and then she prayed for God to forgive her and strengthen her Christian testimony in the home.

A week later she was back with rejoicing, telling Moody how she had gone home and apologized, first to her husband, then to her children, then to the servants, and finally to the neighbors. They all prayed and cried together and the outcome was that the husband turned to God for salvation.

Nagging, critical, bossy wives find it exceedingly difficult to win—or even witness to—unconverted husbands. Not so, those who follow God's blueprint.

There is an amazing illustration of this beautiful truth in the *Autobiography of George Muller*. Writing in his journal during 1835, he recorded this incident:

> March 18. This afternoon we arrived at Basle, where we were very kindly received by the brethren.—During my stay there I attended one day a meeting at which a venerable pious clergyman expounded the Greek New Testament to several brethren, who purposed to give themselves to missionary service. The passage to which this dear aged brother had them come, in the original of the New Testament, was I Peter 3:1,2, which in our English translation reads thus: *"Likewise, ye wives, be in subjection to your own husbands; that, if any obey not the Word, they also may without the Word be won by the conversation of the wives; while they behold your chaste conversation coupled with fear."*
>
> After this aged brother had expounded the passage, he related a circumstance which had occurred in his own days, and under his own eyes at Basle, which has appeared to me so encouraging for those children of God who have unbelieving relatives, and especially for sisters in the Lord who have unbelieving husbands; and which at the same time is such a beautiful illustration of I Peter 3:1, that I judge it desirable to insert the narrative of this fact here. I will do so as exactly as I remember it.—
>
> There lived at Basle an opulent citizen, whose wife was a believer, but he himself feared not the Lord. His practice was to spend his evenings in a wine-house, where he would often tarry till eleven, twelve, or even one o'clock. On such occasions his wife always used to send her servants to bed, and sat up herself to await the return of her husband. When at last he came, she used to receive him most kindly, never reproach him in the least either at the time or afterwards, nor complain at all on account of his late hours, by which she was kept from reasonable rest. Moreover, if it should be needful to assist him in undressing himself, when he had drunk to ex-

cess, she would do this also in a very kind and meek way. Thus it went on for a long time.

One evening, this gentleman was again, as usual, in a wine-house, and having tarried there with his merry companions till midnight, he said to them: "I bet that if we go to my house, we will find my wife sitting up and waiting for me, and she herself will come to the door and receive us very kindly; and if I ask her to prepare us a supper, she will do it at once without the least murmur, or unkind expression, or look." His companions in sin did not believe his statement. At last, however, after some more conversation about this strange statement (as it appeared to them), it was agreed that they would all go to see this kind wife.

Accordingly they went, and, after they had knocked, found the door immediately opened by the lady herself, and they were all courteously and kindly received by her. The party having entered, the master of the house asked his wife to prepare supper for them, which she, in the meekest way, at once agreed to do; and, after awhile, supper was served by herself without the least sign of dissatisfaction, or murmur, or complaint.

Having now prepared all for the company, she retired from the party to her room. When she left the party, one of the gentlemen said: "What a wicked and cruel man you are, thus to torment so kind a wife." He then took his hat and stick, and, without touching a morsel of the supper, went away. Another made a similar remark, and left, without touching the supper. Thus one after another left, till they were all gone, without tasting the supper.

The master of the house was now left alone, and the Spirit of God brought before him all his dreadful wickedness, and especially his great sins toward his wife; and the party had not left the house half and hour, before he went to his wife's room, requesting her to pray for him, told her that he felt himself a great sinner, and asked her forgiveness for all his behaviour towards her. From that time he became a disciple of the Lord Jesus.

Observe here, dear reader, the following points in particular, which I affectionately commend to your consideration: (1) The wife acted in accordance with I Peter 3:1. She kept her place as being in subjection, and the Lord owned it. (2) She reproached not her husband, but meekly and kindly served him when he used to come home. (3) She did not allow the servants to sit up for their master, but sat up herself, thus honouring him as her head and superior, and concealed also, as far as she was able, her husband's shame from the servants. (4) In all probability a part of those hours, during which she had to sit up, was spent in prayer for her husband, or in reading the Word of God, to gather fresh strength for all the trials connected with her position. (5) Be not discouraged if you have to suffer from unconverted relatives. Perhaps very shortly the Lord may give you the desire of your heart, and answer your prayer for them; but in the meantime seek to commend the truth, not by reproaching them on account of their behaviour towards *you*, but by manifesting towards *them* the meekness, gentleness, and kindness of the Lord Jesus Christ.

Sometimes Christian women say, "This submission does not

mean obedience to the husband; it is only a mutual understanding." The *U.S. News and World Report* quoted the executive director of the family life department of the liberal National Council of Churches as advocating this position. The item referred to Rev. William Genne, discussing Paul's instruction for wives to be subject to husbands, and said: "While 'some Protestant churches stress the authority of the husband and father in the family' he added many others regard a partnership as 'a better working arrangement.' " But no one can come up with a "working arrangement" in the home better than the one ordained by Almighty God.

If there is any doubt as to whether the submission means obedience to the husband, listen to Genesis 3:16, where God said to the woman: "I will greatly multiply thy sorrow and thy conception; in sorrow thou shalt bring forth children; and thy desire shall be to thy husband, **and he shall rule over thee.**" Or consider Titus 2:4,5: "That they may teach the young women to be sober, to love their husbands, to love their children, to be discreet, chaste, keepers at home, good, **obedient to their own husbands, that the word of God be not blasphemed.**"

Sometimes foolish women, who do not want to obey the Bible anyway, ask silly questions like, "What if my husband wants me to go out and get drunk?" In the first place, if a wife follows the instructions about submission and obedience outlined in the Bible, in all probability her husband will respect her convictions. If she lives according to the high Bible standard for wives, there should be no problem.

On the other hand, if the husband is so degenerate that he will not respect his wife's spiritual convictions, the same rule would hold true as with commands regarding the Christian's responsibility to government. For example, Romans 13:1 says, "Let every soul be subject unto the higher powers. For there is no power but of God: the powers that be are ordained of God." Christians ought to be good citizens and obey the laws of the land. We believe a Christian is always safe to obey a clear command of the Bible, and trust the Lord to bring the result out right.

That is why Peter explained his position in refusing to stop preaching the Gospel, "we ought to obey God rather than men" (Acts 5:29). The obedience of the wife to the husband must conform to the instructions of Colossians 3:18, "As it is fit in the Lord."

B. The Reason

Why is the wife to be submissive to her husband? It is because the husband's leadership is like Christ's. As verse 23 says, *"For the husband is the head of the wife, even as Christ is the head of the church: and he is the saviour of the body."*

This headship is in no way a dictatorship and we do not condone all the abuses which have been heaped upon wives, using this text as justification. We do not recommend what Norman Copping did to his wife Dorothea when she dropped an electric battery. It so angered him he ordered her to crouch under a table and repeat seven times, as an apology: "My dearest and most wonderful Norman, please forgive me for my inconceivable thoughtlessness, stupidity and thoroughly irresponsible carelessness in allowing that battery to fall from my hands." Mrs. Copping was pregnant at the time. On another occasion the German-born wife fled from their home in London after a quarrel. He sent her a postcard recommending that she commit suicide!

Bizarre and novel actions such as these do not nullify the truth of the husband's leadership over the wife. In I Timothy 2:11-14, the apostle explained:

"Let the woman learn in silence with all subjection. But I suffer not a woman to teach, nor to usurp authority over the man, but to be in silence. For Adam was first formed, then Eve. And Adam was not deceived, but the woman being deceived was in the transgression."

The same theme of the husband's headship, offering the same proof, is given by Paul in I Corinthians 11:3, "But I would have you know, that the head of every man is Christ; and the head of the woman is the man; and the head of Christ is God." He even interpreted the coverings for the head on this basis, saying in I Corinthians 11:7, "For a man indeed ought not to cover his head, forasmuch as he is the image and glory of God: but the woman is the glory of the man."

In spite of equal rights amendments, women's lib, and all the other voices to the contrary, researchers are discovering more and more the truth that God's plan works best. In a major article in the *Waterloo* (Ia.) *Courier,* family-relations expert Clark W. Blackburn said that social scientists had discovered that a dominant, but not too domineering, husband generally produces a better-adjusted family. That is exactly the kind of a husband the Bible pictures.

In the widely-circulated newspaper feature, "Mirror of Your Mind," written by Dr. Edward H. Pinckney and Cathey Pinckney, this question was asked: "Should the husband be the head of the house?"

The answer given by the Pinckneys was:

> Yes, most authorities agree that the recently popular 'partnership formula' for happy marriages doesn't work. Extensive information compiled by researchers indicates that marital equality in decision-making, money matters, sex, and family responsibility is not the best way to run a marriage.
>
> In the most successful marriages, according to McGill University's department of psychiatry, the husband is emotionally stronger than the wife, and there is a clearcut division of authority and responsibility between them. It was noted that marriages, in which wives were emotionally dependent on their husbands, almost always produced happier, better-adjusted children.

Incidentally, the husband who doesn't take his rightful place in marriage will not be helped by divorcing and remarrying. According to a husband-wife relationship study at the University of California at Los Angeles, the husband possesses his greatest family power in his first marriage. It reported that, for reasons not yet plain, his influence in a second marriage is not as great as in his first one.

C. The Degree

To what extent should a wife be submissive to her husband?

Note the strong descriptive statements Paul gives in this passage. In verse 22, he says "as unto the Lord." In verse 24 it is "as the church is subject unto Christ." Also in that verse it is "in every thing." In the final verses of the passage, Paul implores the wife to "reverence" her husband.

The truth of the matter is that wives are not to have authority over their husbands in anything. God never intended the woman to be over the man. In I Corinthians 14:34,35, we are told: "Let your women keep silence in the churches: for it is not permitted unto them to speak; but they are commanded to be under obedience, as also saith the law. And if they will learn any thing, let them ask their husbands at home: for it is a shame for women to speak in the church."

Seventh-day Adventism, Christian Science, Theosophy, Spiritism and other false religious movements stand as sad memorials of the error into which people slide when they fail to follow the Bible's plan of procedure. And there is great trouble whenever a woman does not submit to the man in a marriage relationship.

I recall a young couple whom I united in marriage during a Texas pastorate. He was a military man, and both were very nervous. When I suggested that if it be their intent to be united in the holy bond of matrimony to signify by joining right hands, the bridegroom looked startled for a moment, then suddenly snapped to attention and held his right hand high. The embarrassed bride looked at me, looked at her sweetheart, then looked back at me and snapped to attention along with him, raising her right hand. I was tempted to say, "Do you swear to tell the truth, the whole truth, and nothing but the truth, so help you God?" In thinking about it later, such a swearing, with left hands on a Bible, might not be a bad addition to the marriage ceremony.

Before leaving this section which relates to the wife's submission to her husband, it might prove helpful to quote from an experience of Mrs. Jonathan Goforth, wife of the noted Canadian Presbyterian missionary to China, related in her book, *Climbing,* the "Memoirs of a Missionary's Wife." Discussing her custom of memorizing Scripture during her morning watch, she wrote:

> The following is the most notable incident connected with this habit of memorizing Scripture. I give it, for, judging by the effect it has had upon men and women to whom I have told this story, it touches a vital point in the relation of husband and wife. It certainly brought to my husband and myself a lesson never forgotten.
>
> Our children were all away at school. We were together carrying on aggressive evangelism at a distant out-station. The room given to us was dark and damp, with the usual mud floor. The weather turned cold, and there was no place where one could get warm. I caught a cold. It was not a severe one, but enough to make me rather miserable.
>
> The third or fourth day, when the meetings were in full swing and my organ was taking an attracting part, I became possessed by a great longing to visit my dearly loved friend, Miss H., living at the Weihuifu Station, some hours' run south on the railway. But when I told my husband what I had in mind, he strongly objected and urged against my going. I would not listen, even when he said my going would break up at least the women's work. But I was determined to go and ordered the cart for the trip to the railway. As the cart started and I saw my husband's sad, disappointed, white face, I would have stopped, but I wanted to show him I must have my way *sometimes!*
>
> Oh, what a miserable time I had till my friend's home in Weihuifu was reached! Miss H. gave one glance at my face and exclaimed: "Whatever is the matter, Mrs. Goforth! Are you ill?"
>
> My only answer was to break down sobbing. Of course I could not tell her WHY. Miss H. insisted on putting me to bed, saying I was ill! She made me promise to remain there until after breakfast.
>
> The following morning, while waiting for breakfast, I opened my Testament and started to memorize, as usual, my three verses. Now it happened I was at that time memorizing the Epistle to the Ephesians and had reached the 5th chapter down to the 21st verse. The 22nd, the first of the three to be memorized that morning, read: *"Wives, submit yourselves unto your own husbands, as unto the Lord."* I was, to say the least, startled! Somehow I managed to get this bravely memorized. Then going on to the 23rd verse, these words faced me: "For the husband is the head of the wife, even as Christ is the head of the church: and he is the saviour of the body."
>
> For a moment a feeling of resentment, even anger, arose. I could not treat this word as a woman once did, putting it aside with the remark: "That is where Paul and I differ." I believed the Epistle to the Ephesians was inspired, if any portion of Scripture was. How could I dare cut out this one part to which I was unwilling to submit? How I managed to memorize that 23rd verse. . .I do not know, for all the while a desperate mental struggle was on. Then came the 24th verse: "Therefore as the church is subject unto Christ, so let the wives be to their own husbands in every thing."
>
> I could not memorize further: my mind was too agitated. "It just comes to this," I thought, "am I willing FOR CHRIST'S SAKE, to submit my

will (in all but matters of conscience) to my husband?" The struggle was short but intense. At last I cried, **"For Christ's sake, I yield!"**

Throwing a dressing gown about me, I ran to the top of the stairs and called to my friend, "When does the next train go?"

"In about half an hour," she replied, "but you couldn't catch it and have your breakfast."

"Never mind; I'm going to get that train!"

My friend insisted on accompanying me to the station; we ate as we almost ran. With what joy I at last found myself traveling northward!

On reaching my destination, imagine my surprise to find my husband, with a happy twinkle in his eye, standing on the platform!

"Why, Jonathan," I cried, "how did you know I was coming?"

His reply was simply a happy, "Oh, I knew you would come."

Later I told my husband frankly all I had passed through. What was the result? From that time, he gave me my way as never before, for does not verse 25 of the chapter quoted go on to say: "Husbands, love your wives, even as Christ also loved the church, and gave himself for it." A new realization of the need of *yieldedness* came to us both, which brought blessed results in our home life.[1]

II. GOD'S IDEAL HUSBAND!
Vss. 25-31

One husband showed his love to his wife by writing poems. The celebrated German statesman, writer and poet, Karl Wilhelm, Baron von Humboldt (1767-1835), composed a 100-line poem in honor of his wife, Karoline von Dachroden, every day during the thirty-eight years of their married life. Even after her death, until his own death six years later, he continued to write the daily poem and deposit it on her grave each morning. He did not miss a single day in his devotion, either during his marriage or during his widowerhood.

Paul gives the instruction for the husband:

"Husband's, love your wives, even as Christ also loved the church, and gave himself for it; That he might sanctify and cleanse it with the washing of water by the word, That he might present it to himself a glorious church, not having spot, or wrinkle, or any such thing; but that it should be holy and without blemish. So ought men to love their wives as their own

---

[1] From CLIMBING by Rosalind Goforth, Copyright © 1940, 1968 by Zondervan Publishing House. Used by permission.

bodies. He that loveth his wife loveth himself. For no man ever yet hated his own flesh; but nourisheth and cherisheth it, even as the Lord the church: For this cause shall a man leave his father and mother, and shall be joined unto his wife, and they two shall be one flesh."

A. The Command!

"Husbands, love your wives"! The value of this action in a Christian home is inestimable, not only in the husband-wife relationship, but for the entire family. As one preacher, writing in the *Omaha World Herald,* expressed it: "The most important thing a father can do for his children is to love their mother."

It is strange, is it not, that Paul would find it necessary to give such a command? It is true, of course, that physical love is a vital part of the husband's love for his wife. In fact, it now appears that a little early morning smooching with the wife is every bit as important to a profitable day as a good breakfast.

Selecta, a West German medical magazine, published an article saying that a husband who kisses his wife every morning before leaving for work will have better health, live longer and earn more money than one who doesn't. The research for the article was conducted by several dozen physicians and psychologists over a two-year period.

Dr. Arthur Szabo, a professor of psychology at the University of Kiel, who collated the research, summed it up:

> Husbands who leave home in the morning without kissing their wives do so either because the couple has had a spat, or because they have grown apart. In either case, the husband begins the day with a negative attitude. He tends to be moody and depressed. He is disinterested in his work and surroundings.
>
> While a great many men feign indifference to their wives, nearly all of them are deceiving themselves. Even if a man has ceased to love his wife, he is still influenced by her attitude toward him. Our research proves this—and conclusively so.
>
> A husband who kisses his wife every morning before he goes to the office begins the day with a positive attitude. His feeling of harmony is reflected physiologically as well as mentally.

Dr. Szabo called the kissing husband a safer driver on his way to work, a more efficient employee, and better liked in his professional surroundings. As for living longer, the report showed that—based upon actuarial studies of the life insurance companies—the kissing husbands can be expected to live five years longer than those who don't, all other things being equal!

However, the idea of "love" in the Ephesians passage is far more than physical. In fact, it is the same word as "love" in John 3:16; it is a holy, spiritual, sacred kind of love.

It is a love without bitterness. Colossians 3:19 explains, "Husbands, love your wives, and be not bitter against them." Peter tells us it is a love with honor and therefore a key to the husband's prayer power. He says: "Likewise, ye husbands, dwell with them according to knowledge, giving honour unto the wife, as unto the weaker vessel, and as being heirs together of the grace of life: that your prayers be not hindered" (I Pet. 3:7).

How *much* is compressed in this little four-letter word, *love!* Just as a reconnaissance plane can fly miles high in the sky to take a photograph of the earth, then, when it is developed, a whole section of the country is reduced to an 8"x10" glossy, so a thousand and one facets of responsibility are wrapped up in the word "love" for a husband.

B. The Degree

While the wife's submission to her husband is of tremendous magnitude ("as unto the Lord"), so is the husband's love for his wife: *"Even as Christ also loved the church."* This, obviously, is self-sacrificial love. Our Lord gave Himself for the church, paying the tremendous price at Calvary. This answers the man who feared he was drifting into idolatry, loving his wife too much and therefore displeasing the Lord. While it is certainly wrong not to love the Lord enough, there is no possibility of any husband loving his wife too much! To do this, he would have to love her more than Christ loved the church—something totally impossible.

Admittedly, husbands do not measure up very well to this noble, lofty standard. It is as the skeptic in Hyde Park, London, shouted to the Salvation Army preacher: "We've nothing against this Jesus of Nazareth, but we do against you Christians. You ain't up to sample!" Most husbands are not up to sample.

Someone tells of a young Jewess who went to a Christian lady and asked for help. She said, "I have been reading the New Testament and I am puzzled about when Christians began to be so different from Christ." One thing is for sure: *the average husband's love for his wife is certainly different from the love of Christ to the church!* It ought not to be, at least to such an extent as in the average home.

Paul continues explaining the degree of a husband's love to his wife, saying he should love her as he loves his own body. He declared: *"So ought men to love their wives as their own bodies. He that loveth his wife loveth himself. For no man ever yet hated his own flesh; but nourisheth and cherisheth it, even as the Lord the church"* (vss. 28,29).

We can all understand this degree of love since self-love is one of the greatest forces in the universe. A man who loves his wife as he loves himself will treat her with the same care and consideration he treats his own body. This certainly rules out any dictatorial type of authoritarianism in the home, and it also convincingly shows that a husband flaunting his leadership does not have the scriptural kind at all.

No husband need arise in the morning and, as he looks at his likeness in the mirror while shaving, heatedly declare, "I am the boss. You have got to listen to me and do what I say. You must obey my every order today." That is not necessary. Neither is it necessary for a husband to use kindred language with his wife. The man who considers that his authority is dependent upon such talk or such treatment really does not *possess* the headship.

There is still another idea in Paul's instruction to the husband. Self-love is able to see virtues, possibilities and talents lying dormant which others cannot observe. The husband who loves his wife in this sense will be able to discern hidden virtues and possibilities others will not and could not perceive. Quite the contrary to love being blind, it has the best vision of all.

Well over a half-century ago, an anonymous writer in the

Jackson (Mich.) *Citizen Patriot* expressed this truth in the words:

> Is love blind? Our cynical friends tell us it is. But I do not agree. Love is the only thing that sees. Where would you be today if someone who loved you did not see things in you that nobody else saw? Who but your mother thought you were the finest baby ever born? And why did she have faith in you when no one else did? Because love saw.
>
> Then the best girl in the world said she'd marry you—even though her friends asked one another, 'What did SHE see in HIM?" Love saw. When things were so black you even lost faith in yourself, a great-hearted man or woman became your friend and pulled you through. Why? Because love saw.
>
> There is something fine and big in every one of us, but only those who love can see it. Who can say love is blind?

C. The Explanation!

Why is a husband's love to be so great, so noble? Paul says: *"For we are members of his body, of his flesh, and of his bones. For this cause shall a man leave his father and mother, and shall be joined unto his wife, and they two shall be one flesh."*

The same kind of a spiritual union which binds believers with Christ unites husband and wife. Just as the child of God has become one with the Son of God, so marriage blends two separate and distinct lives into a single entity.

The husband's responsibility is by far the greater of the two. This is only right since the woman has voluntarily taken the place of submission, severed her ties with home and family, given up her maiden name, and assumed a life goal dedicated to being a helpmate to the husband.

No wonder the old preacher called it a venture! And no wonder the standard marriage ceremony warns it is "not by any to be entered into unadvisedly or lightly; but reverently, discreetly, advisedly, soberly, and in the fear of God."

III. THE GREAT MYSTERY: CHRIST AND THE CHURCH!

Paul closes the passage: *"This is a great mystery: but I speak concerning Christ and the church. Nevertheless let every one of you in particular so love his wife even as himself; and the wife see that she reverence her husband"* (vss. 32,33).

A. Like Marriage: Permanent, Indissoluble

The union of believers with Christ is like marriage in the sense it is a union that binds. Just as when husband and wife are "joined" they become "one flesh," so in even a far greater manner the sinner who comes to Christ and claims Him as Saviour is united with Him in a permanent, indissoluble union. Paul expresses it in Romans 8:38,39: "For I am persuaded, that neither death, nor life, nor angels, nor principalities, nor powers, nor things present, nor things to come, Nor height, nor depth, nor any other creature, shall be able to separate us from the love of God, which is in Christ Jesus our Lord." He, seemingly, left nothing out; there is absolutely *nothing* that can break the union of the believer with God.

While marriage has its double exceptions of fornication (Matt. 5:32) and death (Rom. 7:2), the union of the believer and Christ has none. As our Lord assured His disciples in John 10:27-29: "My sheep hear my voice, and I know them, and they follow me: And I give unto them eternal life; and they shall never perish, neither shall any man pluck them out of my hand. My Father, which gave them me, is greater than all; and no man is able to pluck them out of my Father's hand."

B. Like Marriage: A Union of Mutual Obligation

On the part of the church, that responsibility, as with the wife to her husband, is obedience. *"Christ is the head of the church"* (vs. 23). *"The church is subject unto Christ"* (vs. 24). This submission is to be complete and entire, "in every thing." Whatever our Lord commands, this is exactly what the believer is to do. He does not make his own choices; those options are made by the One who owns him, having purchased him through the shedding of His blood (I Cor. 6:19,20).

The obligation on the part of Christ to the believer, like the husband to his wife, is one of love. Note again how this is illustrated by Paul: *". . .Christ also loved the church, and gave himself for it; That he might sanctify it and cleanse it with the washing of water by the word, that he might present it to himself a glorious church, not having spot, or wrinkle, or any such thing; but that it should be holy and without blemish"* (vss. 25-27).

This is the very highest, noblest form of love. "Greater love hath no man than this, that a man lay down his life for his friends" (John 15:13). Yet the extent of the love of Christ for us was so great we are told: "But God commendeth his love toward us, in that, while we were yet sinners, Christ died for us. . . For if, when we were enemies, we were reconciled to God by the death of his Son, much more, being reconciled, we should be saved by his life" (Rom. 5:8,10).

C. A Warning!

Paul does not end this section until he has warned believers not to lose sight of the literal meaning of the passage. While it is true that he is speaking of a great mystery concerning Christ and the church, he implores them: *"Nevertheless let every one of you in particular so love his wife even as himself; and the wife see that she reverence her husband"* (vs. 33).

The spiritual interpretation about Christ and the church does not detract in any sense from the force of the teaching about responsibility in marriage. Quite the contrary, it *adds* to it. You might describe it as the spark of fire which touches off the dynamite of its truth!

Conclusion

Can you visualize what Christian homes would be like if the truths of Paul's instruction in this passage were put into practice in a real and practical manner? How it would eliminate strife and dissension! When it comes right down to it, most things which cause problems in Christian homes are really not worth arguing about. Do you recall the things we mentioned at the start of this message which had broken homes? How foolish, how silly, how trifling were these disruptions. Yet most broken homes can trace the source back to the fountain of something just as foolish and incidental.

Dr. James T. Jeremiah, chancellor of Cedarville College, tells of a couple with two small children who had a number of adjustments to make when the husband decided to enter graduate school after working for several years. They moved into one of those "temporary" apartments which had been hastily constructed and whose walls were paper thin. He quotes the husband as confessing, "What was hardest was finding a way to keep our arguments private. We solved that by turning on the washing machine." The thrashing clatter of that appliance helped drown out and make indiscernible to the neighbors their heated discussions.

But he added, smiling sheepishly, "After a while we found that most of the things we had been disagreeing about weren't worth the effort of hunting up a load of clothes."

We think others, if they faced the issues honestly, would discover the same.

Before leaving this subject, perhaps a word would be in order emphasizing that the responsibilities set forth in this Ephesian passage are valid for husband and wife *regardless of what the mate in the union does or does not do!* So often the other party is blamed. Wives say, "I would obey my husband in everything if he would just love me like he is supposed to love me." But the wife's responsibility in the area of submission does not hinge upon the husband's love or lack of love. It is her obligation, regardless.

In like manner, husbands sometimes complain, "I would find it easy to love my wife as I should if she would not be so bossy and rebellious all the time." But, again, the wife's failure does not excuse the husband. He will one day answer to God at the Judgment Seat of Christ for the manner in which his love was manifested toward his wife.

We suggest to any wife or husband whose mate is failing that he or she try honoring God and following His way *for just one month* and discover whether it pays or not. We are confident that such a one will be pleasantly surprised with the changes in attitude of the mate, not just alone in the personal blessing resulting from obedience to God.

An Absolute Imperative

We must not close this message without warning any who desire a happy home of a basic prerequisite: *You must be right with God first yourself!*

With our telephone bill one month came the following proverb:

> If there is right in the soul,
> There will be beauty in the person;
> If there is beauty in the person,
> There will be harmony in the home;
> If there is harmony in the home,
> There will be order in the nation;
> If there is order in the nation,
> There will be peace in the world.

There is absolutely no possibility of harmony in the home without "beauty in the person." That beauty is available only through a salvation experience whereby the individual is born into the family of God.

Asahel Nettleton was a greatly used evangelist in the East during the early part of the nineteenth century. During a crusade in one town he felt suddenly prompted, while taking a walk, to approach a door and ring the bell. When a young lady responded, he inquired politely: "Does Jesus Christ live here?"

The girl was tremendously embarrassed at first, then she became angry and answered indignantly, "No, He doesn't!" And with that she slammed the door in Nettleton's face.

A few years later, when he returned to the same town for another preaching mission, a lady came to him at the close of a service, cheeks stained with tears. She asked, "Do you remember going to a door one day and asking if Jesus Christ lived there?"

Dr. Nettleton answered, "Why, yes, I do; and I have prayed for the girl who answered the door ever since."

The lady responded, "I am that girl and I want to tell you I couldn't get away from your words. I told my parents what had happened and, some weeks later, I surrendered to Christ. He has been honored in our home ever since and if you were to come to our door now and ask the same question, we could say, 'Yes, Jesus Christ *does* live here!' He has made our home a taste of Heaven."

What if someone were to come to your house today and ask Dr. Nettleton's question? Does Jesus Christ *live* there? We are not talking about crucifixes on the wall, images made of plaster of Paris on the mantel, or even mottos which say that He is the silent listener of every conversation, the unseen guest at every meal. We are talking about whether He is honored, His Word obeyed, and His will performed. If not, why not first turn over your life and then your home to Him without delay?

> God give us homes!
> Homes where the Bible is honored and taught;
> Homes with the Spirit of Christ in their thought;
> Homes that a likeness to Heaven have caught.
> God give us homes!
>
> God give us homes!
> Homes with the father in priest-like employ;
> Homes that are bright with a far-reaching joy;
> Homes where no world-stain shall come to annoy.
> God give us homes!
>
> God give us homes!
> Homes where the mother is queen-like in love;
> Ruled in the fear of the Saviour above;
> Homes that to youth most inspiring shall prove.
> God give us homes!
>
> God give us homes!
> Homes with the children to brighten the hours;
> Budding and blooming with beautiful flowers;
> Places of sunshine—sweet, sanctified bowers.
> God give us homes!
>
> Home, home, sweet, sweet home;
> A likeness to Heaven—
> God give us such homes!

Heavenly Orders for Home and Business

Children, obey your parents in the Lord: for this is right.

Honour thy father and mother; which is the first commandment with promise;
That it may be well with thee, and thou mayest live long on the earth.
And, ye fathers, provoke not your children to wrath: but bring them up in the nurture and admonition of the Lord.

Servants, be obedient to them that are your masters according to the flesh, with fear and trembling, in singleness of your heart, as unto Christ;
Not with eyeservice, as menpleasers; but as the servants of Christ, doing the will of God from the heart;

With good will doing service, as to the Lord, and not to men:

Knowing that whatsoever good thing any man doeth, the same shall he receive of the Lord, whether he be bond or free.

And, ye masters, do the same things unto them, forbearing threatening: knowing that your Master also is in heaven; neither is there respect of persons with him.—Ephesians 6:1-9.

That these are areas of grave problems is beyond dispute. In the field of labor, our country is beset with strikes, turmoil, unrest, distrust, deceit, dishonesty and bitter hatred. The Russian national anthem of red radicalism, the *Internationale,* sung by dedicated communists from Moscow's Red Square to New York's

Union Square, begins:

> "Arise, ye prisoners of starvation;
> Arise, ye wretched of the earth."

It ends with the promise to all workers everywhere, "The International Soviet shall free the human race." But we do not believe that this is the solution to our labor problems.

There are grave difficulties also in the family circle. What should we say of rebellious children, parents without natural affection, the wave of drugs and alcohol blighting every age level, the tendency for the government to exert more and more influence on the children while permitting less and less parental guidance and control, serious talk of "Kiddie Lib," and even bills being introduced into governmental legislative bodies which would, in fact, accomplish the destruction of the American home as we have known it for the past two hundred years?

The United Nations Educational Scientific and Cultural Organization (UNESCO), in its release, *The Influence of Home and Community,* suggests: "Removal of conventional pressures, of religious and legal taboos, of family antipathy toward those who are slightly atypical would probably be equally effective as aids to emotional stability and to better marital and parental adjustment." But we do not believe that irreligious, illegal and immoral actions are the solution.

Once again, however, *the Bible has the answer!* What a Book is this!

We think it is of more than passing significance that Paul put these two subjects respecting children and employment together. Undoubtedly, one of the reasons God planned it that way was that He knew, as we approach the end of the age, it would become increasingly popular for couples: (1) not to have children; (2) both work outside the home in secular jobs. Those days are upon us.

One psychiatrist, in a report to the National Conference on Family Life, declared: "The value of the child is diminishing. . . Prestige value of a new automobile is much greater than a new baby. . .Soon, perhaps, letters of sympathy will be in order with the coming of a new baby."

But the Bible says:

"Lo, children are an heritage of the Lord: and the fruit of the womb is his reward. As arrows are in the hand of a mighty man; so are children of the youth. Happy is the man that hath his quiver full of them: they shall not be ashamed, but they shall speak with the enemies in the gate."—Ps. 127:3-5.

Of the two subjects, the family is by far of the most consequence. As the late Dr. Pat Neff, former university president and governor of Texas, once said, "Tear down the church and the schools, and the homes will build them back; but tear down the homes, and everything will crumble."

Children are not only a blessing from God, they are a tremendous responsibility. Dr. Cortland Meyers quotes a ship's surgeon about a boy falling overboard. The crew launched an all-out rescue effort immediately, got him back on board the ship, used artificial respiration and other life-saving techniques, but all to no avail. The surgeon said he arrived just as they were turning away, giving up hope. When the physician asked if he could be of any assistance, they replied in the negative, saying the lad was beyond help.

As the doctor turned to leave he sensed a sudden impulse to see if there might not be something he could do after all. He went over to the body, turned it over, and chills went up and down his spine as he looked into the face of his own son. He told Dr. Myers, "Well, you may believe I didn't think the last thing had been done. I pulled off my coat and bent over that boy; I blew in his nostrils and breathed into his mouth; I turned him over and over; and simply begged God to bring him back to life. For four hours I worked, until, at sunset, I began to see the least flutter of breath that told me he lived."

It *does* make a difference when your own child or your own family is involved. We need, therefore, to approach this passage in the light of our own circumstances, our own family, our own job.

What orders does Heaven have in these areas for us today?

I. ON THE HOME FRONT!
Vss. 1-4

Ernestine Schumann-Heink, noted grand opera soprano in a previous generation, gave a beautiful definition of a home:

> What is a home? A roof to keep out the rain. Four walls to keep out the wind. Floors to keep out the cold. Yes, but home is more than that. It is the laugh of a baby, the song of a mother, the strength of a father. Warmth of living hearts, light from happy eyes, kindness, loyalty, comradeship. Home is first school and first church for young ones, where they learn what is right, what is good and what is kind. Where they go for comfort when they are hurt or sick. Where joy is shared and sorrow eased. Where fathers and mothers are respected and loved. Where children are wanted. Where the simplest food is good enough for kings because it is earned. Where money is not so important as loving kindness. Where even the teakettle sings from happiness. That is home. God bless it.

A. Heavenly Orders for Children!

The apostle writes: *"Children, obey your parents in the Lord: for this is right. Honour thy father and mother; which is the first commandment with promise; That it may be well with thee, and thou mayest live long on the earth."*

1. Obey Your Father and Mother

Obedience is the first step in the realm of service and this is why its spirit needs to be fervently and permanently instilled in the heart and life of the young. During the past century the obedience philosophy has been under tremendous attack. Progressive educators, psychologists and psychiatrists have argued that *self-expression* is more important than *self-control*. A negative approach to character building is all wrong, we were told, since everything should be positive and constructive.

Of late, however, some of these self-styled "experts" have come to the conclusion that the teachings of John Deweyism have produced disastrous results in our society. The noted syndicated columnist, Amy Vanderbilt, for example, said:

> The parents who permit their children to literally walk all over them, with the mistaken notion that this is modern rearing, are understandably tense. Modern parents convinced that corporal punishment (except in great emergencies as, for example, when a child through carelessness

threatens his own life or that of others) should not be resorted to, often are at a loss to find disciplines that stick.

She referred to disciplinarian measures in her own household, then continued:

> I am always pleased to see that whenever such discipline must be enforced, the children are actually more affectionate than ever, once their initial disappointment has been expressed.

Dr. Harry Bakwin, a past president of the American Academy of Pediatrics, wrote an article in *Parade,* " 'Old-Fashioned' Parents Are Right!" A subtitle said: "A Medical Authority Says 'Modern' Child-rearing Too Often Overlooks a Basic Goal: Character Building." Among other timely, thoughtful things in the article was this paragraph:

> Now this may be an old-fashioned idea—that teaching honesty, generosity, the difference between right and wrong, respect for authority and other character attributes is the most important job of parents. Old-fashioned or not, character is the quality we prize most in people. The fact that it has taken second place today—or has been forgotten entirely—is a sad commentary on modern child-rearing.

Where is this character primarily to be developed? The place to teach it is in the home. Children who do not learn obedience at home will refuse it at school and eventually, in society in general.

When we were young in the ministry and had accepted the call to a church where it was necessary to take a second secular job, we hired on as a school bus driver. One of our fellow drivers was a man everyone affectionately called "Pop" Zornes. His easy-going attitude made him ideal for driving the energetic, irresponsible grammar school students. However, just a few weeks before the end of a school year he was forced to put a six-year-old boy off the bus for continued willful misbehavior. The upset mother excitedly called school authorities and "Pop" was forced to sit in on a conference with the mother, the principal of the school, the boy's teacher, and the playground director. The mother excitedly insisted that her son couldn't possibly be any worse than any other child, so the driver obviously was harrassing him.

"Pop" explained to her that he transported over 150 students a day and, of that number, about six were chronic troublemakers. He patiently and quietly declared that her boy was without doubt the worst of the six and that not a single day had passed since the previous September but what he had been forced to reprimand him either going or coming. The schoolteacher explained that the boy was a constant troublemaker in class; then the playground director testified the child was the nemesis of the schoolyard, constantly throwing sand in the girls' hair and otherwise keeping the recreational activities in a turmoil.

Yet, in the face of all this testimony, the mother told "Pop" he did not understand children, that he ought to take a course in "child psychology," and that he should be more understanding and less harsh. "Pop," slightly angered by this time, rightly told the mother that if she could not train her child sufficiently so as to behave for ten minutes on a school bus, she was the one who needed special instruction in child psychology!

The place to teach obedience is in the home. *"Children, obey your parents."* Yet this forgotten and forsaken commandment is one of the features of our times. It is also listed in that awful description of vile depravity in Romans 1:28-32.

Reason and logic agree, history backing them up with ample evidence, that "children who do not obey their parents never amount to much in life." As another has wisely written, "A disobedient child is a nuisance for society, a burden for the state, and a stumbling block for the church."

Luke 2:51 is a verse deserving to be read and reread, then meditated upon at great length. Speaking about the youth of our Lord in His relation to Joseph and Mary, it says, "And he went down with them, and came to Nazareth, and was subject unto them: but his mother kept all these sayings in her heart." If our Lord needed to be "subject" to His human parents, how much more do children today.

Paul emphasizes in his heavenly orders to children: "Obey your parents **in the Lord.**" There is a sense in which the child obeying his parent is obeying God, and obedience to God supercedes any and all other obligation. The companion passage in Colossians 3:20 says, "Children, obey your parents in all things: for this is well pleasing unto the Lord." The obedient child is one in whom the Almighty is delighted.

Note again: *"for this is right."* Disobedient children are on the side of wrong, on the side of sin, of Satan and of Hell. So much is this true that the Word of God contains solemn warnings to disobedient children. In Deuteronomy 27, listing God's special curses, verse 16 declares: "Cursed be he that setteth light by his father or his mother. And all the people shall say, Amen."

The importance of obedience to parents is highlighted in that same book, when God instructed the people of Israel:

"If a man have a stubborn and rebellious son, which will not obey the voice of his father, or the voice of his mother, and that, when they have chastened him, will not hearken unto them: then shall his father and his mother lay hold on him, and bring him out unto the elders of the city, and unto the gate of his place; And they shall say unto the elders of the city, This our son is stubborn and rebellious, he will not obey our voice; he is a glutton, and a drunkard. And all the men of his city shall stone him with stones, that he die: so shalt thou put evil away from among you; and all Israel shall hear, and fear."—Deut. 21:18-21.

That is how exceedingly serious God considers disobedience to parents.

Other Scriptures highlight the matter. Exodus 21:17 says, "And he that curseth his father, or his mother, shall surely be put to death." The Israelites were told in Leviticus 20:9, "For every one that curseth his father or his mother shall be surely put to death: he hath cursed his father or his mother; his blood shall be upon him." Proverbs 20:20 warns, "Whoso curseth his father or his mother, his lamp shall be put out in obscure darkness." And Proverbs 30:17 says, "The eye that mocketh at his father, and despiseth to obey his mother, the ravens of the valley shall pick it out, and the young eagles shall eat it."

2. Honor Your Father and Mother

Someone has said, "We can love our equals, but we honor our superiors." Yet there is a real sense in which true honor, at least with regard to parents, is impossible apart from love. It works both ways, of course. The child who loves his parent should honor him. And honoring a parent is one method of manifesting love.

As children mature into adulthood, part of the honor is in making sure no parent suffers lack with regard to life's necessities. Jesus emphasized this interpretation to the hypocritical Pharisees in Mark 7:9-13, saying:

"Full well ye reject the commandment of God, that ye may keep your own tradition. For Moses said, Honour thy father and thy mother; and, Whoso curseth father or mother, let him die the death: But ye say, If a man shall say to his father or mother, It is Corban, that is to say, a gift, by whatsoever thou mightest be profited by me; he shall be free. And ye suffer him no more to do ought for his father or his mother; Making the word of God of none effect through your tradition, which ye have delivered: and many such like things do ye."

Paul told the young preacher, Timothy, "If any widow have children or nephews, let them learn first to show piety at home, and to requite their parents: for that is good and acceptable before God." Then he added in verse 8, "If any provide not for his own, and especially for those of his own house, he hath denied the faith, and is worse than an infidel."

The command to honor father and mother was the first "with promise" to be written by the very finger of God upon the tables of stone. That promise, Paul reminds us, is that "it may be well with thee, and thou mayest live long on the earth" (vs. 3). Actually, it is more than a guarantee of length of days, **it is a promise of delightful blessing throughout the length of those long years!** Surely God's way in this matter, as in every other, is the best way.

B. Heavenly Orders for Parents!

Paul says: *"And, ye fathers, provoke not your children to wrath: but bring them up in the nurture and admonition of the Lord"* (vs. 4). While both parents are vitally involved in training the children, the father, because of his place of leadership, is given the specific instructions.

"Provoke not your children to wrath." The apostle says the same in his instruction to the saints at Colosse, adding the explanation there: "Fathers, provoke not your children to anger, lest they be discouraged" (Col. 3:21). In other words, be fair. Be reasonable. This is one reason why discipline executed in anger often does so much harm.

J. Wilbur Chapman tells of being in Tiffany's famous New York emporium and hearing a salesman tell a lady a particular pearl was worth $17,000. The great evangelist mused about that a little bit and then observed:

> As I looked around that beautiful store, I imagined them bringing all their stock up to my house, and saying, "We want you to take care of this tonight." What do you think I would do? I would go as quickly as I could to the telephone and call up the Chief of Police and say, "I have all Tiffany's stock in my house, and it is too great a responsibility. Will you send some of your most trusted officers to help me?" You would do the same, wouldn't you?
>
> But I have a little boy in my home, and for him I am responsible. I have had him for nine years, and some of you may have just such another little boy. I turn to this old Book and I read this word: "What shall it profit a man if he gain the whole world and lose his own soul?" It is as if he had all the diamonds and rubies and pearls in the world, and held them in one hand, and just put a little boy in the other, and the boy would be worth more than all the jewels.
>
> If you would tremble because you had $17,000 worth of jewels in the house, one night, how shall you go up to your Father and your son be not with you?

The average parent, we fear, does not begin to realize the depth of his responsibility.

1. Bring Them Up in the "Nurture" of the Lord

Nurture means discipline, chastening. Why whip children? Because they need it. George Washington is greatly honored today as the Father of our country—and a wonderful *national* father he was—but when it came to the children in his own home, he was not very successful. Although he had no children born to him, when he married Martha Custis he adopted the boy and girl of her previous marriage. The boy, especially, resented discipline and Washington's manner of trying to cope with the problem was to shower him with gifts. When everything else failed, he gave the boy a tour of Europe with a tutor, but the lad came back every bit as arrogant as before. Washington confessed in a letter to a friend, "I can govern men, but I cannot govern boys." His failure was one of discipline.

It is very interesting that when Elizabeth Taylor was a tender eight years of age, her father wrote in *Parents* magazine: "We believe children should be encouraged to develop on their natural lines." Elizabeth Taylor developed in that atmosphere of self-expression and the world knows the result. We think no mother with spiritual discernment would want her daughter to turn out like Elizabeth Taylor. Character is developed by restrictions.

How this truth is emphasized in the Word of God! Proverbs 19:18 says, "Chasten thy son while there is hope, and let not thy soul spare for his crying." We are told in Proverbs 29:15, "The rod and reproof give wisdom: but a child left to himself bringeth his mother to shame." And Proverbs 13:24 points out, contrary to today's philosophy that a parent may "love his child too much" to whip him, "He that spareth his rod hateth his son: but he that loveth him chasteneth him betimes."

2. Bring Them Up in the "Admonition" of the Lord

Admonition is teaching, training, example. While we cannot and would not minimize the importance of *nurture,* the issue of *admonition* is far more vital and weighty.

In the meeting of an evangelist friend of mine, a six-year-old lad came forward and said, "My brother wants me to be saved."

"Why does your brother want you to be saved?"

The tender youth pitifully responded, "Because we don't want to grow up and be like Daddy. Will you pray that my daddy will come home and leave that other woman?"

We find it remarkable that a lad in such early "flower of youth" would be so advanced in maturity as to know he ought not follow his daddy in his sin. Yet most boys will grow up to be like their father and most girls will grow up to be like their mother.

That is why *admonition* is more vital than *nurture.* As someone has explained, "The business of the farmer is to raise corn, not to kill weeds. Killing weeds is incidental; growing a good crop of corn is the main thing."

What kind of example does it take to develop proper character? A survey of high school students in Northern Indiana listed these qualities as the ones most desired by children in fathers: (1) understanding; (2) common sense; (3) active interest in family affairs; (4) loyalty to all family members, without favoritism; (5) gentlemanly conduct; (6) leadership—he talks things over with his family, but the final word is his.

To these we would add the spiritual qualities of personal devotions, family devotions, a burden for souls, faithful and regular church attendance, plus all the manifestations of the fruit of the Spirit.

How fortunate was Timothy in his youth. Paul reminded him, while admonishing him, in II Timothy 3:14,15: "But continue thou in the things which thou hast learned and hast been assured of, knowing of whom thou hast learned them; And that from a child thou hast known the holy scriptures, which are able to make thee wise unto salvation through faith which is in Christ Jesus."

If children are to be properly instructed in things relating to salvation and the holy Scriptures, they will have to get those lessons at home. The public schools are probably one of the strongest anti-God, anti-Bible forces in today's society.

A distraught mother wrote the late Walter Maier how her thirteen-year-old daughter's eighth-grade teacher had told the class that "only simple-minded people still believe the Bible." It was this teacher's habit to regularly make studied attacks on the Word of God, belittling God and everything holy.

Maier went on:

> In the Bodleian Library at Oxford. . .is a significant document containing these words: "It is impossible for the Word of God as written in the book of nature and God's Word written in the Holy Scripture to contradict

one another." This remarkable declaration was signed, not by eighth-grade schoolmasters but by British university professors and research experts, and not by a mere handful, but by 800 foremost scientists. One of them, Sir David Brewster, whose academic degrees, decorations, honors, and memberships require thirteen lines, exclaims: "Oh, is it not sad that not all are content with the beautiful simple plan of salvation—Jesus Christ only?. . .What can the highest intellect on earth do but bow to God's Word and God's mind thankfully?. . .I depend on God's Word." But the child will not get his spiritual development in today's public school; it must be instilled in the home.[1]

Home training tells how the child will turn out. Do you not find it sad, yet significant, that Herodias' daughter, responsible for the death of that great prophet and man of God, John the Baptist, had her actions explained in Matthew 14:8, "She, being before instructed of her mother"?

A judge in Gary, Indiana, when passing sentence on young culprits, said, "I wish it were possible to put the parents of these children in the penitentiaries for allowing them to grow up like this." Home training tells!

Another Indiana judge declared that in future truancy cases he would sentence parents to one day in the county jail for each day their children missed school without good reason. Truly, a greater Judge than these in Indiana will hold parents accountable for the manner in which they neglect the spiritual instruction and training of their children.

Remember again, *example* is more vital than *exhortation*. We recall reading of a father who was explaining to his little boy the definition of a Christian. When he got through, the lad innocently looked up into his eyes and inquired, "Father, have I ever seen a Christian?" He did not recognize anyone he knew as fitting the category the father had described. *What a rebuke!*

No one starts his child's instruction too soon! Billy Sunday said:

> We wait too long. We wait until they stagger home drunk before we teach them, "Look not upon the wine when it is red." We wait until oaths and curses fall from the mouth before we teach them, "Thou shalt not take

---

[1] From AMERICA, TURN TO CHRIST! by Walter A. Maier, © 1944 by Concordia Publishing House. Used by permission.

the name of the Lord thy God in vain." We wait until they are on the way to prison before we teach them, "Thou shalt not steal." It's too late to take swimming lessons after the ship begins to sink. It's too late to insure your house after the flames burst through the roof.

II. ON THE BUSINESS FRONT!
Vss. 5-9

Actually, if the heavenly orders are followed on the home front, the problems on the business front will evaporate like fog under the blaze of the morning sun. Those who develop good character in the home will manifest good character on the job.

A. Heavenly Orders for Labor!

Paul says:

"Servants, be obedient to them that are your masters according to the flesh, with fear and trembling, in singleness of your heart, as unto Christ; Not with eyeservice, as menpleasers; but as the servants of Christ, doing the will of God from the heart; With good will doing service, as to the Lord, and not to men: Knowing that whatsoever good thing any man doeth, the same shall he receive of the Lord, whether he be bond or free."—Vss. 5-8.

1. "Obedient Unto Masters"

"Be obedient to your masters." In other words, obey orders! We have seen this as a divine command for wives, for children, and now for employees. While the natural man chafes at taking orders—just as do natural wives and natural children—the Christian employee is to be careful to do exactly as he is told.

In fact, he is instructed to be obedient *"with fear and trembling."* This thought is not one of a pup curling up with his tail between his legs and his head between his feet, expecting a beating for disobedience, but it signifies an earnest desire to do the job right. Paul, whose business was preaching, described it: "I was with you in weakness, and in fear, and in much trembling" (I Cor. 2:3). He was simply seeking to do his very best.

This obedience is to be *"in singleness of your heart."* In other words, promoting the welfare of the one for whom you work and making it the principal business of your labor. How rarely this characteristic is seen in today's employee. Do you, as a Christian, seek to benefit the company for whom you work with your service? Or is it simply a job, a means to a paycheck and a livelihood?

Paul even goes so far in his instruction as to say a Christian's labor should be *"as unto the Lord."* In other words, we are to realize that we are, first and foremost, responsible to God. Whatever we do, we are doing it in His name as Christians.

2. *"Not With Eyeservice, As Menpleasers"*

We have all seen employees of this caliber. Dr. John Geary, of the University of Maryland, summed up their philosophy in a humorous vein:

> We shouldn't work on Fridays because everyone is thinking about the weekend and no one gets anything done. We shouldn't work on Mondays because everyone is too tired from the weekend. If we don't work on Fridays then Thursday will be the day before the weekend, so we shouldn't work on Thursdays. If we don't work on Mondays then Tuesday is the first day after the weekend, so we shouldn't work on Tuesdays. That leaves Wednesday. But who wants to have to get up early and get all dressed up just one day a week to drive/bus/walk/bike all the way to work, so we shouldn't work on Wednesdays. Instead, we could come for half an hour on the first Wednesday of every month. . .to pick up our paychecks.

Such is the philosophy of today's workers.

While we are not discussing unions here either pro or con—they have done some good and some harm, as both its friends and enemies will attest—we must lay at the door of unions the credit for causing a real problem. Instead of turning out all the work possible in an 8-hour day, unions have taught their employees to slow down production. It has even reached the place where the National Labor Relations Board ruled, in a 3-to-1 decision, that it is perfectly permissible for a union to fine its members for working too rapidly.

This was not the philosophy upon which unions were founded. Samuel Gompers (1850-1924), a native of London who migrated to this country with his family in his youth, took a leading part in launching the Federation of Organized Trades and Labor Unions, becoming its first president. When the American Federation of Labor was constituted in 1886, he was elected president and was re-elected annually thereafter until his death, with the exception of a single year. So highly revered by labor that he is affectionately called the father of modern American unionism, it might be well to remember what he said about this matter of *initiative* in labor. In a speech less than ten years before his decease, Gompers declared:

> Doing for people what they can and ought to do for themselves is a dangerous experiment. In the last analysis, the welfare of the workers depends upon their own initiative. Whatever is done under the guise of philanthropy or social morality which in any way lessens initiative is the greatest crime that can be committed against the toilers. Let social busybodies and professional 'public morals' experts and their fads reflect upon the perils they rashly invite under this pretense of social welfare.

The Apostle Paul warned Christians that their labor was not to be the kind effective only when someone in authority was looking on. The child of God is to do his very best on the job, no matter whether anybody acknowledges it—or even knows about it.

A sculptor preparing a statue to be erected in a Grecian temple was asked why he took such pains with the backside, since it would be against the wall and no one would notice. He is reported to have responded, "The gods will see it." While we do not believe in a plurality of gods, the Christian knows his Heavenly Father is watching and observing all of his labor, whether in the church, the home, or on a secular job. Because of this, he strives to do his best, always.

3. "As the Servants of Christ"

What a contrast this is to mere "eyeservice, as menpleasers." Christians should stand out in factories, in stores, on farms, or wherever they labor, through the manner in which they perform their duties. This, note carefully, is the "will of God."

Spurgeon is said to have declined an invitation to preach at a gathering where he was promised an exceptionally large hearing, explaining, "I have no ambition to preach to ten thousand people, but to do the will of God." That is the ambition of any Christian—doing the will of God.

Notice also, doing the will of God is further enjoined to be *"from the heart."* Certainly this includes a conscientiousness regarding every phase of service. Probably it includes being cheerful as well, gladly doing the work assigned without complaining.

4. With Good Will, As to the Lord

We will never have any trouble if we keep this in mind. Paul repeats his instruction in verse 7, saying, *"With good will doing service, as to the Lord, and not to men."* All of our work is to be done with the solemn realization that one day we will give an account to our Lord about how we performed our secular job.

5. The Main Payday!

This is going to come from our Lord Jesus Christ, not through a weekly or monthly paycheck. Verse 8 expresses it, *"Knowing that whatsoever good thing any man doeth, the same shall he receive of the Lord, whether he be bond or free."*

The story is told of a man who appealed for help to the Duke of Earlington. The Duke inquired, "On what grounds?"

"On the ground that I am your brother, Sir."

The Duke reportedly put his hand into his pocket, took out an English penny, and said, "Get all your other brothers to give you as much as that and you will be a richer man than I."

So, today, one who looks to any man for his riches will be disappointed. If the boss is a skinflint, the child of God still has heavenly promises regarding provision—and the assurance from his Father that he will eventually come out on top. Galatians 6:7 is still true, "Be not deceived; God is not mocked: for whatsoever a man soweth, that shall he also reap." This is not only saying that one who sells out to sin will receive the bitter harvest of sin's fruits, it is also assuring us that when one plants a good and noble crop, he receives that kind of a harvest.

It pays to do right on the job.

B. Heavenly Orders for Management!

Paul says, *"And, ye masters, do the same things unto them, forbearing threatening: knowing that your Master also is in heaven; neither is there respect of persons with him."*

1. "Do the Same Things!"

In other words, employers ought to follow the principle of the Golden Rule. The instructions God gave for employees are equally pertinent for employers.

Just as the servant is to handle his duties as one who is primarily answerable only to God, so should those connected with management. They are to follow the same Christian principles: operating in fear and trembling, doing their job as unto Christ and as His servants, performing from the heart all other duties within the will of God.

2. "Forbearing Threatening"

How easy, how tempting it is for one in authority to threaten those under him. The position of power has always brought the possibility of a curse. Yet the Christian master is to do nothing unkind, or cruel, or selfish, or discourteous.

What would this mean? It would involve proper working conditions for the employees. It would necessitate paying fair and honest wages. The virtues of patience and temperance would certainly be included.

The entire thought is one of treating employees as brothers, not as slaves. Paul's letter to Philemon, regarding his runaway slave Onesimus, is pregnant with suggestive thought in this area. Onesimus was to be received "not now as a servant, but above a servant, a brother beloved" (vs. 16); yea, even "more than" that (vs. 21).

3. The Heavenly Explanation!

Paul explained why Christian employers are to have such an attitude toward employees, noting: *"Your Master is in heaven; neither is there respect of persons with him."* The Christian who is a boss is still an employee, a servant to God.

Conclusion

One thing that is so obvious in these heavenly orders relates to how everything revolves around being "in the Lord." It is important that children know Jesus Christ as personal Saviour in order to be obedient to parents, honoring father and mother properly. So parents, in order to rear their children properly in the nurture and admonition of the Lord, must have a personal relationship to the Lord Jesus Christ. It is the same with the employee and the employer. To make these high, grandiose principles operate in the realm of daily reality, a vital experience with God is a fundamental prerequisite.

In other words, these lofty principles cannot be accomplished through the arm of the flesh. This is why the Christian's foundational duty is not in the area of labor reforms, it is in the realm of getting people saved. When people come to know Christ as personal Saviour, the problems relating to labor and management will be happily solved.

Christians at War!

Finally, my brethren, be strong in the Lord, and in the power of his might.

Put on the whole armour of God, that ye may be able to stand against the wiles of the devil.

For we wrestle not against flesh and blood, but against principalities, against powers, against the rulers of the darkness of this world, against spiritual wickedness in high places.

Wherefore take unto you the whole armour of God, that ye may be able to withstand in the evil day, and having done all, to stand.

Stand therefore, having your loins girt about with truth, and having on the breastplate of righteousness;

And your feet shod with the preparation of the gospel of peace;

Above all, taking the shield of faith, wherewith ye shall be able to quench all the fiery darts of the wicked.

And take the helmet of salvation, and the sword of the Spirit, which is the word of God:

Praying always with all prayer and supplication in the Spirit, and watching thereunto with all perseverance and supplication for all saints;

And for me, that utterance may be given unto me, that I may open my mouth boldly, to make known the mystery of the gospel,

For which I am an ambassador in bonds: that therein I may speak boldly, as I ought to speak.

But that ye also may know my affairs, and how I do, Tychicus, *a beloved brother and faithful minister in the Lord, shall make known to you all things:*

Whom I have sent unto you for the same purpose, that ye might know our affairs, and that he might comfort your hearts.

Peace be to the brethren, and love with faith, from God the Father and the Lord Jesus Christ.

Grace be with all them that love our Lord Jesus Christ in sincerity. Amen.—Ephesians 6:10-24.

On November 1, 1861, President Abraham Lincoln appointed General George B. McClellan to the position of General-in-Chief of the Union Army, replacing General Winfield Scott. It proved to be a poor choice, not because the Democrat Party eventually nominated him to oppose Lincoln in the 1864 elections, but because of McClellan's inefficiency. He repeatedly ignored Lincoln's orders for a general Union offensive and, when he did obey, he proceeded with such inexcusable caution that the war effort was greatly hindered.

After putting up with the disobedience and inefficiency as long as he could the Great Emancipator wrote McClellan the following note:

> My dear McClellan:
> If you don't want to use the army, I should like to borrow it for awhile.
> Yours respectfully,
> A. Lincoln.

Surely no one would criticize the Lord if He reacted in the same manner. Christians seemingly do not realize they are at war; they seem indifferent to the fact that today's church is in midst of the conflict of the ages. It is a battle between Heaven and Hell, light and darkness, righteousness and iniquity, God and Satan.

.What is at stake? It is not the rich oil fields of the Middle East, not the strategic Suez or Panama canals, not some vital mid-Pacific airbase. No, no! It is something far more valuable: *the precious souls of men, women, boys and girls!* Ephesians 5:14 fits in well here, "Wherefore he saith, Awake thou that sleepest, and arise from the dead, and Christ shall give thee light."

Just as the children of Israel, after crossing the Jordan River into the Promised Land, were forced to wage vigorous warfare to drive out the enemy and possess the possession Jehovah had given them, so sinners saved by grace and entering the Canaanland of the Christian life find they have a strenuous battle on their hands. There are foes to be conquered, battles to be fought, victories to be won, strongholds to possess.

I. THE CALL TO ARMS DECLARED!

A. A Call for STRENGTH: Offensive Power!

Verse 10 says, *"Finally, my brethren, be strong in the Lord, and in the power of his might."* Paul is careful to note, at the very start, that the secret and source of strength for battle against sin is *"in the Lord."*

There is an old legend about Felix of Nola being pursued by murderers, taking refuge in a cave. As soon as he entered the haven of safety, a band of spiders immediately wove their webs over the opening. When the killers arrived at the spot they saw the webs and passed on. The saint then said, "Where God is not, a wall is but a spider's web; where God is, a spider's web is as a wall." While the story may be false, the application is certainly true.

This is why the believer must turn to Him for his strength. Paul told the Ephesians what he had learned through experience, "I can do all things through Christ which strengtheneth me" (Phil. 4:13). Our strength in spiritual warfare or service is only "through Christ." This harmonizes with what our Lord said in John 15:4,5: "Abide in me, and I in you. As the branch cannot bear fruit of itself, except it abide in the vine; no more can ye, except ye abide in me. I am the vine, ye are the branches: he that abideth in me, and I in him, the same bringeth forth much fruit: for without me ye can do nothing."

A Christian advancing into battle against Satan apart from the strength of Jesus Christ would be as handicapped as a David facing Goliath in Saul's armor. The believer who goes out to fight the Devil in his own strength is certain to be defeated.

Jehovah warned His earthly people:

"Woe to them that go down to Egypt for help; and stay on horses, and trust in chariots, because they are many; and in horsemen, because they are very strong; but they look not unto the holy One of Israel, neither seek the Lord!. . .Now the Egyptians are men, and not God; and their horses flesh, and not spirit. When the Lord shall stretch out his hand both he that helpeth shall fall, and he that is holpen shall fall down, and they all shall fail together."—Isa. 31:1,3.

A writer in a book dealing with hymns and hymn writers says that Martin Luther and his associates frequently became discouraged over the manifold dangers they constantly faced. On such occasions Luther would say to Melanchthon, "Come, Philip, let us sing the 46th Psalm!" Then they would sing Luther's version:

> A sure stronghold our God is He,
> A timely shield and weapon;
> Our help He'll be, and set us free
> From every ill can happen.
>
> And were the world with devils filled,
> All eager to devour us,
> Our souls to fear shall little yield,
> They cannot overpower us.

What an expression Paul used regarding being strong in the Lord! He spoke of strength which is wrapped up *"in the power of his might."* This was the power manifested when He spoke and universes sprang into being, the power that upholds them today by His right hand. The "power of his might" performed the miracles in the contest of Moses against Pharaoh, brought down the walls of Jericho, and routed the Midianite army for Gideon and his little band of three hundred. This is the power to which the Ephesians were reminded in the opening chapter: "The exceeding greatness of his power to us-ward who believe, according to the working of his mighty power, which he wrought in Christ, when he raised him from the dead, and set him at his own right hand in the heavenly places" (1:19,20).

Paul referred often to this power. In Colossians 1:11 he spoke of being "strengthened with all might, according to his glorious power, unto all patience and longsuffering with joyfulness." To the Corinthians he enthused:

"For though we walk in the flesh, we do not war after the flesh: (For the weapons of our warfare are not carnal, but mighty through God to the pulling down of strongholds;) Casting down imaginations, and every high thing that exalteth itself against the knowledge of God, and bringing into captivity every thought to the obedience of Christ."—II Cor. 10:3-5.

Yes, and this is the same power described in Acts 1:8, where the departing Redeemer told His remaining disciples, "But ye shall receive power, after that the Holy Ghost is come upon you: and ye shall be witnesses unto me both in Jerusalem, and in all Judaea, and in Samaria, and unto the uttermost part of the earth."

Paul is an example of one who exhibited in life and service this "power of his might." Describing his ministry at Corinth, he said in I Corinthians 2:4,5, "My speech and my preaching was not with enticing words of man's wisdom, but in demonstration of the Spirit and of power: that your faith should not stand in the wisdom of men, but in the power of God."

Peter, John and the other apostles are also examples of those who fought in this same "power of his might." In Acts 4:33 we read of them, "And with great power gave the apostles witness of the resurrection of the Lord Jesus: and great grace was upon them all." Their—and our—Commander-in-Chief had promised, "All power is given unto me in heaven and in earth. Go ye therefore. . ." (Matt. 28:18,19).

Well might William Cowper write,

> Oh, I have seen the day,
> When with a single word,
> God helping me to say,
> "My trust is in the Lord."
> My soul has quelled a thousand foes,
> Fearless of all that could oppose.

B. A Call for STEADFASTNESS; Defensive Power!

In verse 11 Paul says, *"Put on the whole armour of God, that ye may be able to stand against the wiles of the devil."* Note the words: *"be able to stand."* In verse 13 he adds, *"and having done all, to stand."* Then he says in verse 14, *"Stand therefore."*

Great is the Christian who can take everything Satan is able to hurl at him and still remain unmoved, never giving ground, never retreating. As a host of commentators have pointed out, there is no covering for the back in the Christian's armor. For him to retreat is to expose himself to Satan's fiery darts.

Paul also tells the Ephesians they need to "be able to withstand in the evil day." That is, they should be ready to encounter and soundly defeat Satan at any time. A Christian ought always be on guard against the wiles of the Devil.

This is followed up with "having done all, to stand." In other words, be able to *hold* the ground after winning it. Be ready, be prepared for Satan's next charge, his next attack. There is no such thing as so decisively defeating Satan that he gives up. Every victory won by the believer is only temporary.

This is why we must put on the "whole armour of God." To do anything less is to go into battle only partially prepared, incompletely armed.

II. CONFLICT WITH ENEMY DEFINED!

Here it is in verse 12: *"For we wrestle not against flesh and blood, but against principalities, against powers, against the rulers of the darkness of this world, against spiritual wickedness in high places."*

A. Not a Physical Warfare, but Spiritual

It is a war against principalities and powers. It is a battle against the forces of Hell as marshaled by Satan himself. In this respect, how comforting it is to know the position of our Commander-in-Chief. Ephesians 1:20,21 assure us: "Which he wrought in Christ, when he raised him from the dead, and set him at his own right hand in the heavenly places, Far above all principality, and power, and might, and dominion, and every name that is named, not only in this world, but also in that which is to come."

It is a warfare against the rulers of the darkness of this world. Paul is not necessarily speaking of this world's rulers, although sometimes they are the believer's enemies, but of a warfare against the rulers of "the darkness." This is not a battle against the President of the United States of America, or the Prime Minister of England, or the Emperor of Japan, or the King of Iran, or the Premier of Russia. No, even the most evil and wicked of these earthly rulers are at most, in the spiritual warfare, merely pawns whom Satan uses to move around on the world's chessboard.

The phrase "spiritual wickedness in high places" defines it best, perhaps, because it literally means "wicked spirits in the heavenlies." This conflict is *spiritual* combat.

B. Not an Easy Warfare

Paul describes it as military operations facing the very "wiles of the devil." This speaks of his cunning arts, his deceits, his trickery. Actually the word *wiles* means *stratagems*. He has mapped out his battle plans and we ought to be familiar with them. Second Corinthians 2:11 warns, "Lest Satan should get an advantage of us: for we are not ignorant of his devices."

One must know his enemy if he is to conquer him. Unfortunately, the average individual thinks of Satan as an ugly, horrible-looking creature with cloven hooves, horns, pitchfork tail, and wearing a suit of bright red underwear. Quite the contrary, II Corinthians 11:14,15, inform us: "Satan himself is transformed into an angel of light. Therefore it is no great thing if his ministers also be transformed as the ministers of righteousness; whose end shall be according to their works."

Dr. H. A. Ironside well commented:

> It would be a very simple thing if the adversary of our souls came to us honestly and said, "Good morning. I am the devil, and I want you to get into something that is going to cause you a lot of misery and wretchedness, and which will dishonour your Saviour; and if you will only listen to me and obey me, I will be able to accomplish this." We would have no difficulty in saying to him, "Get thee behind me, Satan: for thou savorest not the things that be of God, but the things that be of men" (Mark 8:33). But he does not come that way. He is transformed into an angel of light, and he seeks to deceive us.[1]

Know your enemy!

III. CLOAK OF ARMOR DESCRIBED!

Here is the armor as Paul describes it in verses 14-20:

"Stand therefore, having your loins girt about with truth, and having on the breastplate of righteousness; And your feet shod with the preparation of the gospel of peace; Above all, taking the shield of faith, wherewith ye shall be able to quench all the fiery darts of the wicked. And take the helmet of salvation, and the sword of the Spirit, which is the word of God: Praying always with all prayer and supplication in the Spirit, and watching thereunto with all perseverance and supplication for all saints; And for me, that utterance may be given unto me, that I may open my mouth boldly, to make known the mystery of the gospel, For which I am an ambassador in bonds: that therein I may speak boldly, as I ought to speak."

A. Girdle of Truth

Paul lists the girdle first because it was the initial piece placed on the body of a warrior preparing for battle, basic to all the rest. It was made of leather or linen, then covered with copper or scales or iron. Since the girdle was foundational for the warrior, we can well understand why it relates to "truth" in the Christian warfare.

---

[1] From IN THE HEAVENLIES by H. A. Ironside, Published by Loizeaux Brothers, Inc. Used by permission.

When we mention truth, the average Christian probably visualizes three things. First of all, he thinks of Jesus Christ. The Saviour said in John 14:6, "I am. . .the truth." Second, complete integrity in speech comes to mind. If anyone ought always to tell the truth, the Christian is that one. He is commanded in Ephesians 4:25, "Wherefore putting away lying, speak every man truth with his neighbour: for we are members one of another." Third, there is the Word of God, described in II Peter 2:2 as "the way of truth."

All three aspects of truth are no doubt involved here. Before one can effectively fight in the army of God, he must know Jesus Christ as personal Saviour, he must be truthful in his speech, and he must become familiar with the Bible. Yet of the three, the third element is probably the one primarily intended.

Someone objects, "No, the Word of God is listed later in the armor as a sword." But there it is an *offensive* instrument; here it is part of *the defense.* The idea seems to be that the first step in fighting for God is for the Christian to know his Bible. This is important in understanding "the wiles of the devil," as well as in giving strong protection from Satan's attacks. "The truth" here is a counterpart of "the faith" in Jude 3.

John had much to say about *truth.* In his brief second epistle, he spoke of "the truth" three times and "in truth" twice in the opening four verses. In III John 3,4, he declared: "For I rejoiced greatly, when the brethren came and testified of the truth that is in thee, even as thou walkest in the truth. I have no greater joy than to hear that my children walk in truth." Later he spoke of Demetrius as having a good report "of the truth itself" (vs. 12).

This girdle of truth went about the loins—a place of strength. Our strength, wrapped in His truth, is fundamental for fighting effectively.

B. "Breastplate of Righteousness"

We are, of course, clothed in Christ's perfect righteousness. Second Corinthians 5:21 assures us, "For he hath made him to be sin for us, who knew no sin; that we might be made the righteousness of God in him." First Corinthians 1:30 tells us Christ Jesus is of God "made unto us. . .righteousness." In Philippians 3:9, Paul spoke of giving up all the things in which he formerly trusted that he might "be found in him, not having mine own righteousness, which is of the law, but that which is through the faith of Christ, the righteousness which is of God by faith." Surely Satan has no place in a heart protected by Christ and His righteousness.

However, there is also a righteousness which we are to "put on." This follows the example of our Lord in Isaiah 59:16,17:

"And he saw that there was no man and wondered that there was no intercessor: therefore his arm brought salvation unto him; and his righteousness, it sustained him. For he put on righteousness as a breastplate, and an helmet of salvation upon his head; and he put on the garments of vengeance for clothing, and was clad with zeal as a cloak."

This is an outward manifestation of righteousness. It is exemplified in a Henry Clay saying, "I would rather be right than be President." Such should be the attitude of every Christian.

Unless we wear this breastplate, we will not win many battles, conquer many strongholds, defeat many foes, or win many souls to our Lord Jesus Christ. Well did Shakespeare have one of his characters exclaim,

> What better breastplate than a heart untainted!
> Thrice is he armed that hath his quarrel just;
> And he but naked, though lock'd up in steel,
> Whose conscience with injustice is corrupted.

C. The Shoes of "the Preparation of the Gospel of Peace"

Shoes are important in warfare. How precarious is the position of a soldier who does not have sure footing when he seeks to wield his sword! Just as no experienced mountain climber in the Alps would think of attempting to scale some summit lacking proper shoes with sharp, strong spikes to bite into the steep terrain, so no Christian should attempt to go into battle without his feet properly shod.

The "preparation" here signifies readiness, or preparedness, as in II Timothy 4:2: "Preach the word, be instant in season, out of season, reprove, rebuke, exhort with all longsuffering and doctrine." It is a Paul telling the Romans, "So, as much as in me is, I am ready to preach the gospel to you that are at Rome also" (Romans 1:15). A believer shod in this manner is ready for the conflict!

One thinks here of the words in the Song of Solomon, "How beautiful are thy feet with shoes, O prince's daughter" (7:1). Even more quickly does Romans 10:15 come to mind: "And how shall they preach, except they be sent? as it is written, How beautiful are the feet of them that preach the gospel of peace and bring glad tidings of good things."

Will you join Frances R. Havergal in praying,

> "Take my feet, and let them be
> Swift and beautiful for Thee"?

D. "The Shield of Faith"

Dr. R. E. Neighbour expressed the need of faith in warfare when he said, "There is no use for anyone to fight against the wiles of the devil, if his hands are hanging down, and his knees trembling in unbelief." That noted man of faith who wrought such miracles in this realm, George Muller, said:

> Just in the proportion in which we believe that God will do just what He has said in His Word, is our faith strong or weak. Faith has nothing to do with feelings, or with impressions, with improbabilities or with outward appearances. If we desire to couple these with faith, then we are no longer resting on the Word of God, because faith needs nothing of the kind. Faith rests on the naked Word of God. When we take Him at His Word, the heart is at peace.

In other words, **"Believe God!"** His promises are true, they "in him are yea, and in him Amen, unto the glory of God" (II Cor. 1:20).

Some time ago a thirteen-year-old English lad received two United States one dollar bills as a Christmas gift. It was shortly after Congress had passed the law requiring the motto "In God

We Trust" to appear on all United States currency. One of the bills he received had the motto and the other, obviously printed before the ruling, did not. Curious, he wrote to the *Manchester Guardian* to inquire: "Has the United States just **started** to trust in God or **stopped** trusting in Him?" Observing the current crop of professing Christians in our churches today, one might easily wonder if Christendom has just started or just stopped trusting Him.

Paul describes faith as a shield and, to the warrior, a shield is an instrument of defense and protection. How often the Lord is spoken of as our shield, especially in the Psalms. It is the shield of faith in Him which alone can stop and quench the fiery darts of the wicked one. In Hebrews 11, more than a score of examples are given as proof that it works. Faith's shield will prove adequate protection for you in your battle against Satan and his cohorts.

E. "Helmet of Salvation"

This, like the shield of faith, is something to "take." It is something to accept as a gift. The reference to this helmet is not one of a salvation experience. If it were, it would have been mentioned first in the Christian armor. Quite the contrary it speaks of one already saved.

The key is in the reference to the helmet. Since it is a covering for the head, obviously it speaks of *a knowledge* of salvation. Many an individual has been born into the family of God, yet for some reason or another has lacked assurance. Paul is simply pointing out that a man not sure he is saved will make a poor soldier, indeed.

The philosopher Carlyle had a neighbor with a rooster which crowed loudly every morning at daybreak, invariably waking Carlyle. When he complained to the neighbor about the rooster, he said, "I scarcely sleep all night."

Immediately the man queried, "How can that be? He doesn't crow until daylight."

Carlyle's classic answer was, "Oh, if you only knew what I suffer all night, *waiting* for that thing to crow!"

The same kind of anxiety fills the soul of many a Christian who is unsure of his or her salvation. And that concern prevents the poor child of God from enjoying the resting in Christ which should be his portion. How pertinent and comforting is I John 5:13, "These things have I written unto you that believe on the name of the Son of God; **that ye may know that ye have eternal life,** and that ye may believe on the name of the Son of God."

F. "Sword of the Spirit"

Here is the portion of the Christian's armor which turns him into a victorious conqueror. *The Prairie Overcomer* commented about a contest conducted by the Wilkinson Sword Company. The advertisement describing it glowed: "Fifty lucky persons will win an authentic Wilkinson Infantry Sword. The same sword used in Royal Parades and the Trouping of the Colours. Just think what it will mean to a lucky winner when this sword hangs over the fireplace or on a rec room wall!"

The magazine caustically observed:

> We refer to this offer not to promote this type of lucky draw, but to call attention to the fact that swords are really not for display. Swords are for battle, but many people who would shrink back from the rigours of the battlefield are pleased to display a sword over the fireplace.
>
> Thus it is with regard to the Sword of the Spirit, the Word of God. It is for defence, not display. Fellow Christians, you can have the same sword as that used by our Lord Jesus Christ, and by Paul, and by Peter. But, remember, it is for use in battle. Heed the psalmist's appeal to the saints of God: "Let the high praises of God be in their mouth, and a twoedged sword in their hand" (Ps. 149:6).

It was with the Sword of the Spirit that Christ won in His warfare against Satan. With each temptation, our Lord responded through a potent thrust of "It is written!"

Actually, however, when Paul speaks of the Word of God as being the Sword of the Spirit, he is not referring to the Bible as a single unit. The Greek word used here is not the usual *logos,* but *rhema,* which means "a saying." In other words, instead of being a single sword, it is an entire arsenal. Whenever Satan comes to tempt the Christian soldier, the saintly warrior is to select a saying from the arsenal and smite the adversary with it.

G. "Praying Always With All Prayer"

It is interesting to read the lives of successful warring saints and note how high a priority each placed upon prayer. Charles Finney once kept a huge crowd waiting for more than an hour before going to the platform. When someone sought him out to tell him it was past time, he heard the voice of Finney coming from behind a closed door, "I won't go out there unless You go with me." John Knox's biographer says he dismissed his congregation at St. Giles Cathedral one Sunday morning because he felt he had no message for the people.

1. How Should Soldiers Pray?

Verse 18 says, *"Praying always with all prayer and supplication in the Spirit, and watching thereunto with all perseverance and supplication for all saints."* They are to pray at all times: *"always."* They are to pray *"with all prayer and supplication."* They are to pray *"in the Spirit."* They are to pray *"watching thereunto with all perseverance and supplication."* In other words, the child of God should make his petition, then watch for the answer.

> Worry? Why worry? What can worry do?
> It never keeps trouble from overtaking you.
> It puts a frown upon the face, and sharpness in the tone,
> We're unfit to live with others, and unfit to live alone.
> Worry? Why worry? What can worry do?
> It never keeps trouble from overtaking you.
>
> Pray? Why pray? What can praying do?
> Praying really changes things, arranges life anew.
> It puts a smile upon your face, the lovenote in your tone,
> Makes you fit to live with others, and fit to live alone.
> Pray? Why pray? What can praying do?
> It brings God down from Heaven to live and work with you.

2. For Whom Should Soldiers Pray?

The Christian soldier should pray for his fellow warriors: *"all saints."* We remind our readers again that saints are simply sinners saved by grace. Pope Paul VI recently inaugurated machinery to cut centuries off the time limit it formerly took the Roman Catholic Church to make a saint. However, the Bible offers "instant sainthood" to any and all who receive Jesus Christ as personal Lord and Saviour.

Pope Paul VI followed up his first announcement with a second, this time seeking to make sainthood "less expensive." He ordered church officials to eliminate the extravagant frills which have heretofore been associated with canonization and beatification. The commission he appointed to study the matter advised him that costs could be reduced by as much as $8,000 for canonization and nearly $4,800 for beatification.

Vatican observers pointed out that the cost of sainthood is such that "only orders or other wealthy sponsors can afford it." So the Pope's economy-minded commission made a series of recommendations, which included: (1) "Doing away with the practice of giving relics of a new saint or blessed, encased in costly containers, to cardinals and other dignitaries." (2) "Eliminate some payments made to involve officials above their regular salaries." (3) "Making members of the Sistine Choir perform free at beatification and canonization rites." (4) "Augmenting costs for a 'particularly important' canonization with church funds."

No doubt this seems rather absurd to those who understand the simple Bible plan of salvation. It offers not only "instant sainthood," but *it is all absolutely free!* It does not cost anyone one single penny to become a saint. The moment Christ is received as Saviour, sainthood is automatic and without charge or fees. It is "the gift of God" (Rom. 6:23).

Soldiers ought not to pray alone for fellow soldiers, but for their commanding officers. We think especially of preachers. Paul said in verses 19 and 20, *"And for me, that utterance may be given unto me, that I may open my mouth boldly, to make known the mystery of the gospel, For which I am an ambassador in bonds: that therein I may speak boldly, as I ought to speak."*

How should a Christian soldier pray for his commanding officers? He should pray that their preaching might please God and win souls. Notice the quintet of petitions Paul mentions: "That utterance may be given unto me," "that I may open my mouth boldly," "to make known the mystery of the gospel," "that therein I may speak boldly," and, "as I ought to speak." What preacher who is worth his salt does not want and long for this? We know that such is the cry of our own heart!

IV. CONCLUDING MESSAGES!
Vss. 21-24

A. A Word About Tychicus

In verses 21 and 22, Paul says: *"But that ye also may know my affairs, and how I do, Tychicus, a beloved brother and faithful minister in the Lord, shall make known to you all things: Whom I have sent unto you for the same purpose, that ye might know our affairs, and that he might comfort your hearts."*

The character of Tychicus was such that it combined two rare characteristics. He was both *a beloved brother* and *a faithful minister.* He was gracious and gentle, yet he did not compromise the truth in any way. He was faithful to the Word of God, but he was not harsh and unloving in the stand he took. Sometimes modernists are noted for their graciousness, yet they compromise; on the other hand, fundamentalists are famous for their faithfulness to the Bible, but some are anything but gracious in their ministry. How wonderful when a servant of Christ possesses *both* characteristics.

When Paul sent Tychicus to Ephesus, he had a dual purpose in mind. For one thing, he wanted him to present a missionary report on Paul's work in Rome. True, Paul was in prison, "an ambassador in bonds," but he was serving God as acceptably and, perhaps, as effectively there as on any other mission field where God had placed him previously. Circumstances are not keys to effective service.

Paul's other purpose in sending Tychicus to Ephesus was to "comfort your hearts." He wanted this young preacher to be a blessing to them, even as he had no doubt been a blessing to Paul.

B. A Word About Christian Graces

In the last two verses of this blessed epistle, Paul says, *"Peace be to the brethren, and love with faith, from God the Father and the Lord Jesus Christ. Grace be with all them that love our Lord Jesus Christ in sincerity. Amen.*

1. Peace!

"Peace to the brethren," Paul said. He did not refer to the "peace with God" of Romans 5:1, since this was a present possession of the Ephesian saints. No, he spoke of the "peace of God" as described in Philippians 4:7, where he had declared, "And the peace of God, which passeth all understanding, shall keep your hearts and minds through Christ Jesus." Such peace is possible only for "brethren."

2. Love!

"Love with faith." Here was another reminder that Paul intended Christ's wish to be fulfilled in them, "By this shall all men know that ye are my disciples, if ye have love one to another" (John 13:35).

3. Faith!

Did you note the connection of faith with love? This is the love described in the great love chapter which "believeth all things, hopeth all things" (I Cor. 13:7).

All three in this trilogy—peace, love, faith—are "from God the Father and the Lord Jesus Christ." They are not things to be worked up; they are characteristics to be appropriated through growth in grace. In fact, that is the next thing Paul mentions.

4. Grace!

Like his mention of grace at the start of the epistle, this is not God's grace in salvation. This is the "grace wherein we stand" (Rom. 5:2). It is something needed fresh with each passing day, especially for those who battle in the ranks of Christ's army.

5. "Amen!"

The epistle closes with the familiar, *"So be it!"* In the words of the poet,

> Like Scottish calls from glen to glen
> Across the spheres rings each "Amen";
> Then God is glad, He knows men's parts
> If prayers and hymns come from their hearts.

Conclusion

As we have been thinking about putting on the whole armor of God and vigorously contending for the faith, it may be that one reading these lines is a deserter. Are you a soldier in God's army, one who has put on the uniform, professing to be a warrior of Jesus Christ, yet refusing to fight? If so, some sort of a "re-enlisting" ceremony would be in order.

Since failure to fight and stand for truth would be sin, I John 1:9 is certainly appropriate: "If we confess our sins, he is faithful and just to forgive us our sins, and to cleanse us from all unrighteousness."

Will you join in sincerely saying,

> Forward then, with Jesus sharing
>   In the warfare here below!
> Forward! In His Name unfearing,
>   Boldly meeting every foe.
>
> Count it never a disaster,
>   When the shame for Him you bear,
> But rejoice that such a Master,
>   Gives you in His Cross a share.
>
> Unto sin be daily dying,
>   That His life may through thee shine;
> Find thy strength in lowly lying
>   At the pierced feet divine.
>
> Soon the earthly conflict over,
>   Christ will come to claim His own;
> Oh, the grace—the grace, my brother!—
>   If He then shall say "Well done!"

Finally, we simply call attention to Paul's closing words: *"All*

them that love our Lord Jesus Christ in sincerity."
Do you love Him in sincerity?

Other Books by Dr. Sumner

ARMSTRONGISM

Some of the most influential and greatly-used leaders in Christendom have highly commended this authoritative study of Herbert and Garner Ted Armstrong's evil cult. For example, consider some of the following:

"... detailed, thorough, and comprehensive. It will do much good ... May God give it wide circulation."
—*Dr. Jack Hyles*

"We recommend this scholarly and important big book. It is true to the Scriptures, and it will be a tremendous revelation to honest readers."
—*Dr. John R. Rice*

"... an excellent volume! ... will result in opening the eyes of many ... I am in hearty agreement with you ..."
—*Dr. Lee Roberson*

"I am now happy to recommend this book which will answer every question concerning the false teachings of both Herbert and Garner Ted Armstrong."
—*Dr. Jack Van Impe*

"... well written, well documented, thorough, even kind."
—*Dr. Bob Moore*

".. the largest, the most informative and the most comprehensive book on the American-based cult ..."
—*Dr. G. Archer Weniger*

"... very large and detailed book ... a masterpiece."
—*Dr. Tom Wallace*

"The most documented, thorough examination and expose' of any cult I have ever read ... superb and extremely helpful ... a classic work on one of the most insidious cults of our time and should be read by all pastors and Christian workers."
—*Dr. C. Sumner Wemp*

"... the finest of this type written ... clear and scholarly ... honest, sincere, factual and documented ... God's answer to one of the greatest religious deceptions of all time. It ought to be in every Christian home, in the library of every Bible-believing preacher and in every fundamental college. I am extremely proud to possess a copy of my own."
—*Dr. Tom Malone, Sr.*

ONLY $7.95

15 Chapters, 424 Pages

Biblical Evangelism In Action!

"... ONE OF THE MOST HELPFUL BOOKS ON SOUL WINNING TO APPEAR IN THIS GENERATION ... LOADED WITH WORKABLE IDEAS ... BEARS OUR UNCONDITIONAL RECOMMENDATION."

—Dr. G. Archer Weniger

"We do not know of any book similar in nature which is as practical and thorough."—THE BAPTIST BULLETIN

"I WOULD LIKE TO GIVE MY FULL COMMENDATION ... IT IS INTERESTING READING AND CONVINCING IN ITS PRESENTATION ..."

—Dr. Lee Roberson, Chancellor, Tennessee Temple Schools; Pastor, Highland Park Baptist Church, Chattanooga, Tennessee.

"HOW I REJOICE IN THE APPEARANCE UPON THE STAGE OF CHRISTIAN LITERATURE OF THIS GREAT BOOK..."

—Dr. Tom Malone, President, Midwestern Baptist College; Pastor, Immanuel Baptist Church, Pontiac, Michigan.

Only $5.50

EVANGELISM: The Church on Fire

This book comprises a series of ten lectures on evangelism delivered by the author at the Grand Rapids Baptist Bible College & Seminary. The publishers have summed up this significant volume with the words: *"In forceful, practical, stimulating style, Mr. Sumner describes the need for New Testament evangelism, the meaning of New Testament evangelism, personal and pulpit qualifications of New Testament evangelists, regular and special evangelism in the New Testament church, evangelistic preaching, good manners in evangelism, and conserving the results of evangelism."*

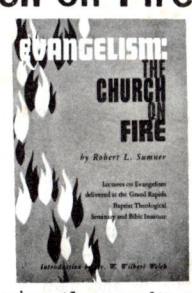

"... a very challenging book. My own desire to win the lost was intensified by reading it."—Dr. John G. Balyo, Cedar Hill Baptist Church, Cleveland, Ohio.

"Several features make this one of the most important books written on evangelism in the last twenty-five or more years." —Evangelist John R. Rice.

220 Pages

$4.75

"... if churches ever need a book like this and the message it contains, the time is now!"—Dr. Walt Handford, Southside Baptist Church, Greenville, South Carolina.

Hell Is No Joke

This is a book of six strong evangelistic messages dealing with the subjects, *Hell Is No Joke, The Unmocked God, Slipping into Hell, Have You Counted the Cost? Do You Think You Will Go to Heaven When You Die?* and, *Heaven: Home, Sweet Home, of God's Children.* The Pathway Book Club, in offering it as its main monthly selection, said of it: *"The messages are Bible-centered, easy to understand, and are made vivid through the use of interesting illustrations. Each of these messages should provide the reader with a number of 'sermon starters' or add to one's materials for sermon building."*

Reviewers Say:

"We cannot recommend too strongly that every home possible should own this book. These sermons will inspire and start fires burning and give suggestions and illustrations and outlines for preachers. They are full of Bible truth, heart-warming illustrations. They read easily and leave a lasting impact.

"A wonderful way to win souls would be to buy this book and lend it among unsaved friends, in each case pressing the matter of salvation after one had read these sermons."—*The Sword of the Lord.*

"Six evangelistic sermons on Hell, judgment and Heaven by a widely-known evangelist. The messages are expository, clear in outline, rich in illustration and make a strong appeal for the reader or hearer to turn to God."—*Baptist Record.*

"Plain, pointed and practical preaching here! While the themes are as old as time itself, there are no platitudes here. 'Old-fashioned' preaching that rebukes sin and exalts the Lord."—Dr. Robert Lee Braden, Phoenix, Arizona.

"Here are six typical Sumner sermons, pungent, succinct, Scriptural and evangelistic."—*Baptist Bulletin.*

"This book of six sermons carries the same sober urgency suggested in the title. As in any of Sumner's works, the material is clearly marked by those attributes which equip him for his multifarious duties... Mr. Sumner has a presentation of pathos and force. The messages are bibliocentric and worthy of a place in your library."—*Baptist Bible Tribune.*

"... a great warning to men of the danger that confronts them who neglect the Word of the Lord and the salvation He has provided... It should be read with great and careful interest by both saint and sinner. Its warnings are very timely and essentially needful."—*The Ohio Independent Baptist.*

$3.25

Identification in Jesus Christ

1. By the Letter
   A. Rom. 6
   B. Rom. 7
   C. Rom. 8

2. By the Spirit
   A. Eph 1:16-18
   B. Rom 1:1-2
   C. Eph 3:16-19
   D. Rom 8:13
   E. I Thess. 5:23
   F. Jude :20
   G. I Thess 5:17
   H. Eph 6:18

3. By Experience
   A. Gal 2:20
   B. Rom 8:29-30
   C. Luke 14:25-33
   D. Mark 10:28-31
   E. Luke 9:23-27
   F. Matt. 25:31-44
   G. Matt. 19:27-30
   H. Matt 10:37-39
   I. Matt. 7:16-20
   J. Matt 7:24-29
   K. Jude :20
   L. I Cor. 5:17